GET INTO MEDICAL SCHOOL

Write the Perfect UCAS Personal Statement

Effective techniques & over 100 examples of personal statements

2026 entry

Olivier Picard, Byam Rosewell, Jaiden Townsend

Published by ISC Medical
97 Judd Street, London WC1H 9JG
Tel: 0203 507 0001

First Edition: May 2025
ISBN13: 978-1-905812-28-8
A catalogue record for this book is available from the British Library.
© Interview Skills Consulting Limited 2010–2025. All rights reserved.

No part of this publication may be reproduced, stored in a retrieval system, or transmitted in any form or by any means, electronic, mechanical, photocopying, recording or otherwise, without prior permission of the publishers.

The moral right of Olivier Picard, Byam Rosewell and Jaiden Townsend to be identified as the authors of this work has been asserted in accordance with Sections 77 and 78 of the Copyright, Designs and Patents Act 1988.

Printed and bound by CPI Group (UK) Ltd, Croydon, CR0 4YY

Contents table

		Page
1	Introduction	4
2	How to use this book	5
3	Starting work on your personal statement	7
4	Format and expectations	9
5	Section 1: Why medicine?	11
6	Section 2: Qualifications and studies	15
7	Section 3: Extracurricular	34
8	Refining your personal statement	53
9	Making your statement fit	61
10	Editing and checking your statement	62
11	Examples of personal statements	65
12	Power words	280

1 Introduction

Competition for spots at medical school is incredibly tough. Many aspiring students believe that getting an interview is just a matter of luck, but that's far from the truth. There's a lot you can do to increase your chances of standing out, securing an interview, and ultimately earning a place. It all begins with your personal statement.

Your personal statement is one of the few chances you'll have to set yourself apart from the thousands of other applicants. While your grades and references show that you're academically qualified, and entrance exams will certainly play a role, it's your personal statement that could make the difference between landing an interview or not. This is especially true at schools where most candidates have excellent grades and the competition is fierce. Some medical schools, like Bristol, have a ratio of 12 applicants for every available place.

The space for your personal statement on the UCAS application is limited – about one typed page in Arial font size 10. You'll need to divide this into three sections, each answering a different question. It can be tricky, especially if you haven't done much creative writing since your GCSEs. Writing about yourself in a confident and concise way is something most people aren't used to, and it can be challenging.

Unfortunately, many strong candidates miss out on interviews simply because they don't fully understand what their personal statement should convey. They may not focus enough on the key experiences and skills that will make their application stand out, leading to a statement that doesn't reach its potential.

This guide will take you step by step through the process of crafting a standout personal statement, providing you with helpful structures and techniques to organise your thoughts and present yourself in the best possible light. We've also included over 100 personal statement examples. Since this is the first year the new three-question UCAS format is being used, all of these examples are based on real personal statements from successful candidates, which we've adapted to fit the new format. This will give you insight into the different approaches that have worked for others, helping you create a unique and compelling statement of your own.

2 How to use this book

Reflecting on and writing about yourself

This book provides all the information and advice you need to create a strong and successful personal statement. The first few chapters will help you understand exactly what admissions tutors are looking for and offer guidance on suitable content and structure. You'll find detailed advice on how to approach writing your personal statement, along with examples of good and bad practices.

The example statements are designed to showcase the variety of writing styles and approaches that can work. They differ greatly in tone and content; some are more narrative and storytelling-based, while others are concise and factual.

As you read through the examples and gather inspiration for your own personal statement, remember that there are many different ways to write a strong one. Everyone has their own unique style, and it's crucial to stay true to yourself. Don't try to change your personality or force it into a particular mould. Instead, use the techniques in this book to reflect on what you have to offer, and adapt them in a way that suits your individual style.

Plagiarism/similarity detection

The examples in this book are meant to serve as a guide and reference only. They should never be copied, either in whole or in part.

Similarly, when reading other people's personal statements, be cautious not to be tempted to borrow sections that sound impressive. UCAS uses a similarity detection service called Copycatch, which can spot similarities and instances of plagiarism – plainly copied content.

Each personal statement submitted to UCAS is checked against a database of previously submitted statements, as well as sample statements from websites and other sources. Once a personal statement is processed, it is added to this library.

If a personal statement is found to have 10% or more similarity, it will be flagged by the UCAS similarity detection service team. If necessary, the university you are applying to will be notified and will decide how to handle the situation based on the significance of the similarity.

So, while it's perfectly fine to draw inspiration from the examples in this book, always ensure that your personal statement is entirely your own work. Avoid the temptation to copy and make sure that everything you submit is original.

Using AI to write your statement

There are two ways in which you can use AI. It can help you rewrite a piece of text that you have written yourself; it can also help you generate ideas. When used correctly, it can be a powerful tool.

UCAS updates its policies regularly. You will find its current guidance on this page:

https://www.ucas.com/applying/applying–university/writing–your–personal–statement/guide–using–ai–and–chatgpt–your–personal–statement

Alternatively, use the QR code below:

3 Starting work on your personal statement

Your personal statement may only be 4,000 characters long – around 800 words – but creating a standout version will take more time and effort than you might expect. So it's important to start early. Set aside ample time to brainstorm ideas, write your draft, get feedback, and revise it multiple times before arriving at your final version. It's never too early to start working on your personal statement, but leaving it to the last minute because you underestimated the amount of work involved could hurt your chances.

You can begin thinking about the personal qualities you want to highlight well in advance – perhaps even during the summer holidays. Take the time to ask friends, colleagues, or others you work with for their feedback. Ask questions like, "Do you think I'm a good team player?" or "How would you describe my ability to listen, empathise, and communicate?" Reflect on situations where you have demonstrated these attributes. Getting others' perspectives will help you create an honest and credible personal statement that genuinely reflects who you are.

As you begin considering the content, jot down any ideas or feedback you receive. These don't need to be fully fleshed-out ideas at this stage – simple bullet points or headings will work. The goal is to capture your thoughts so you can refer back to them when it's time to start developing your personal statement in more detail.

A countdown for your personal statement

For 2026 entry, UCAS applications for medical school open on 3 September and close on 15 October. Ideally, you should aim to submit your application as early as possible within that time frame to build a buffer and avoid a last-minute panic. For example, if your aim is to submit your application on 30 September, you might want to follow a timetable that looks like this:

1 September	Start brainstorming for ideas and look at different examples of personal statements.
10 September	Begin composing your first draft, reviewing and editing as you go along.
15 September	Give your draft personal statement to your friends, relatives and teachers for their comments. Continue to revise and edit your statement, taking into consideration the comments and advice received.
20 September	Ask your friends, relatives and teachers for their final comments on your draft personal statement. Upload your personal statement into your UCAS application and do your final editing and proofreading, but don't send it yet.
30 September	Submit your application.

This extra time will give you a cushion, just in case something unexpected comes up and you're not ready to submit on the first day. However, don't treat this as an excuse to procrastinate – time has a way of slipping away faster than you'd expect!

Of course, it doesn't mean you can't start earlier if you're eager. The earlier you start, the more time you'll have to refine and perfect your personal statement.

4 Format and expectations

The personal statement and its new format

A personal statement is a concise résumé of your personal and academic achievements, along with a reflection of your aspirations and goals. It's your chance to explain to the university or college why you're well suited for the course you're applying for, and to showcase your passion and commitment.

The statement must be no more than 4,000 characters in total, including spaces. This limit is intentional – it's meant to keep it brief; it's a résumé rather than a full autobiography.

In previous years, personal statements would consist of a single long piece of text where you would write about yourself, your achievements and why you were applying to the subject. For 2026 entry, this format has shifted from a single longer text to three smaller separate sections, each posing a different question designed to help guide the focus of your answers.

The questions you need to answer are:

1. Why do you want to study this course or subject?
2. How have your qualifications and studies helped you to prepare for this course or subject?
3. What else have you done to prepare outside of education, and why are these experiences useful?

Each section needs to contain a minimum of 350 characters (including spaces) while maintaining the overall character count of 4,000.

Although the personal statement is now being split into three sections, those three sections will be read by the same person, meaning they will be assessed as one entity. You will need to bear that in mind when you write the statement because it means you cannot repeat information.

What admissions tutors are looking for

The admissions tutors will be looking for evidence that:

- You have demonstrated a genuine interest in and motivation for pursuing medicine.

- You are well informed about the demanding nature of a career in medicine and the specific requirements needed to succeed.

- You can show compassion and a commitment to helping and caring for others through relevant work or personal experiences.

- You actively participate in a broad range of activities and have diverse interests.

- You have contributed to various school, college, or community activities, demonstrating teamwork, leadership, communication skills, and a willingness to take on responsibility.

- You have developed skills during your academic experiences that are applicable to a medical career.

- You have achieved personal accomplishments not related to exams, awards, or other formal recognitions.

Your personal statement will be scored according to the criteria set by the admissions team. This, combined with your reference, will form the overall assessment of your personal attributes.

It's all about you!

Before you begin, remember that your personal statement is all about **you**. It's not about writing an autobiography or listing all the amazing things you've done, as the admissions tutors aren't looking for that. Instead, they want to know why you specifically want to pursue a career in medicine, how you've demonstrated your interest in the field, and how you've proven that you possess the right qualities for the profession.

5 Section 1: Why medicine?

Section 1 asks, "Why do you want to study this course or subject?" This is your chance to clearly explain your reasons for applying to study medicine and the personal journey that led you to this decision. While the motivation to pursue medicine may seem obvious to you, it is not immediately clear to the admissions tutors.

In this section, you have the opportunity to share your personal story – why medicine appeals to you, what inspired your decision, and how your experiences have shaped your desire to become a doctor. Whether it's a personal experience, a specific moment that sparked your interest, or the values that draw you to healthcare, make sure to highlight what genuinely drives you toward this career.

To answer this, you need to consider two questions:

- What experiences prompted your interest in medicine?
- Do you have an idea of what you want to do once you've qualified?

What experienced prompted your interest in medicine?

Your decision to pursue medicine may have been influenced by a variety of factors:

1. **A topic that inspired you and helped you develop an understanding of medicine, taken from a range of sources:**
    - Reading medical journals or articles (e.g. 'Student BMJ')
    - Taking online courses on medical topics (e.g. FutureLearn)
    - Watching documentaries or medical series
    - Reading books by or about doctors
    - Researching a medical condition a friend or relative has
    - Following current events and health news
    - Engaging with medical blogs or social media accounts
    - Attending public lectures, webinars, or watching TED Talks
    - Listening to medical or healthcare-related podcasts
    - Exploring scientific research papers or medical case studies online

2. **A role model who has impacted your life:**
   - Famous people in medicine throughout history
   - A relative or friend working in healthcare
   - Someone whose approach to patient care or advancing healthcare was inspiring

3. **An experience of working/volunteering in a healthcare environment:**
   - Charity work
   - Volunteering at a hospital, hospice, care home, etc.
   - Entertaining people at a retirement home
   - Caring for a neighbour or an acquaintance
   - Volunteering for a mental health helpline
   - First aid volunteer (e.g. St John Ambulance, Red Cross)
   - Participating in a health education or awareness campaign

4. **Your own exposure to health issues:**
   - Direct personal experience of health issues. You may have lived with a condition throughout your childhood, like asthma, epilepsy, diabetes, cancer, sleep disorders, ADHD, mental health challenges, or allergies. Alternatively, you may have experienced an injury, such as a broken limb or an accident, which allowed you to witness the work of healthcare professionals first-hand.

   - You may have cared for or been affected by someone else's health issues, such as a neighbour, family friend, or relative. This could include caring for a parent with an illness, such as those mentioned above, or others like dementia, Parkinson's disease, frailty, sensory loss, or eating disorders. It may also involve supporting someone struggling with addictions, such as alcohol, smoking, medication, gambling, or technology.

   - You may also have dealt with the loss of a loved one and the aftermath, leading you to desire improvements in how such situations are handled.

5. **An interest in the challenges of medicine:**
   - Lifelong learning
   - Academic curiosity
   - Compassionate and caring approach
   - Balance of critical thinking and communication

Do you have a career in mind once you've qualified?

As you consider applying to medical school, it's worth starting to think about what kind of doctor you might want to become. Some applicants already have a clear sense of the career path they hope to follow after qualifying. You might be drawn to a hands-on field like surgery, a core medical specialty, or one of the vital support specialties such as anaesthetics, radiology, or pathology. Others are inspired by broader fields like general practice or emergency medicine, which offer variety and continuity of care. You might even be passionate about areas beyond the clinic—such as public health, global health, policy, or medical research.

It's completely normal not to have everything figured out yet. However, showing awareness of different specialties—and an openness to exploring them—can strengthen your application. It demonstrates that you've thought carefully about what a career in medicine involves and how your own experiences and qualities align with the profession.

If you already have a particular area of interest, think about what draws you to it. Often, career choices are influenced by personal or family experiences. For instance, someone who has lived with asthma or has a loved one affected by COPD or sleep apnoea may feel connected to respiratory medicine. A personal or family history of cancer might lead to an interest in oncology. Similarly, someone who has experienced mental health challenges—either personally or through supporting someone else—might feel called to psychiatry.

Equally important is reflecting on your skills and how they may suit certain specialties. If you enjoy working with your hands or have a knack for crafts, instruments, or other dexterous hobbies, surgery might be a great fit. If you're someone who enjoys solving puzzles, working with data, or thinking analytically, you might gravitate toward radiology, pathology, or internal medicine.

It's also worth knowing that medicine offers many paths beyond the traditional hospital or GP setting. Some doctors work in the military as army medics, while others join humanitarian organisations, provide healthcare in prisons, or become involved in expedition or wilderness medicine. These roles require resilience, adaptability, and a strong sense of purpose—but for the right person, they can be incredibly fulfilling.

Ultimately, medical school will expose you to a wide range of specialties and opportunities. What matters most at this stage is curiosity, self-awareness, and a willingness to learn. Admissions teams aren't expecting you to have your entire career planned out—but they will value thoughtful reflection on what kind of doctor you might become, and why.

Warning about using work experience in Section 1

Section 1 asks about what motivated to study medicine as a career. Strictly speaking, this refers to anything that has happened before you have made your decision to study medicine. You need to keep this in mind when talking about your experiences, and particularly work experiences.

If you've had work experience from a young age, for example you've been with the ambulance service since you were 13–then that's definitely relevant for section 1, as it shows part of your journey discovering medicine as a career. However, anything you've done more recently, like volunteering or work experience to strengthen your application after deciding to pursue medicine, would be better placed in section 3.

That being said, nothing stops you from including recent work experience in Section 1, as long as you reflect it as a primary driver for your decision and on the proviso that it does not severely deplete section 3.

Section 2: Qualifications and studies

Section 2 asks, "How have your qualifications and studies helped you to prepare for this course or subject?"

This is your chance to reflect on how the subjects you've studied, the knowledge you've gained, and other aspects of your education connect to a career in medicine. Broadly speaking, think about those four themes:

- Knowledge and skills gained from your subjects
- Demonstration of strong academic performance (aside from grades)
- Projects or activities undertaken in an educational context
- Leadership and positions of responsibility

Knowledge and skills gained from your subjects

This is your chance to explain how your A level subjects, or any other qualifications, relate to a future in medicine. Admissions tutors want more than just good grades; they're interested in how your subjects have helped you build relevant skills, knowledge, and ways of thinking.

Show how your subject choices reflect both your academic strengths and personal qualities. Biology and chemistry provide a foundation in core medical topics like physiology and pharmacology, while physics supports problem-solving and an understanding of medical technology.

Modern foreign languages can enhance communication and cultural awareness, vital in today's diverse healthcare environments. Subjects like philosophy or religious studies encourage ethical thinking, and practical or creative subjects like art or design and technology can show precision and manual dexterity—useful in hands-on medical roles.

By linking your subject choices to skills needed in medicine, you'll present yourself as a thoughtful, well-prepared applicant. The following pages outline how common subjects support your readiness for medical school.

CHEMISTRY

Understanding of biochemistry and pharmacology: A solid foundation in biochemistry is essential for understanding physiological processes and pharmacology. Studying chemical reactions, organic molecules, and metabolic pathways helps understand how drugs affect the body and how biochemical reactions drive human health and disease.

Analytical and quantitative skills: Chemistry requires a high level of accuracy in measurements, calculations, and interpretation of results. Precision and being comfortable working with data is vital for dosage calculations, analysing results, and interpreting information.

Laboratory skills and scientific techniques: Techniques such as titration, chromatography, and spectrophotometry are relevant to medical laboratory and research settings. Chemistry provides good training on following protocols rigorously and working with precision.

Problem-solving and critical thinking: Chemistry involves complex problem-solving, from balancing equations to predicting reaction outcomes. This strengthens critical thinking, a trait essential for diagnosing conditions, interpreting patient data and troubleshooting.

Understanding of chemical safety: Chemistry teaches the importance of safe handling of chemicals. It is also a good introduction to risk management and the importance of safety protocols.

Resilience and perseverance: Chemistry is a topic that requires an accumulation of a lot of knowledge and the ability to apply it to practical problems, some of which can be challenging. Answering a question may require multiple attempts and failures, in the same way this can be found in medicine when diagnosing complex conditions or doing research.

Interdisciplinary thinking: Chemistry overlaps with biology and physics, helping you understand medicine from an integrated scientific perspective. This interdisciplinary knowledge mirrors the holistic approach in medicine where understanding the biochemical, physical, and biological aspects of the body is crucial for treating patients.

BIOLOGY

Foundation in human biology: Exploring cell biology, human physiology, genetics and systems like the cardiovascular or immune system has given you an appreciation for the complexity of the human body and a better understanding of health and disease. This foundation is essential for diagnosing and treating conditions, helping identify how various systems interact and how diseases manifest across different levels.

Understanding of pathophysiology: Studying conditions at a cellular and systemic level is invaluable for understanding pathophysiology and disease mechanisms. This insight helps recognise abnormal biological processes and their effects on health, making it easier to formulate appropriate treatments and interventions in a medical context.

Lab skills, scientific rigour and research skills: Lab skills play an important role in medicine. That includes the ability to use lab equipment, use microscopy and chromatography, plan and evaluate experiments, record results, analyse data, and convey your findings.

Lab skills also provide a good understanding of safe laboratory processes. As you encountered new biological concepts and challenges, you became well-versed in the scientific method, learning how to formulate hypotheses, design experiments, and draw meaningful conclusions from real data. Through your biology studies, you will have gained proficiency in data analysis, a skill vital not just in scientific research but also in areas like statistics and data-driven decision-making, i.e. evidence-based medicine.

Ethics and empathy for living organisms: Some curricula delve into topics relating to biomedical ethics, e.g. use of animals in research, genetic screening, genome engineering. All of these issues bear a direct relevance to medicine.

Appreciation of complexity and connectivity: Biology reveals how various systems are interconnected, from ecosystems to organ systems. This understanding is valuable in medicine, where treating one area often affects others and clinicians often need to work on a multidisciplinary basis and not remain confined to their own speciality.

PHYSICS

Scientific understanding and curiosity: Physics deepens your understanding of fundamental scientific principles, which aligns with the scientific foundation of medicine. For example, concepts in mechanics and energy relate to how the human body functions, from muscle movements to circulatory dynamics.

Problem-solving and critical thinking: Physics involves analysing real-world problems, applying theories, and conducting experiments, which are all skills directly relevant to the clinical reasoning required in medicine. Physics trains you to tackle complex problems logically and critically, just as you would analyse symptoms, test results, and patient histories to form a diagnosis.

Data management skills: Physics requires precision in calculations and experimental measurements, which are also vital in medicine. Learning to measure accurately, interpret results, and work with precise data will have prepared you for the careful handling of patient information and test results in a medical setting. On the other hand, some aspects of physics require making approximations for particular quantities. This can also be the case in the study of medicine.

Familiarity with technology and innovation: Physics plays a crucial role in medicine by underpinning technologies like medical imaging (MRI, CT scans, ultrasound) and radiation therapy. Understanding the principles of these technologies enhances the ability to operate, troubleshoot, and innovate in medical diagnostics and treatment, ensuring effective patient care.

Experimental skills and scientific methodology: Physics involves formulating hypotheses, conducting experiments, and analysing outcomes. These skills mirror the scientific method used in medical research and diagnostics.

Resilience and patience: Physics, much like medicine, is complex and often requires persistence to grasp difficult concepts or troubleshoot experiments.

MATHS

Problem-solving and analytical thinking: Mathematics fosters strong problem-solving skills. Whether tackling algebraic equations or understanding geometric relationships, mathematical study sharpens the ability to approach problems methodically and logically. This skill is invaluable in medicine, where medical professionals must diagnose and treat complex conditions, often requiring the synthesis of multiple pieces of information. Logical thinking aids in identifying patterns, interpreting symptoms, and making informed decisions about patient care.

Data analysis and evidence-based medicine: Mathematics aids in analysing medical research, clinical trials, and patient outcomes. Skills in statistics and probability enable medical professionals to interpret trends, assess treatment effectiveness, and make evidence-based decisions in clinical practice.

Medical imaging and diagnostic technology: Mathematics, particularly in areas like calculus and geometry, is fundamental to the operation of medical imaging technologies. These imaging techniques rely on complex mathematical principles to reconstruct images and analyse body structures. A solid grasp of mathematics helps medical professionals understand how these technologies work and ensures accurate interpretation of imaging results, leading to better diagnoses.

Pharmacokinetics and dosage calculations: Further mathematics plays a significant role in understanding pharmacokinetics, the study of how drugs move through the body. Calculations related to drug dosage, concentration, and timing require knowledge of mathematical formulas and concepts like rates of change, logarithms, and proportions.

Research and medical advancements: Medical research frequently involves statistical analysis, experimental design, and modelling biological systems. Further mathematics provides the tools necessary for conducting rigorous research and analysing experimental data. With an increasing emphasis on personalised medicine, where mathematical modelling of genetic information is crucial, further math studies enable medical professionals to contribute to innovative research and advancements.

LANGUAGES

Communication skills: Studying a modern language develops advanced communication skills, crucial in medicine for interacting with diverse patients and colleagues. It improves clarity, adaptability, and the ability to explain complex ideas simply. Adapting speech across languages builds flexibility, while grammar study enhances logical thinking and clear expression.

Cultural awareness and empathy: Learning a language immerses you in the culture and perspectives of another society, promoting cultural sensitivity and empathy – qualities essential in a healthcare setting. This effect is deepened when language study is combined with travel or time spent abroad, offering first-hand experience of cultural differences. Understanding how challenging it can be to communicate in a foreign language also fosters patience and empathy towards patients who may struggle with English, ultimately improving trust and quality of care.

Listening skills and patient-centred care: Language learning places strong emphasis on attentive listening and considered responses, which align closely with patient-centred care in medicine. These skills teach you to listen actively to "read between the lines", and to tailor your responses to the needs of others – an essential ability when building rapport with patients and responding to their concerns. This attentiveness helps ensure that patients feel heard and understood.

Problem-solving and adaptability: Communicating in a foreign language often means finding alternative ways to express yourself when the right words elude you. This builds problem-solving and adaptability – skills invaluable in medicine, where you must simplify complex ideas or navigate communication barriers. Regularly rephrasing sharpens creativity and flexibility, helping you respond effectively to diverse clinical situations.

Memory and cognitive skills: Language learning involves memorising vocabulary, grammar, and idioms, which strengthens memory, cognitive flexibility, and mental agility. Regularly recalling and applying linguistic rules improves your ability to retain and organise complex information – an essential skill in medicine, where you must absorb vast amounts of knowledge and apply it accurately in dynamic clinical environments.

HISTORY

Critical analysis and evaluation: History demands the careful examination of sources, narratives, and interpretations. This has developed your ability to critically assess complex information – just as a doctor must do when evaluating symptoms, patient histories, and clinical evidence. Emphasise how forming reasoned conclusions in history mirrors the diagnostic process in medicine.

Evidence-based reasoning: History teaches you to build arguments rooted in solid evidence, avoiding assumptions or bias. This aligns closely with evidence-based medicine, where treatment decisions must be backed by the best available research and clinical data. You can highlight how this approach has shaped your thinking and prepared you for a scientific and research-oriented field.

Communication skills: Writing essays and participating in discussions has developed your ability to construct clear, persuasive arguments and explain complex ideas – skills vital for communicating with patients and colleagues in medicine. Explain how history has trained you to present information clearly and sensitively, something essential when discussing diagnoses or treatment options.

Understanding of ethics and human behaviour: History provides insights into human motivations, cultural shifts, and ethical dilemmas across different times and societies. This helps build empathy, cultural awareness, and an appreciation for the ethical dimensions of medicine. You could say that learning about historical injustices, healthcare developments, or ethical debates in history has deepened your understanding of the social responsibilities of doctors.

Analytical thinking and pattern recognition: History sharpens your ability to spot patterns, causes, and consequences, while also making decisions from limited or conflicting evidence – much like diagnosing in medicine. Analysing historical case studies has trained you to piece together complex information, think critically, and adapt to uncertainty. These skills are vital when interpreting symptoms, test results, and patient histories to make informed clinical decisions.

ART

Attention to detail and observation skills: Art trains you to observe details closely, from colour and texture to subtle nuances in expression and form. Studies have suggested that art can be utilised to teach observational skills in medical students, a skill that is integral to patient examination but seldom taught directly within medical curricula.

Creativity and problem-solving: Making art involves innovative thinking and finding creative approaches to convey ideas. In medicine this can be useful in troubleshooting problems and when trying to explain complex topics to patients or colleagues.

Hand–eye coordination and manual dexterity: Art, especially drawing, painting, or sculpting, develops fine motor skills and hand–eye coordination, which are essential for procedures in medicine.

Empathy and understanding of human emotion: Art often explores themes related to human experience and emotion, fostering empathy and understanding. Aside from the obvious relations to medicine, the very fact you've chosen art as a topic could be used to demonstrate that you have a well-rounded nature.

Patience and perseverance: Few projects give immediate results. In medicine you will experience that frustration during preparation for your exams, when confronted with a difficult clinical case, when doing research that seems to be taking longer than it should, etc.

Non-verbal communication and visual interpretation: Art teaches you to communicate ideas visually and interpret meaning beyond words. In medicine you often need to interpret non-verbal cues, body language and facial expressions. This is turn helps in building rapport with people.

Open-mindedness: Art sparks debate over techniques and meaning, encouraging appreciation for alternative perspectives and respect for others' views. This mindset is valuable in medicine, where symptoms and test results can be interpreted differently, and doctors may disagree on the best course of action, especially when evidence is unclear.

RELIGIOUS STUDIES

Understanding human experience: Religious studies explores diverse beliefs, values, and worldviews, fostering cultural sensitivity and empathy – both essential in medicine. It also provides insights into human motivations and the search for meaning, helping you better understand the emotional and psychological needs of patients. This awareness allows you to connect with patients on a deeper level, particularly when they face life-changing diagnoses or challenges.

Ethical reasoning: Religious studies often explores complex ethical questions, teaching you to approach moral dilemmas thoughtfully and impartially. In medicine, where ethical considerations are frequent, from end-of-life care to consent issues, this invaluable skill will prepare you to navigate ethical challenges in a balanced and compassionate manner.

Communication and active listening: Religious studies emphasises understanding and interpreting others' perspectives, which requires strong listening and communication skills, useful when discussing sensitive topics respectfully.

Critical thinking and analytical skills: Analysing religious texts and philosophical arguments develops critical thinking and analytical abilities. This is comparable to analysing symptoms, making evidence-based decisions, and critically assessing research during daily practice.

Open-mindedness: Religious studies encourages an open mind and respect for varied perspectives, which is vital in a diverse healthcare setting. Encountering these different worldviews will have taught you resilience in understanding complex issues, a skill that helps when working with patients from all backgrounds in a compassionate and non-judgemental way.

Logical argumentation and reflection: Religious studies trains you to develop coherent arguments, reflect on deep questions, and challenge assumptions. Explain how this skill has prepared you for the reflective practice in medicine, where learning from experiences, adapting to feedback, and continually reassessing your approach is vital for professional growth.

PSYCHOLOGY

Understanding human behaviour and mental health: Studying topics such as mental health disorders, developmental psychology, and stress responses prepare you to understand the psychological aspects of patient care and recognise the mind–body connection in health.

Communication and interpersonal skills: Psychology emphasises active listening, empathy, and clear communication. Studying psychology teaches you to communicate effectively around difficult and sensitive topics. These skills enable you to build trust with patients and approach their concerns with empathy.

Research skills and evidence-based practice: Psychology involves analysing research studies, interpreting data, and applying evidence-based principles. This background prepares you to assess clinical studies, evaluate treatment effectiveness, and approach patient care with a scientific, research-informed mindset.

Analytical and critical thinking: Psychology encourages evaluating complex theories, critiquing research, and interpreting experimental findings. Critical thinking is essential for diagnosing patients, understanding research findings, and making evidence-based decisions.

Understanding of stress and coping mechanisms: Psychology explores the effects of stress and coping strategies, which is valuable in understanding patient experiences and managing your own well-being. This understanding helps you empathise with patients under stress and develop resilience in handling the emotional demands of a medical career.

Ethics and confidentiality: Psychology places strong emphasis on ethical principles like confidentiality and informed consent. This foundation helps prepare students for the ethical responsibilities expected in medicine.

Cultural sensitivity and awareness: Psychology often explores how cultural factors influence behaviour and mental health. This awareness is invaluable in a medical setting, as it allows for appreciation of diverse backgrounds of patients.

DESIGN TECHNOLOGY

Problem-solving and innovation: Design technology involves identifying problems and creating practical solutions, a process similar to diagnosing and treating medical issues. Developing prototypes or solutions strengthens problem-solving skills and prepares you to think creatively and adapt solutions for individual patients in medical practice.

Attention to detail and precision: Design technology requires precision in planning, measurements, and execution. Mention how this skill translates to patient care, where accuracy in procedures, data interpretation, and documentation can impact patient outcomes.

Manual dexterity and hand–eye coordination: Design technology involves working with tools and materials, improving fine motor skills that are directly applicable to medical procedures, such as suturing or handling medical instruments.

Research and evidence-based approach: Design technology requires researching materials, user needs, and functionality to create effective designs. Evidence-based practice involves evaluating clinical research, understanding patient needs, and finding effective treatments.

Project management and time management: Projects are managed from concept to completion, developing skills in organisation, time management, and prioritisation. Balancing studies, clinical duties, and patient care requires careful planning.

Resilience and adaptability: Projects often require overcoming design flaws or revising plans – teaching resilience and adaptability. Working through setbacks during projects prepares you for the challenges in medicine, where resilience and adaptability are key to handling difficult cases and learning from clinical experiences.

Understanding of your clients' needs: Designing with the end user in mind nurtures empathy and awareness of individual needs. Relate this to patient care, explaining how creating user-centred designs has prepared you to consider each patient's unique circumstances and needs.

COMPUTING

Analytical and logical thinking: Structured problem-solving and logical reasoning are required to develop algorithms and debug code. These skills are transferable, where diagnosing patients and interpreting complex data involve a systematic, analytical approach.

Data analysis and interpretation: You will have learned to analyse data sets and extract meaningful insights. These skills will allow you to interpret clinical data, such as lab results and patient records, and make informed, data-driven decisions in patient care.

Understanding of health technology and software: Computing has likely exposed you to software and possibly to areas like AI or data management, which are increasingly relevant in modern medicine. Your background in technology will help you adapt to electronic health records, telemedicine, and future innovations that improve patient care.

Attention to detail and precision: Writing code requires high precision and careful attention to detail, as small errors can lead to significant issues. This can be related to medicine, where accuracy is essential in diagnostics, treatment planning, and patient safety.

Problem-solving and troubleshooting: Solving issues and optimising code require perseverance and adaptability. These skills are applicable in medicine, where you'll need to troubleshoot complex patient cases, adapt to changing conditions, and continuously learn from clinical experiences.

Project and time management: Projects often involve setting goals, planning workflows, and meeting deadlines, developing time management skills. This experience helps you to handle the demands of medical school and the ability to prioritise and manage tasks in a high-pressure environment.

Ethics and data confidentiality: Computing emphasises responsible data management and cybersecurity, which align with the ethics and confidentiality standards in medicine. Understanding data security prepares you to handle patient information with care and confidentiality.

GEOGRAPHY

Analytical and problem-solving skills: Geography requires analysing complex systems, whether related to physical environments or human populations, and understanding how various factors interact. This analytical mindset is crucial, where diagnosing patients involves assessing multiple factors such as symptoms, medical history, and lifestyle.

Data interpretation and geographic information systems: You'll have worked with data, maps, and geographic information systems. The ability to interpret and analyse data is essential, especially when reviewing patient information, interpreting test results, or evaluating the effectiveness of treatments. Your ability to handle and interpret geographical data will prepare you for similar tasks in medical practice.

Understanding of public health and environmental factors: Geography examines the relationship between environments and human health. Studying environmental issues, such as pollution or climate change, will deepen your understanding of how environmental factors affect health.

Communication and collaboration: Geography often involves collaborative projects and presenting findings clearly. In medicine, effective communication with colleagues and patients is crucial. Presenting findings will strengthen your ability to explain complex ideas clearly, something vital for patient consultations and teamwork in healthcare settings.

Global and cultural awareness: Studying topics such as global development, population dynamics, and urbanisation equips you with a broader awareness of the disparities in healthcare access and quality across the world. Understanding the cultural context of a patient's life can inform more empathetic and effective care.

Critical thinking and decision-making: Geography encourages critical thinking when assessing how human activities impact the environment, requiring careful evaluation of evidence and consideration of multiple perspectives. This is key when assessing patient conditions, considering different diagnostic options, and making informed decisions regarding treatment plans.

Demonstration of strong academic achievements

You can showcase your academic strengths not only through your subject choices, but also through specific educational achievements. These accomplishments reflect your academic potential, strong work ethic, and your ability to manage the intellectual demands of a medical degree.

While UCAS advises applicants not to mention specific grades in the personal statement (as these are recorded elsewhere on the application form), there are still many effective ways to demonstrate strong academic performance.

Consider the following:

1. **Class rankings and year position**
   If you've consistently placed among the top students in your year group or within a particular subject, this can be a powerful way to demonstrate academic excellence. While personal statements should not mention specific grades (as per UCAS guidelines), referring to your ranking or relative position provides a clear, quantifiable measure of your success without breaching that rule.

   Being ranked top in your year for a subject like biology or chemistry, or placing within the top 5% of your class, shows not only strong academic ability but also consistent effort, discipline, and motivation. If your school publishes internal rankings, uses performance bands, or awards positions based on assessments or cumulative performance, these can all be valid forms of evidence.

   This kind of achievement also demonstrates your ability to perform well under pressure—whether in exams, timed coursework, or practical assessments—and suggests that you're academically prepared for the challenges of a medical degree.

   Even if you weren't always at the very top, placing highly in a competitive environment or being recognised for significant improvement can also be compelling. It's especially worth highlighting if your school or college has a strong academic reputation, or if you've excelled in a particularly rigorous cohort.

   Ultimately, referencing your class ranking helps demonstrate that your academic performance stands out not just in isolation, but in comparison with others, an important factor in the highly competitive field of medicine.

2. **Awards and recognition**
   If you've received any awards, prizes, or formal commendations during your education, this is an excellent opportunity to highlight them. These recognitions serve as external validation of your academic performance and work ethic, and help reinforce your credibility as a high-achieving, committed student.

   Examples might include subject-specific prizes, such as awards for excellence in biology, chemistry, or mathematics; broader honours like headteacher's commendations, academic excellence awards, or honours for consistently high performance. Some schools or colleges also offer internal distinctions such as "Student of the Year" or awards for most improved performance, which can also be valuable to mention—especially if they reflect resilience, progress, or determination.

   If you've been named to a dean's list or equivalent academic honour roll, be sure to include it. Even nominations for prestigious awards or scholarships can demonstrate your standing among your peers. When referencing these achievements, try to briefly explain what the award was for, whether it was based on exam results, coursework, overall contribution, or teacher recommendation.

   Including these recognitions in your personal statement shows that your efforts have been noticed and appreciated by your school or academic community, and that you have consistently demonstrated the kind of excellence and discipline expected in medicine.

3. **Competitive exams and external achievements**
   Taking part in academic competitions, such as the UK biology Olympiad, chemistry challenge, senior maths challenge, or similar subject-specific contests, demonstrates much more than subject knowledge. It shows initiative, intellectual curiosity, and a genuine enthusiasm for learning beyond the classroom syllabus.

   These competitions are typically voluntary and often require independent preparation, which reflects your ability to take ownership of your learning, an essential skill for medical students. Engaging with advanced, unfamiliar content also indicates critical thinking, problem-solving ability, and resilience, especially when facing complex or unfamiliar questions.

   If you achieved a certificate, bronze/silver/gold award, or a distinction, make sure to mention it, as these achievements are nationally recognised and highly regarded by admissions tutors. However, even if you didn't place or win, your willingness to participate still says a great deal about your ambition and academic motivation.

You can also reflect briefly on what you learned or how the experience influenced your interest in medicine. For instance, the problem-solving aspects of the Maths Challenge might have strengthened your analytical thinking, while a chemistry competition could have sparked an interest in drug design or biochemical processes.

These kinds of experiences show that you're not just meeting academic expectations, you're actively seeking out opportunities to grow, challenge yourself, and engage with your chosen subjects on a deeper level. All of this helps build a compelling case for your readiness for medical study.

4. **Early or advanced subject study**
If you've taken on a subject early, such as sitting a GCSE or A level before your peers, or have chosen an unusually demanding or diverse subject combination, this can be a strong indicator of academic maturity, self-discipline, and motivation. Medical schools look for applicants who are not only high achievers but also willing to challenge themselves and go beyond what is expected.

Studying a subject early often requires working independently or at a faster pace, which mirrors the self-directed learning style needed in medical school. For example, completing GCSE biology a year early, or taking further mathematics alongside three science A levels, shows you're capable of handling complex material under time pressure. Likewise, combining science subjects with a contrasting discipline such as English literature, philosophy, or a modern language demonstrates intellectual breadth and the ability to manage a diverse workload.

These decisions also reflect good time management and the capacity to prioritise, which are critical skills for a future doctor. If you undertook advanced study through an external course, online programme, or extension module (e.g. a university taster course or MOOC in medical sciences), it shows genuine passion for learning and a proactive approach to your development.

Even if these efforts didn't result in formal awards, your willingness to stretch yourself academically speaks volumes about your mindset and your preparation for the rigour of medical training.

Projects or activities undertaken in an educational context

If you focus solely on how your subjects connect to medicine, your personal statement may end up sounding similar to others. To make your statement stand out, consider including any special projects or activities you've been involved in that bring those subjects to life. These could include:

- Conferences, talks, masterclasses, extracurricular courses
- Extended Project Qualifications (EPQs)
- Essays
- Research projects
- Scholarships
- School projects
- Presentations
- Participation in debating societies
- Contribution to the school newsletter articles
- Involvement in school health initiatives
- Young enterprise schemes

You can mention any projects you led or took part in, as long as they were part of your educational experience and not external activities. For each of these experiences, reflect on what you learned, the skills you applied in managing the project, and the personal qualities you demonstrated along the way.

Here are some skills or personal qualities you could highlight in your statement:

Communication skills
- Clearly and confidently articulating ideas (verbally and in writing)
- Developing persuasive speaking skills through debates or presentations
- Engaging diverse audiences through conferences, talks, or written work
- Listening and responding thoughtfully in discussions or debates

Time management
- Balancing academic work with extracurricular commitments
- Meeting deadlines and managing multiple responsibilities

Attention to detail
- Ensuring accuracy and precision in research, writing, and presentations
- Recognising nuances that influence decision-making

Research & data analysis
- Collecting, synthesising, and evaluating information
- Researching and applying findings to practical challenges
- Analysing data and using insights to inform decisions in healthcare

Project management & organisation
- Planning and executing long-term projects or assignments
- Managing multiple tasks and deadlines while maintaining standards
- Setting clear goals, tracking progress, and adapting plans as needed

Teamwork & collaboration
- Working with others on group projects or school initiatives
- Sharing responsibility and supporting teammates
- Providing constructive feedback and managing conflict effectively

Problem-solving & adaptability
- Identifying solutions to challenges in research, projects, or debates
- Thinking creatively to find innovative solutions
- Adapting to changes and finding alternative approaches
- Responding flexibly to situations and overcoming obstacles

Critical thinking & analysis
- Evaluating complex information to draw evidence-based conclusions
- Challenging assumptions and identifying biases in research/projects
- Analysing findings logically and systematically
- Addressing ethical dilemmas and navigating moral challenges

Leadership & initiative
- Leading and guiding peers, making informed decisions
- Making decisions under pressure or in difficult situations
- Motivating others and encouraging team collaboration
- Taking responsibility for successes and setbacks

Resilience & stress management
- Managing tight deadlines or limited resources effectively
- Staying solution-focused during adversity
- Adapting to unforeseen challenges and learning from setbacks
- Handling failure constructively
- Using mistakes as learning opportunities

Leadership and positions of responsibility

Positions of responsibility, inside and outside the classroom, can say a great deal about your character, maturity, and readiness for the challenges of medical school and a career in healthcare. Medicine is not only academically demanding but also requires strong interpersonal and leadership skills. If you've held any roles that demonstrate these qualities, it's important to include them in your personal statement and reflect on what you learned from the experience.

Here are some examples of relevant roles:

- **Head student, deputy head, or prefect:** These roles often involve representing the student body, helping to maintain school values, supporting peers, and sometimes even contributing to policy discussions with staff. They demonstrate your ability to take initiative, communicate effectively, and act as a role model.

- **Student council member or house captain:** Positions that involve speaking on behalf of your peers, organising events, or coordinating activities show that you can collaborate, listen, and lead.

- **Subject ambassador or peer mentor:** Acting as a mentor to younger students or helping with tutoring shows responsibility, patience, and a willingness to support others – skills vital for anyone entering the medical profession.

- **Organising or leading clubs and societies:** Whether you founded a science club, led a debate team, or organised a language exchange group, these initiatives display creativity, commitment, and leadership. They're especially valuable if related to health, science, or service.

- **Sports captain or team leader:** Leadership in sport reflects teamwork, discipline, motivation, and resilience. These qualities are transferable to clinical environments, where working as part of a team under pressure is often required.

- **Volunteer coordinator or charity fundraiser:** If you've taken the lead in organising a volunteering initiative, charity drive, or awareness campaign, this shows compassion, project management, and community engagement – all qualities aligned with the values of medicine.

7 Section 3: Extracurricular

Section 3 asks: "What else have you done to prepare outside of education, and why are these experiences useful?"

In this section you need to address anything you've done outside of a school environment that may be relevant and has helped you acquire skills that are transferrable to a healthcare environment. This will include:

- Work experience in or outside of healthcare settings
- Volunteering roles
- Participation in community activities
- Caring for others
- Exposure to medical conditions
- Attending relevant courses or conferences
- Reading medical books, journals, or articles
- Holding leadership or responsibility roles
- Proficiency in additional languages
- Achievements and awards
- Hobbies, interests, and activities
- Plans for a gap year

For each point, you'll need to describe the experience or achievement and reflect on the skills you demonstrated or developed, highlighting their relevance to a career in medicine.

Given that you have approximately 2,000 characters for section 3 and that around 1000 characters may need to be devoted to your medical work experience, you might not be able to include everything you've done in your social life. Therefore, choose the experiences or achievements that are most impressive or best highlight your personal qualities. Remember, it's not about quantity but about showing the depth and relevance of your experiences. Admissions tutors are looking for quality, not superhuman accomplishments!

The following sections will dive deeper into each of these points.

7.1 Work experience related to healthcare

Why do you need work experience?

Medical schools expect applicants to demonstrate relevant work experience, either by observing healthcare professionals or through hands-on involvement in a caring role. This helps to show admissions tutors that you have an understanding of what a career in caring for others entails, and that you hold a realistic view of the challenges and demands involved in working in healthcare.

Different medical schools apply different criteria when it comes to work experience. Some prefer a combination of observational and practical experience, while others value ongoing involvement over one-off placements. With this in mind, when deciding what to include, aim to present a range of settings and experiences to meet as many expectations as possible.

What work experience should you include?

Many applicants mistakenly think that work experience must include either working with a doctor in a hospital or shadowing their local GP, but this is not strictly true. This type of work experience is not always available and can be hard to find in a healthcare environment. Volunteer placements in hospitals, general practices and other clinical settings are often limited due to confidentiality concerns. Don't worry if you haven't had the chance to shadow a GP or meet patients on a hospital ward; there are many other areas related to medicine where you can demonstrate worthwhile experience. Some of these are described below.

Shadowing a doctor in a hospital
This is the most sought-after form of work experience, though securing a hospital placement can be quite challenging. Some applicants are fortunate enough to arrange placements shadowing doctors from various specialties across multiple wards. If you are lucky enough to shadow a doctor on the wards, you will gain first-hand insight into how multidisciplinary teams work together to meet the complex needs of patients.

Teamwork and communication will likely be among your key learning points, and you may observe how sensitive and delicate situations, such as breaking bad news, are handled by the healthcare team. These moments may affect not only the patients and their families, but also the doctors and other healthcare professionals involved in delivering the news.

Shadowing a GP in a practice
As with hospital placements, securing experience in primary care can be difficult, often due to concerns around patient confidentiality – particularly if you're seeking a placement in a local GP surgery. You'll notice that the doctor–patient relationship in general practice is significantly different from that in hospitals. Consultations tend to be one-to-one, and GPs often build long-term relationships with their patients.

While the dynamic of a multidisciplinary team differs from that in a hospital setting, you'll still see how healthcare professionals collaborate in general practice – offering services such as physiotherapy, counselling, minor surgery, immunisations and more.

GP surgeries also function as small businesses, employing non-clinical staff such as practice managers, receptionists and telephonists, all of whom play key roles in keeping the practice running efficiently. You may have the chance to observe practice or management meetings and gain a valuable glimpse into the operational side of general practice, which some applicants may initially overlook as less relevant to a medical career.

The variety of experiences you'll gain in general practice can greatly enrich your personal statement. Be sure to include detailed reflections on what you observed and learned.

Working with other associated healthcare professionals
Doctors are just one part of a wider healthcare team. Gaining experience with other professionals, such as biomedical scientists, haematologists, nurses, or healthcare assistants, can offer valuable insight, which is well worth including in your personal statement.

Even volunteering in a non-clinical capacity, such as running the tea and coffee trolley, chatting with patients and their families, and offering comfort, can give you an important understanding of the patient experience and the emotional impact of care. In a GP practice, for example, you might assist a practice nurse with clinics for asthma or diabetes.

It may be easier to obtain a placement at a GP reception desk, but try to ensure that you gain meaningful exposure to the clinical side of medicine and avoid being limited to administrative tasks like filing or photocopying.

Working in residential or care homes and hospices
There are many valuable caring environments outside of hospitals and surgeries where you can gain relevant experience, such as residential homes, care homes or hospices, in a voluntary or paid capacity.

In these environments, you may observe doctors adapting their consultation styles based on patients' needs and conditions. The emotional depth of these experiences can be profound, and for many students, time spent in a hospice or care home is a significant turning point in confirming their desire to pursue a medical career.

Volunteering
Volunteering is a popular and relatively accessible form of work experience. It can be arranged through a variety of organisations and offers many opportunities to develop key skills relevant to a career in medicine. Examples include:

- Working with the elderly in the community. There are many ways to support elderly individuals, whether through helping with shopping, cleaning, entertainment, or basic personal care tasks. Your experience might take place in a care home or involve home visits and meal services for older people living independently. Such work offers valuable insight into the social care needs of an ageing population.

- Working in youth centres, schools or summer camps. Demonstrating an ability to engage with a wide age range is important, and working with children and young people, whether in a youth club, school, or summer camp setting, is another common and useful form of work experience. Supporting children with learning difficulties or regularly caring for young people with specific conditions (such as autism) can help to develop your empathy, patience and communication skills.

- Working in other care centres. There are many other settings where you can gain experience with individuals requiring support, including centres for people with physical or learning disabilities, as well as those supporting disadvantaged or vulnerable groups. Volunteering with community organisations, faith-based groups, or charities that work with the homeless or disabled can also be highly relevant. These experiences help to build your understanding of the diverse challenges faced by people in different circumstances and highlight your commitment to caring for others.

In all of these roles, you should aim to reflect on what you have learned, particularly in relation to key qualities such as compassion, resilience, and communication, and consider how these experiences have shaped your motivation to pursue a career in medicine. In addition, if you've volunteered in environments where resources are limited, such as a food bank, homeless shelter, or community organisation, you'll have developed adaptability, resilience, and the ability to think creatively to solve problems. You also gain insight into the social determinants of health, as well as the ability to interact with individuals from diverse backgrounds, an important skill when working in healthcare.

First aid
Volunteering for St John Ambulance and the British Red Cross is an extremely popular form of work experience which many prospective medical school students consider. First aid is also a useful skill to acquire regardless of your intentions to study medicine or not and will teach you some basic life-saving and triage techniques.

Charity and fundraising work
This may sound like unlikely relevant work experience potential, but providing you can explain the relevance of this to your application for medical school, it can sound as interesting as shadowing a doctor. If you want to mention charity and fundraising activities as relevant work experience to give you an insight into the medical world, make sure that you show the link to your motivation.

For example, collecting money at a train station for a charity would not, by itself, constitute a strong motivation factor unless you had previously been given the chance to meet some of the beneficiaries of the charity or felt particularly strongly about the lack of care these people received. In that case the motivation factor for medicine would be the awareness that you had developed of the fact that some members of society are less catered for than others.

7.2 Work experience unrelated to healthcare

Some medical schools place particular value on candidates who show an ongoing commitment to work experience. In fact, they may regard a regular Saturday job at a supermarket more favourably than a one-off week spent filing paperwork at a GP surgery. Therefore, if you have undertaken any consistent paid or voluntary work, it is well worth including, even if it's something as straightforward as stacking shelves. This can demonstrate your sense of responsibility, reliability, and, in many cases, your ability to communicate effectively with people from a wide range of backgrounds. It also provides evidence of your capacity to work under pressure in a busy, real-world environment.

Customer service role (retail, hospitality, call centre)
These roles help you develop excellent communication skills and the ability to stay calm under pressure. You'll become more confident when interacting with patients, colleagues, and other healthcare professionals, allowing you to build strong relationships and provide effective care. You'll also enhance your ability to manage multiple tasks at once and prioritise effectively, which is crucial in the fast-paced environment of healthcare.

Hospitality or restaurant work (waitstaff, barista, chef)
This kind of work helps you stay organised under pressure, collaborate effectively within a team, and manage patient or colleague inquiries – skills that are essential in a medical career. You'll be able to provide high-quality care in fast-paced environments, work well with multidisciplinary teams, and communicate clearly with patients and healthcare professionals.

Working in administration (e.g. receptionist, office assistant)
Administration roles help you develop strong organisational and time management skills, which are crucial when handling patient records, appointments, and medical paperwork. You'll also learn to manage confidential information, communicate effectively with patients and staff, and prioritise tasks in a busy environment.

Manual work (gardening, warehouse work, delivery)
Manual work can demonstrate your work ethic, discipline, and ability to stay focused under demanding conditions. It helps you develop resilience and perseverance, qualities that are crucial in the healthcare environment.

7.3 Personal interests and achievements

The third section of your personal statement offers the opportunity to discuss the personal attributes and skills you have developed through various life experiences relevant to a career in medicine, even if they are not directly within a medical field.

Doctors must be able to communicate effectively on various levels with patients and their families, colleagues, medical students, and NHS managers. Effective communication involves not only the ability to speak clearly but also to listen attentively, empathise, and give and receive feedback. Your personal statement will be particularly valued if you can demonstrate experience in communicating with different groups, especially if this involved overcoming communication barriers.

Working in medicine also requires a high level of teamwork. You should aim to demonstrate in your personal statement that you can work well in a team and that you are a reliable and responsible individual who can actively contribute. It is important to show that you can support and respect others and understand the impact your actions have on those around you. You can provide examples of teamwork from experiences outside of school/college or university, or from your current career if you are a graduate applicant.

Other personal attributes that can be highlighted here include your leadership skills, particularly through any positions of responsibility you have held outside of the educational environment. You could also showcase your organisational skills and provide examples of when you have shown initiative.

While you are under no obligation to pursue personal hobbies and interests, mentioning them gives you an ideal opportunity to explain how these activities demonstrate your personal drive, ambition, and desire to achieve. You can reflect on how these qualities are relevant to your application to study medicine and your future career as a doctor.

Finally, through your research and understanding of the demands of a career in medicine, you will hopefully have gained an appreciation of the extreme pressures faced by healthcare professionals, and the importance of managing stress through other activities and interests. This is an ideal place to describe how you currently manage your work–life balance and how you would plan to maintain this balance during your time in medical school and beyond. Reflect on the ways you relax and relieve stress, so the admissions tutors can see that you will be able to cope with the pressures and demands that lie ahead.

Here are some examples of what you could include:

Personal life experiences or responsibilities:
If you have faced challenging situations in your personal life, such as caring for a family member, overcoming adversity, or balancing significant personal commitments with your academic studies – it's worth mentioning. These experiences often highlight qualities that are crucial for a medical career, such as empathy, resilience, adaptability, problem-solving, and emotional intelligence. Here are a few more examples of personal experiences that can be relevant:

- **Caring for a family member:** Taking on the role of a caregiver for a family member with a long-term illness, disability, or mental health condition is a significant responsibility. This experience allows you to develop strong empathy and an understanding of the emotional and practical needs of patients and their families. It teaches you how to manage complex care needs, communicate effectively with medical professionals, and balance personal and family obligations, all of which are essential in medical practice.

- **Supporting a sibling or relative with special needs:** If you've helped a sibling or relative navigate life with special educational needs, autism, or another developmental condition, you'll have developed valuable skills in patience, communication, and problem-solving. These experiences can make you more adaptable when working with patients who may face similar challenges, as well as help you understand the importance of individualised care and the need to be resourceful.

- **Overcoming personal health struggles:** If you've had to deal with a personal health issue, such as a chronic illness or mental health challenge, it can provide you with unique insight into the patient experience. Understanding the physical and emotional toll of illness, along with how to navigate the healthcare system, can increase your empathy and resilience. This also demonstrates perseverance and the ability to balance personal difficulties with academic or professional commitments, qualities that are important for a medical career.

- **Balancing work and studies:** Taking on a part-time job while managing your studies demonstrates time management, work ethic, and responsibility. You learn to prioritise and stay organised, as well as how to work efficiently under pressure – skills that will serve you well when juggling the demands of medical school and clinical placements. A role such as a tutor, shop assistant, or delivery driver can also help you develop strong communication and problem-solving abilities, which are vital in medicine.

- **Dealing with personal loss or trauma:** Experiencing personal loss such as the death of a loved one or experiencing a traumatic event can cultivate emotional intelligence and coping mechanisms. It teaches you how to manage grief, support others in emotional distress, and develop the resilience needed to face difficult situations. This emotional maturity is crucial when working with patients who may be going through similar challenges.

- **Taking responsibility in a family or household setting:** If you have taken on significant responsibilities in a family setting, such as managing household duties, budgeting, or caring for younger siblings, you'll have developed organisational and leadership skills. These experiences show your ability to stay focused and handle responsibilities, often in a high-pressure environment, which translates well to managing complex patient cases and working in high-stress medical situations.

- **Navigating cultural or social challenges:** If you have had to navigate challenges related to your cultural or social background, whether moving to a new country, adjusting to a different educational system, or working in a diverse community, highlight the adaptability and cultural sensitivity you developed. These experiences will allow you to better understand patients from diverse backgrounds and provide compassionate, patient-centred care.

- **Managing a personal project or initiative:** Running or starting a personal project – whether a charity initiative, a small business, or a creative endeavour – shows initiative, problem-solving, and perseverance. Balancing the demands of running such a project alongside other responsibilities also highlights your organisational skills and your ability to adapt when faced with challenges. These qualities are essential for a medical student and future doctor.

- **Fostering emotional support for others:** If you've been a source of emotional support for friends or family members during times of hardship, this demonstrates empathy, active listening, and the ability to manage emotionally charged situations. These experiences will help you develop the bedside manner required to build trust and rapport with patients, especially those facing difficult health challenges.

Tutoring or mentoring
Engaging in tutoring or mentoring provides an excellent opportunity to reinforce your own understanding of complex concepts while simultaneously developing key leadership, motivational, and communication skills. As a tutor or mentor, you are often tasked with breaking down intricate ideas or subjects into simpler, digestible explanations, which requires a deep understanding of the material. This ability to clarify complex information is directly transferable to medicine, where you'll regularly need to explain complicated medical concepts to patients, families, or colleagues in a way they can easily understand.

One of the most important aspects of tutoring or mentoring is adapting your communication style to meet the needs of different individuals. Not every person learns or processes information the same way, so being able to adjust your approach—whether that's through analogies, visual aids, or hands-on examples—is a valuable skill in any medical career. In healthcare, you'll often need to communicate with patients from various backgrounds, with differing levels of understanding of medical terminology and concepts. Tailoring your communication to ensure clarity, while remaining empathetic and patient, is essential for effective patient care.

In addition, tutoring or mentoring strengthens your leadership abilities. As a mentor, you're responsible for guiding someone through challenges and motivating them to reach their full potential. This involves not only providing knowledge but also fostering a positive, supportive environment where the individual feels encouraged and empowered. These leadership skills are critical in medicine, where you'll be required to lead, support, and collaborate with multidisciplinary teams to ensure the best possible outcomes for your patients. Whether you're supervising a junior colleague, participating in team-based care, or leading a medical initiative, your ability to inspire and guide others will be fundamental to your success.

Moreover, mentoring and tutoring also teach you patience, resilience, and how to handle setbacks – skills that are highly relevant in healthcare, where challenges and unexpected situations arise regularly. The experience of helping someone overcome a difficult subject or achieve their goals can be incredibly fulfilling and will help develop the emotional intelligence necessary to connect with patients and colleagues in a compassionate, understanding manner.

By showcasing your tutoring or mentoring experience, you demonstrate that you possess not only academic proficiency but also the leadership, communication, and interpersonal skills needed to excel in the collaborative, patient-centred environment of healthcare.

Leadership roles in clubs and organisations

Taking on leadership roles in clubs, societies, or other organisations prepares you for the responsibilities of being a doctor. Whether leading a sports team or organising an event, these experiences demonstrate your ability to guide others, make decisions, and take accountability – skills essential in medicine. Here are some examples of roles that candidates commonly refer to, with an indication of the skills they help demonstrate:

- Team captain: Leadership, motivation, communication, and the ability to bring people together to work towards a common goal.

- Youth group leader: Mentoring ability, empathy, and responsibility in a supervisory or pastoral role.

- Volunteer coordinator: Organisation, time management, delegation, and the ability to inspire others.

- Committee member: Collaboration, planning, and the ability to voice ideas or concerns constructively.

- First aider or cadet leader: Calmness under pressure, a basic clinical understanding, and care for others.

- Organiser for fundraising: Initiative, responsibility, and commitment to causes beyond yourself.

- Youth representative: Advocacy, maturity, and the ability to communicate effectively with peers and adults.

Effective leadership in healthcare goes beyond giving direction. It involves listening, delegating, resolving conflict, and supporting others to achieve common goals. Reflecting on your leadership shows that you understand the importance of collaboration, emotional intelligence, and creating a positive team environment, which are key in multidisciplinary healthcare teams.

This section also offers an opportunity to highlight situations where you stayed calm and took initiative in challenging circumstances, or adapted your approach to different individuals. These insights demonstrate maturity and an understanding of leadership's human side, which is highly valued in clinical practice.

By showcasing how you've led by example, motivated peers, and managed responsibility, you'll present yourself as ready to contribute positively to healthcare, both as a student and as a future doctor.

Participation in clubs and societies

Active participation in clubs and societies is an excellent way to demonstrate that you are a well-rounded individual with the ability to commit to activities beyond your academic studies. It shows that you are curious, motivated, and capable of managing your time effectively.

You might be a long-standing member of a debating society, a sports team, a music ensemble, or a science or medical society. Involvement in these groups can showcase a wide range of transferable skills relevant to a medical career. For example, team sports highlight teamwork, leadership, and resilience under pressure, while debate or public speaking clubs can show that you're confident, articulate, and capable of thinking critically.

Even hobbies like chess, drama, creative writing, or coding clubs can be relevant if you're able to reflect on what they've taught you, whether it's focus, patience, attention to detail, or creative problem-solving. All of these are valuable in a medical setting.

Ultimately, mentioning your involvement in clubs and societies is not just about listing hobbies; it's about using these experiences to show your character, your personal drive, and how you've developed qualities that will help you succeed in medical school and as a doctor.

Social media management or content creation

Engaging in social media management or content creation equips you with valuable skills that can directly transfer to a medical career. It allows you to hone your communication abilities, as it involves conveying information clearly and effectively to diverse audiences. In the context of healthcare, this is especially important, as doctors need to communicate complex medical information to patients, colleagues, and the public in an understandable and compassionate manner.

Managing social media platforms or creating content also enhances your time management skills, as it often requires balancing multiple tasks—such as creating posts, responding to messages, and maintaining engagement—while meeting deadlines. These skills are crucial in the fast-paced environment of medicine, where you must prioritise patient care, manage various responsibilities, and adapt quickly to changing circumstances.

Moreover, content creation encourages creativity and innovation, qualities that can be valuable in problem-solving and presenting information in ways that are engaging and accessible. Being able to stay organised and focused under pressure, while working towards specific goals, mirrors the challenges faced in healthcare, where maintaining patient outcomes and team objectives is paramount.

Additionally, these experiences may demonstrate your adaptability and awareness of modern communication platforms, which are becoming increasingly important in the healthcare field, particularly in areas like patient education and public health campaigns. By highlighting your social media and content creation experience, you can show that you possess the communication, organisational, and time management skills essential for success in a medical career.

Hobbies, personal interests and group activities
Your hobbies and personal interests provide valuable insight into who you are beyond your academic achievements. Including these in your personal statement allows you to show qualities such as dedication, motivation, and a healthy approach to work–life balance, all of which are crucial for managing the demands of a medical career.

Whether you've committed yourself to individual pursuits like learning a musical instrument, hiking, running, or painting, or taken part in team sports, orchestras, or drama groups, these activities can speak volumes about your discipline, resilience, and enthusiasm for learning. Regular involvement in a hobby shows that you can set goals and persevere in developing a skill.

Group activities, such as team sports or theatre productions, are particularly valuable in demonstrating teamwork, communication, and time management skills. You can also use them to highlight your ability to lead, support others, and stay calm under pressure – important qualities in a healthcare setting.

Taking part in niche or academic interest groups like investment clubs, coding circles, or book clubs, reflects intellectual curiosity and analytical thinking. Participation in physical or creative activities showcases your emotional expression, confidence, or commitment to your own well-being.

In addition, time spent on hobbies reflects your ability to maintain a balanced life. Engaging in activities outside of your studies helps you recharge and manage stress, a key factor in sustaining long-term success in medical school and practice.

Ultimately, your engagement in hobbies and group activities helps to paint a picture of someone who is balanced, self-aware, and capable of committing to long-term personal development – the kind of person well suited to a career in medicine.

Community, charity or religious activities
Active involvement in community groups, charitable organisations, or religious activities can provide strong evidence of your commitment to service, empathy, and your ability to work with diverse groups of people.

You might have volunteered at a food bank, participated in fundraising campaigns, or supported the running of events for a local charity. These kinds of activities can demonstrate initiative, organisational skills, and dedication to improving the lives of others.

If you've taken part in faith-based activities, such as assisting with Sunday school, running youth groups, or helping to organise religious festivals, this can show your ability to communicate with and guide others, as well as your ability to manage responsibility in trusted roles. You might also have supported vulnerable members of your community, such as the elderly or newly arrived migrants, through religious or cultural groups, showing compassion and cultural awareness.

You could also reflect on what you learned through these roles – such as patience, teamwork, public speaking, or conflict resolution – and how these skills will help you interact sensitively and effectively with patients from all walks of life.

Overall, your involvement in these activities shows more than just community engagement – it can reflect your values, your motivation to make a positive difference, and your ability to balance personal commitments alongside academic life, all of which are important qualities for medical students and future doctors.

Technological projects
Involvement in technological projects, whether independently or in a group, demonstrates problem-solving, creativity, initiative, and resilience. Creating a website, designing an app, or working with coding, data analysis, or robotics are experiences worth mentioning in your personal statement.

These projects show you can tackle complex challenges, learn independently, and adapt to new technologies – qualities valuable in modern medicine. As healthcare becomes more reliant on digital systems, showcasing technological literacy and a proactive learning approach can help you stand out.

Technological projects also develop analytical thinking and attention to detail – skills that directly apply to clinical settings where precision and logical reasoning are crucial. Collaborative projects highlight communication and teamwork, particularly with diverse groups. Including such work shows you're resourceful, forward-thinking, and committed to developing relevant competencies.

Character-building or simulation exercises
Involvement in activities such as the Duke of Edinburgh's Award or Young Enterprise schemes are commonly mentioned and demonstrate initiative, organisational and leadership skills.

A useful point to mention here is that you will get more credit for your achievements if you give examples of how you demonstrated these personal attributes, than by simply saying something like "through good teamwork, management and leadership, my team and I completed the expedition safely". In other words, describe what you actually contributed personally.

Gap years
A well-structured gap year can be a valuable addition to your personal statement, especially if you used the time to develop skills, gain life experience, or explore healthcare settings. Planning and executing a gap year shows maturity, independence, and initiative. Whether you raised funds,

organised travel, or arranged work placements, these actions demonstrate responsibility and foresight.

If you volunteered, worked, or participated in structured programmes, especially in healthcare, education, or community service, you can highlight attributes like adaptability, resilience, communication, and cultural awareness. These qualities are vital in medicine, where you'll work with people from diverse backgrounds and situations.

Even non-clinical experiences – such as customer-facing roles, teaching abroad, or volunteering – can reflect teamwork, leadership, and empathy. What matters is how you link these experiences to your motivation for studying medicine.

A gap year should be seen not as a break from learning, but as an opportunity to grow and prepare for the challenges of medical school and beyond.

Travel
Travel can effectively demonstrate your awareness of different societies and cultures, particularly if it has shaped your values or influenced your understanding of healthcare and social issues. This doesn't need to be limited to gap-year travel; many candidates travel extensively due to family or parental work commitments.

Such experiences highlight cultural sensitivity, adaptability, and open-mindedness, all essential qualities for a medical student and future doctor. Exposure to diverse healthcare systems and social norms deepens your understanding of how backgrounds influence patients' needs and experiences of care.

Reflecting on your travels in your personal statement shows how they broadened your perspective, increased empathy, or sparked an interest in global health. Practical aspects such as navigating new environments, overcoming language barriers, or handling unexpected challenges, demonstrate resilience, independence, and resourcefulness.

Competitions and awards
Achievements in competitions or awards schemes can offer valuable evidence of your motivation, determination, and ability to excel under pressure. These experiences not only highlight your intellectual or creative strengths but also demonstrate personal qualities such as resilience, self-discipline, and a willingness to challenge yourself.

Here are some examples of competitions and awards and the skills they demonstrate:

- Essay competitions: Critical thinking, the ability to construct arguments, and communicate ideas clearly, skills essential in academic and clinical settings.

- Public speaking or debating: Confidence, clear communication, and the ability to think on your feet and express ideas with clarity and empathy.

- Duke of Edinburgh's Award: Independence, commitment, teamwork, leadership, and resilience in unfamiliar or challenging situations.

- Music performances and prizes: Dedication, discipline, and confidence, especially when performing under pressure or collaborating in group settings such as orchestras or bands.

- Art or photography exhibitions: Creativity, attention to detail, and the ability to express complex ideas or emotions visually.

- Sports competitions: Teamwork, leadership, resilience, and the ability to perform under pressure.

- Martial arts grading: Perseverance, self-control, focus, and commitment to long-term personal development.

Reflecting on how you prepared for and responded to these challenges can help you show maturity, growth, and readiness for the demanding nature of medical training.

Qualifications or certificates

Obtaining certain qualifications and certificates can demonstrate a range of aptitudes and skills relevant to the medical profession. For example:

- **First aid certification** demonstrates the ability to remain calm and think clearly under pressure, an essential quality in medical practice. The training places individuals in simulated high-stress scenarios where rapid, accurate decision-making is critical, closely mirroring the demands of clinical environments. It also develops key skills in prioritisation and triage, teaching how to assess situations quickly, identify the most urgent needs, and act effectively. Beyond the practical aspects, providing first aid requires taking responsibility for someone's well-being at a vulnerable moment, nurturing a strong sense of accountability and duty – core values in the medical profession.

- **Basic Life Support (BLS) training** equips individuals with essential clinical skills, such as performing high-quality CPR, managing airways, and using an automated external defibrillator (AED), all vital in emergency medical care. The training emphasises precision under pressure and reinforces the importance of acting quickly and confidently in life-threatening situations. It also fosters teamwork, as BLS scenarios often involve coordinating with others to deliver effective, time-critical interventions. These experiences not only build technical competence but also develop situational awareness, composure, and a readiness to take initiative – traits that are indispensable in any healthcare setting.

- **Language certifications** highlight strong communication skills, cultural awareness, and the ability to connect with people from diverse backgrounds, all of which are crucial in medicine. Studying a language requires active listening, attention to detail, and the ability to interpret both verbal and non-verbal cues, skills that directly translate to patient interactions and clinical consultations. It also fosters empathy and patience, particularly when navigating conversations where misunderstandings can easily occur. In a healthcare setting, even a basic knowledge of another language can help build trust, reduce anxiety, and make care more accessible, reinforcing the importance of inclusive, person-centred practice.

- **Music theory and performance** cultivate discipline, focus, and resilience, qualities that are directly transferable to the study and practice of medicine. Mastering a musical instrument requires consistent practice, attention to detail, and the ability to stay composed under pressure, especially during live performances or exams. These experiences help develop patience and perseverance, as progress is often gradual and demands long-term commitment, much like the journey through medical training. Music also encourages creative thinking and emotional expression, which can enhance empathy and interpersonal skills, contributing to a more compassionate and well-rounded approach to patient care.

- **Leadership training courses** develop confidence, initiative, and the ability to work effectively within a team – core attributes in any healthcare setting. These experiences teach how to communicate clearly, delegate tasks appropriately, and adapt to the needs of a group, all while maintaining a shared goal. They also encourage reflection, emotional intelligence, and ethical decision-making, which are vital when navigating complex situations in medicine. Importantly, leadership is not only about taking charge, but also about listening, supporting others, and leading by example – qualities essential for working within multidisciplinary teams and delivering patient-centred care. Workplace health and safety

- **Mental health first aid** provides essential skills in recognising, understanding, and responding to mental health crises with compassion and care. This training enhances emotional intelligence, teaching how to approach individuals in distress with empathy and without judgement. It fosters the ability to listen actively and provide initial support while encouraging professional help when needed, skills that are invaluable in healthcare settings where mental health is often intertwined with physical health. Mental health first aid also highlights the importance of reducing stigma and creating an environment where patients feel comfortable discussing their emotional and psychological well-being, ensuring a holistic approach to care.

8 Refining your personal statement

Once you have put together a first draft of your statement, the real work begins. Set it aside for a few hours or overnight, then reread it with fresh eyes. Does it make sense? Does it flow well? Is it too dull? Would some paragraphs read better if they were expanded with examples? Are some paragraphs too long or too short compared with others? Does the statement contain enough personal information, or is it merely a succession of facts? Is the content satisfactory, but you feel it could still be refined?

In this section, we present a number of tips you can follow to improve your statement.

Writing a story

Personal statements often feel generic because they lack a personal touch. One powerful way to add that touch is through storytelling. Stories can be woven into two key sections:

- In the introduction: For example, "Meeting Jason, an 8-year-old autistic boy, was one of the most frightening yet enlightening experiences of my life." This creates a memorable opening!

- In the work experience section: Instead of the usual "It showed me the importance of listening and caring", you could recount a specific moment, like reading to a patient in a hospice, that left a lasting impact.

This approach may not suit everyone, but it can make your personal statement stand out and leave a stronger impression. The story can focus on an experience or observation that highlighted a personal goal or insight into a career in medicine. It doesn't need to be overly emotional or humorous, but it should be meaningful and, above all, genuine. If you decide to include a story, ensure it's something you've experienced personally. Remember, if your story sparks an interview, you may be asked to elaborate, so it must be truthful.

While storytelling can capture the attention of admissions tutors, don't get too caught up in it at the expense of showcasing other essential qualities. They will still expect to see your aptitude and commitment to medicine, relevant work experience, and personal traits that reflect you as a well-rounded candidate – not just someone with a good story to tell.

In this book, you'll find several examples of personal statements where storytelling techniques have been used effectively.

The words aren't coming?

Creative writing comes naturally to some, but not to everyone. Even if you've had a productive brainstorming session and have plenty of ideas for your personal statement, you may still struggle with how to make it sound just right.

If you find yourself stuck, unable to start or experiencing writer's block, a great way to move forward is to look at examples of other personal statements. In this book, you'll find a variety of personal statements, each written in a unique style. Your school or college may also have examples from previous students.

Reading other personal statements can help you understand how others have explained their reasons for pursuing their chosen course. You'll see how they described their interests and skills, and how they incorporated these into their applications. Also, you'll get a sense of the different structures and writing styles used. By "style", we mean the tone, whether it's concise, eloquent, straightforward, descriptive, or more elaborate, not the actual language, as your UCAS application must, of course, be in English!

After reading a few examples, you'll be able to identify what works and what doesn't. You'll notice which explanations and descriptions resonate with you, and soon enough, you'll have a clear idea of what you want to express and how to express it.

However, an important point to remember is: while reading others' personal statements can provide inspiration, never copy someone else's work. You can draw ideas from them, but plagiarism is strictly prohibited.

Creating your own content, language, and style

When writing your personal statement, it's crucial to think about the style, language, and tone you want to use. This may not come naturally at first, and it may take a few drafts to find the right balance. Your first draft could be a mix of styles, but through editing, you'll refine it into a more cohesive and consistent tone. Here are some tips to help you transform your brainstormed ideas into the most effective and persuasive language:

- **Write when you're feeling enthusiastic:** This will help convey energy and passion in your statement, making it more engaging.

- **Use proper English and proofread:** Spelling, punctuation, and grammar are important. Mistakes can leave a negative impression of your attention to detail. Make sure terms like "orthopaedics", "paediatrics", or "gynaecology" are spelt correctly and use British English spelling (e.g., "paediatrics" vs. "pediatrics").

- **Avoid abbreviations or SMS language:** Keep your tone professional, and refrain from using shorthand or casual expressions.

- **Keep your language simple and clear:** You don't need to use complicated language. If you're not confident with complex words, stick to straightforward expressions that come across as more natural.

- **Use positive language:** Focus on what excites you about medicine and highlight the positive aspects of your experiences and skills.

- **Be concise:** Every word should serve a purpose. If something doesn't add value, leave it out. Your space is limited, so use it wisely.

- **Be sincere, not arrogant:** Aim to come across as genuine and humble. When describing work experience with people from different cultural or socio-economic backgrounds, use respectful language. For example, say "populations in disadvantaged areas" instead of "poor people".

- **Don't lie or exaggerate:** Your personal statement must be truthful. You may be asked about it during your interview, and any exaggerations or falsehoods will be quickly uncovered.

- **Stay on topic:** Stick to relevant details. If you find yourself straying off course, take a break and come back with a fresh perspective.

- **Avoid humour:** Humour is subjective, and the admissions tutors may not share your sense of humour. Stick to a professional tone.

- **Keep sentences short and impactful:** Aim for sentences around 15-20 words, varying sentence length to keep the writing dynamic. Focus on conveying one main point per sentence for clarity and impact.

By following these tips, you'll create a personal statement that is professional and engaging, helping you stand out in the admissions process.

Write in the active voice

Whether you realise it or not, unless you have a knack for creative writing and practise it regularly, you will naturally fall into the habit of writing in the passive voice. While this may seem fine at first, it results in sentences that are wordy, dull, and lack the impact that active voice can provide. For example:

Passive voice: "The patient was being cared for by a large team of doctors and nurses, and a wide range of skills was deployed by the team to make sure the patient was safely managed."

Active voice: "A large team of doctors and nurses cared for the patient, deploying a wide range of skills to make sure they managed him safely."

You can easily spot passive voice by looking for forms of the verb "to be", such as "was" or "were".

To reduce your use of passive voice and add more flair to your writing, incorporate some "power verbs" into your vocabulary. A list of suggested power verbs can be found at the end of this book. Review your draft personal statement, identify passive voice sentences, and rewrite them using power verbs to make your writing more compelling.

While it's fine to use some passive voice for variety, make sure to strike a balance between the two styles. The most effective personal statements feature far more active sentences than passive ones.

Avoid clichés

A cliché is an expression or phrase that has been used so frequently that it has lost its original impact and become predictable. The issue with clichés is that admissions tutors will have encountered them countless times, diminishing their effectiveness. If your goal is to create a unique and compelling personal statement, relying on clichés won't help you stand out.

For instance, stating something like, "Ever since I was young, I've wanted to be a doctor to help people" is a prime example of a cliché. It doesn't offer any insight into you as a person because it's a phrase that has been used repeatedly. Notice how vague it is, with no real details or examples to explain why you want to help people, how you like to help people, or who you specifically want to help. Plus, it's obvious that doctors aim to help people, so this isn't new or exciting information. Clichés like this are stale, overly familiar, and can cause the admissions tutor to lose interest quickly, making it hard to regain their attention.

Many clichés are broad generalisations that don't add real value or meaning. To make every word in your personal statement impactful, it's best to avoid these overused phrases.

Some common clichés often seen in medical school personal statements include:

- I am fascinated by the workings of the human brain.
- I am fascinated by the human body.
- I have a fascination with science and how the human body works.
- The functioning of the human body holds a particular fascination for me.
- The study of science is fascinating, particularly the human body.
- I have always been fascinated by the complexities of the human body.
- Science and the human body have always fascinated me.
- The complexities of the human body never cease to amaze me.
- I'm passionate about science.
- My interest in science has led me to pursue a career in medicine.
- Studying medicine will provide me with a challenge.
- I'm enthusiastic about science.
- I'm hardworking and often burn the candle at both ends.
- I like to do things by the book.
- My work has never given cause for complaint.
- I'm excited by the changing face of medicine.

- Studying medicine is a once-in-a-lifetime opportunity.
- Getting a place in medical school would be a dream come true.
- I hit the ground running when I set up a community kids club.
- I can really make a difference.
- I've always been a good communicator.
- My desire to study medicine stems from my childhood.
- I've always wanted to be a doctor.
- I enjoy caring for people.
- I thrive under pressure.
- I love helping people.
- I want to save lives.
- I want to make a difference in the world.
- I was a good science student.
- Medicine runs in my blood.

Put yourself in the shoes of an admissions tutor reading hundreds of personal statements. Many of those statements will likely include the same tired phrases in their opening paragraphs. Would you think, "Wow, this candidate is truly passionate about medicine. I can't wait to read more!" Or would you think, "I've seen this a hundred times. What's different about this candidate?"

What makes a phrase a cliché is that it's often a statement without examples or depth to back it up. Saying, "I'm interested in science" doesn't really say anything until you explain that you enjoy reading specific publications, engaging in school activities like dissections, or other experiences that showcase your genuine interest. Similarly, "I've always been fascinated by medicine" doesn't have much meaning unless you explain how you volunteered at a hospice or trained as a Red Cross volunteer.

In conclusion, only use these standard statements if they are supported with specific examples. If you choose to include them, they work best as part of a concise and impactful conclusion to your personal statement:

"Over the past 10 years, I have demonstrated a strong interest in science and in caring for others through various personal and professional experiences. People often describe me as hardworking, professional, approachable, and supportive. I believe these qualities will help me become a great doctor."

This type of statement may feel overly generic within the body of the personal statement but can be effective as a conclusion that builds on all the specific examples you've shared.

Use power words

When writing your personal statement for medical school, using power words can significantly enhance the impact of your writing. Power words are strong, action-oriented verbs and adjectives that convey confidence, passion, and a proactive approach to challenges. These words not only make your personal statement more engaging but also demonstrate your motivation and readiness for the demands of a medical career.

Instead of relying on vague or passive language, power words help to paint a vivid picture of your experiences and qualities. They create a sense of dynamism and purpose, giving admissions tutors a clearer sense of who you are and what you have to offer.

Here are some tips on how to effectively use power words in your medical school personal statement:

1. **Highlight your achievements**
   Power words can help you demonstrate the impact of your experiences. Instead of simply stating you "worked in a hospital", use words like contributed, coordinated, facilitated, or led. These action words show that you actively participated and had a tangible influence in your role. For example:

   "I led a team of volunteers at a local clinic, where we provided essential support to patients during their treatments."

   "Through my research, I discovered key insights that enhanced the understanding of patient care in a clinical setting."

2. **Show your passion**
   A personal statement for medicine should communicate your genuine interest in the field, and power words can help you convey enthusiasm and drive. Words like passionate, committed, driven, and dedicated show that you are fully invested in your aspirations. For example:

   "I am passionate about improving healthcare access for underserved communities."

   "My experience working with diverse patient populations has deepened my commitment to pursuing a career in medicine."

3. **Demonstrate problem-solving skills**
   As a future doctor, you'll be faced with complex problems that require critical thinking and creativity. Use power words that show how you approach challenges, such as analyse, resolve, strategise, adapt, and innovate. These words convey that you are someone who takes initiative and is capable of finding solutions. For example:

   "When faced with a challenging case, I developed and implemented a new approach that improved the outcome."

   "I adapted to a fast-paced work environment, quickly resolving issues as they arose."

4. **Emphasise leadership and teamwork**
   Medicine is a collaborative field that requires teamwork and leadership. Power words such as collaborated, mentored, guided, empowered, and inspired showcase your ability to work effectively with others and lead teams when necessary. For example:

   "I have guided junior team members through difficult cases, ensuring that all perspectives were considered in decision-making."

   "I collaborated with healthcare professionals from diverse backgrounds to ensure comprehensive patient care."

5. **Be specific and measurable**
   Whenever possible, use power words in conjunction with specific details and measurable outcomes. Numbers, percentages, and quantifiable achievements add weight to your statement and make your accomplishments more tangible. For example:

   "I organised a fundraising event that raised £5,000 for a local healthcare charity."

   "I mentored younger students in biology, helping them to develop effective study habits and achieve top grades in their exams."

A list of 800 power words and action verbs can be found in Chapter 12. You should be comfortable in incorporating these throughout your personal statement to help maximise impact.

9 Making your statement fit

By now, you should have a first draft of your personal statement. Don't stress if it's a bit lengthy; editing it down is much easier than trying to expand a short one. If your statement is on the shorter side but you're confident you've covered everything important, don't worry. It's perfectly fine to submit a concise, well-written statement instead of padding it out with irrelevant details.

Remember to keep an eye on your character limit. UCAS has set this limit for a reason: to help you demonstrate your ability to express your motivations for studying medicine clearly and succinctly. The goal is to convey your passion and drive for a medical career without over-explaining.

Here are a few tips to help reduce your character count:

- Avoid listing hobbies and interests just to fill space.

- Don't repeat information that's already on your UCAS form.

- Don't use headings. While they may make your statement appear well structured, they can waste valuable space and make it seem too rigid.

Next, take a moment to consider the layout of your personal statement. A well-organised, easy-to-read document will leave a stronger impression than one that feels cluttered or rushed. Be sure your paragraphs are well structured, and don't cram too much into each one. For example, try to balance the length of the paragraphs on work experience and personal skills or achievements to ensure a cohesive flow.

Avoid using fancy formatting, such as underlining, bold text, or different colours. UCAS's online system doesn't process these formats, so any extra effort on your part won't show up. Your words should be powerful enough on their own.

Finally, remember that UCAS cannot process text with foreign characters, such as accents. If you've gained experience abroad or want to use words like "cliché", it's best to avoid these characters.

10 Editing and checking your statement

Once you have put together a good first draft, the next thing you should do is read your statement out loud and slowly. This will help highlight any areas which sound disjointed or if you've missed anything out. You will also spot if something doesn't read very well or sounds confusing, because if you find yourself confused about something you read in your personal statement, then it's likely that anyone else reading it will do too. By reading your personal statement out loud, you will also discover if your sentences are too long because you will run out of breath!

Don't rely on automatic spell check

It's highly likely that the word processing program you will be using to draft your personal statement will come equipped with a spell check function. By all means use this and, in fact, you should. But don't rely on it completely because it is not 100% foolproof.

For example, a spell checker will only detect if words are spelt correctly (or incorrectly), but not if they have been used correctly. There are a number of commonly misused words that many spell checkers will not detect, such as advice/advise, their/there, to/too, whether/weather, practice/practise, cite/sight and so on. Take a look at this sentence and spot how many correctly spelt but incorrectly used words there are.

> *"I to developed a better understanding by listening to the advise the consultant gave too all there patience."*

Correctly spelt, this sentence should read as follows:

> *"I too developed a better understanding by listening to the advice the consultant gave to all their patients."*

The spell check may also try to correct words which are already correctly spelt and used, for example 'my self-discipline' may be corrected to 'myself discipline' which, of course, is completely wrong in this context.

Your spell checker can be a useful tool, but its accuracy depends on the language settings you've selected in your word processing software. One common issue is the use of American spellings for certain words, which can make your personal statement seem inconsistent with UK English. Here are some examples of American versus UK spelling differences:

- Customize (UK: customise)
- Realize (UK: realise)
- Specialize (UK: specialise)
- Organize (UK: organise)
- Recognize (UK: recognise)
- Materialize (UK: materialise)
- Behavior (UK: behaviour)
- Color (UK: colour)
- Pediatrics (UK: paediatrics)
- Gynecology (UK: gynaecology)
- Anesthesiology (UK: anaesthetics)
- Fulfill (UK: fulfil)
- Skeptical (UK: sceptical)
- Center (UK: centre)
- Color (UK: colour)
- Humor (UK: humour)

While spell checkers are helpful for an initial edit, they can't replace the importance of thorough proofreading. Be sure to read through your personal statement carefully to ensure that everything is accurate, consistent, and in the correct English style.

Ask for opinions

Getting multiple opinions on your personal statement can be incredibly helpful. It's often hard to spot errors in your own writing because you're so familiar with the content.

Asking family, friends, teachers, or career advisers for feedback can provide valuable insights. Career advisers, in particular, are great because they have experience reading many personal statements and can offer a good perspective on what works and what doesn't. However, don't leave it to the last minute, since they tend to be very busy around this time of year.

When you ask someone to review your draft personal statement, request that they consider the following specific points:

- Is the introduction engaging and attention-grabbing?
- Do I provide a convincing, sincere reason for wanting to study medicine?
- Does the description of my work experience and volunteer work support my desire to pursue a career in medicine?
- Does the statement make sense overall?
- Have I rambled or am I too wordy?
- Does the statement flow logically, or are there areas that feel disjointed?
- Have I included anything irrelevant?
- Is every sentence crucial to my personal statement?
- Have I used unnecessary clichés?
- Are there any spelling mistakes or grammatical errors?
- Am I using active voice and power verbs to make my point?
- Are my sentences clear and easy to read, with the right length?
- Is my conclusion memorable, and does it provide closure?
- Are there any weak areas or sections that need more detail?
- Are there parts that aren't clear or need further explanation?

And ask them directly: "Can you describe what you think this personal statement says about my personality?"

By now, you will have read and reread your personal statement several times and will have input from anyone else you may have shown it to, so you will have quite a few changes and amendments to make to it. Before you start rewriting the bits you're not happy with, make sure you save a copy of the original statement, because you may want to refer back to it. After you've made your changes, repeat the process of reading the statement to yourself and showing it to others for comment. Each time you go back and make more changes, save the previous version of the statement so that you keep a copy of each one for reference.

The final golden rule is to read and reread your personal statement as many times as possible, to check there are no typos. Don't forget that spell check isn't foolproof and you will already have seen instances where this can go wrong on previous pages, so you would be well advised at this point to revert to traditional proofreading techniques. If necessary, ask your friends, family or school teachers to read it and check the spelling for you, because this is vital. There is no point in presenting a beautifully worded and structured personal statement if it is littered with spelling mistakes and errors.

11 Examples of personal statements

In this chapter, you will find 107 examples of personal statements. Each one is a recent successful applicant's real statement, which we have thoughtfully rewritten to reflect the new format adopted by UCAS for 2026 entry.

We have specified whether each statement is for A level (11.1 – 11.78) or graduate entry (11.79 – 11.107) at the beginning of the statement. Next to this, you'll find the total character count for all three sections combined. At the head of each individual section, we have also indicated the character count used for that section.

It's important to note that while these statements aim to be informative and inspiring, they are not always perfectly polished or academically worded. In fact, that's intentional. What they all have in common is that they feel authentic – they sound like they were written by real people with genuine motivations, not machines or professional writers.

When writing your own statement, try not to stress over whether it sounds impressive enough or if every sentence is grammatically flawless. What matters far more is that it reads smoothly and reflects your own voice. Admissions tutors are looking for insight into who you are, not just how well you can write. So, focus on clarity, sincerity, and making sure your personality and values come through.

Don't be afraid to be yourself. This chapter is here to give you ideas and a sense of structure, but your statement should still feel uniquely yours.

11.1 A level entry — 3977 characters

SECTION 1 [1117 characters]

Medicine as a subject area has long sparked my curiosity, not only because of its uniqueness, but because of both the logical and yet innovative thinking it encompasses. What set the clinical environment apart from the research lab during my work placements was the patient contact; it is what attracts me to the career, and witnessing it has cemented my desire to become a doctor. I believe my persistence and motivation will always fuel my drive to continue learning, and hope that my patience will help me to one day become a good doctor. My drive to study medicine stems not only from my interest in human biology, but also from its sheer diversity as a discipline and career. Both a science and an art, medicine remains an inimitable area of knowledge. It is precisely this that attracts me to the course, while my drive to become a doctor has always been rooted in the prospect of caring for others. As a reapplicant, I have had the opportunity to carefully reconsider and better familiarise myself with the career through further work experience. As a result, my desire to become a doctor has been reinforced.

SECTION 2 [1265 characters]

Last year, I had the opportunity to carry out research for my extended essay in school, where I tested the antibacterial properties of five different herbs. This experience not only strengthened my research skills but also deepened my interest in complementary medicine and the role of nutrition in maintaining health. Writing the essay allowed me to explore the scientific basis behind natural remedies and consider their potential benefits as part of a holistic approach to healthcare. This has further inspired my desire to pursue a career in medicine, where I can integrate scientific knowledge with a compassionate, patient-centred approach to care.

Studying psychology at A level has provided me with a deeper understanding of human behaviour and the critical interplay between mental and physical health. Topics such as cognitive processes, mental health disorders, and development have broadened my perspective on patient care, emphasising the importance of addressing both emotional and physical well-being. This has enhanced my empathy and ability to approach healthcare holistically. Additionally, psychology has strengthened my analytical thinking and evidence evaluation skills, preparing me for the critical and reflective mindset required in medicine.

SECTION 3 [1595 characters]

Moving around the world made my childhood unpredictable. This taught me to adapt quickly to new situations. I became accustomed to change, and my international upbringing has allowed me the flexibility to be an independent student. I saw the importance of human psychology in medicine when I spent two weeks at a dermatology clinic in Hamburg, where the doctor's calm, confident and even witty behaviour helped to put the patients at ease. Her fast-paced day also introduced me to the sometimes-stressful reality of the career, which I again witnessed during my week at a London hospital. Having just faced the challenge of speaking a foreign language in a clinical setting, I came to really appreciate the value of adept communication skills in medicine. Most notably, the placement taught me the value of a patient's own understanding; I realised that 'not knowing' can be the most terrifying aspect of a prognosis, and saw how key a doctor's didactic role is to the patient's peace of mind.

Community service was and remains an important focus of my extracurricular activities. To raise money for my school's charity club, I set up a 'Monday Muffins' programme and was in charge of the annual raffle, which helped me with time management and organisational skills. I now look forward to an eventful gap year, which will begin with more hands-on work experience at a German cancer clinic. During times of stress I find cooking very relaxing, and am now saving for a culinary and language course in Florence next spring. I hope to later be able to fund more travelling and voluntary work abroad.

11.2 A level entry — 3610 characters

SECTION 1 [967 characters]

Having medical parents means that I grew up seeing the demands of medicine. However, my first practical insight into the profession began when my friend's father was diagnosed with terminal pancreatic cancer. Diagnosis was difficult, and his end-of-life care demanding. I supported my friend throughout and was moved by the skill and compassion the healthcare team demonstrated during this difficult time.

My parents being doctors might make you think that I'm just following in their footsteps; in reality my decision to pursue medicine as a career has come as a result of a carefully thought-out process. I first thought of studying law because I enjoy the rigour and analytical processes involved, but I felt it would not be as focused on the individual as medicine would be. I investigated finance as a career and discounted it for the same reason. For me, medicine is the only place where I can make a practical difference to people in a truly caring environment.

SECTION 2 [1229 characters]

I was awarded an academic scholarship at age 11 and have achieved gold and silver, as well as 'best in school' awards in UKMT Maths Challenges. My GCSE PE mark was among the top five in the country. All of this resulted from planning and hard work. I enjoy taking on challenges and look forward to complex medical exams. I relish the power of language, have won national prizes for public speaking, story writing, regional prizes for prose reading, and poetry speaking, and achieved Distinction in Advanced Speech (LAMDA Grade 6).

I get on well with people from all walks of life. Being elected Head Girl by both staff and pupils has enriched my experience, developing my leadership, organisational, and communication skills. Leading a team of officials, liaising with the Headmistress, and managing publications, committees, and events taught me to prioritise tasks, delegate responsibilities, and maintain high standards under pressure. Representing the school at external functions has enhanced my confidence and ability to engage with diverse audiences. These experiences have prepared me to take on the challenges of a medical career, where effective leadership and collaboration are essential to providing high-quality care.

SECTION 3 [1414 characters]

During work experience in hospital and primary care, I shadowed doctors and practice staff from many disciplines, appreciating the breadth of the doctor's role. I worked with disabled adults as a Millennium Volunteer and now teach dinghy sailing to physically and mentally disabled teenagers and adults. Their resilience is impressive, and one sailor, autistic, inspired me to explore the autistic spectrum. I have many attributes doctors need: effective communication, leadership, teamwork, compassion, adaptability, integrity, and intellectual curiosity. I enjoy problem-solving and new challenges.

Nominated Managing Director for our Young Enterprise photography company, Shooting Stars, I dealt with clients, resolved problems, and led a team that won awards. As an experienced mountaineer, rock climber, and skier, I assess evidence, make tough decisions, and adapt quickly. I swim and sail competitively and am a qualified Coastal Skipper. Sailing demands self-reliance, discipline, cooperation, and determination, and I've been Under-18 Firefly National Champion and won the CCF National Schools Regatta. I aim to be a well-rounded doctor who contributes to patients' physical and mental well-being.

I balance work and social activities well, as shown by my significant academic workload alongside extracurricular activities. I'm ready for this challenge, with the insights, skills, and motivation to succeed.

11.3 A level entry — 3626 characters

SECTION 1 [781 characters]

For many years my mother has been suffering with anxiety, affecting her ability to perform daily tasks and remember important information. Witnessing the emotional and cognitive toll of this condition made me reflect on the importance of effective medical interventions and mental health support. This has inspired me to explore the field of psychiatry further, by reading books and watching documentaries.

I also spent my Saturdays at a local care home where I kept company with elderly people with conditions such as dementia and Parkinson's disease. My experience volunteering in those community settings gave me the drive to understand the psychological and physiological aspects of anxiety, strengthening my desire to become a doctor who provides holistic patient-centred care.

SECTION 2 [849 characters]

Studying A level psychology gave me a good understanding of anxiety and the way it affects cognition, memory, and decision-making. I learned how heightened stress responses can impair concentration and recall, which has significant implications for conditions like generalised anxiety disorder and PTSD.

As part of my A levels I completed an Extended Project Qualification (EPQ) on a neuroscience-related topic, which greatly enhanced my analytical and critical thinking skills. Through my EPQ, I explored brain structures, including the amygdala's role in emotion and the hippocampus's role in memory. This research honed my ability to critically evaluate sources, manage time effectively, and communicate complex concepts clearly – skills that are crucial for conducting medical research and informing evidence-based practice in clinical settings.

SECTION 3 [1996 characters]

My first time experiencing the reality of working in healthcare was a work placement at St Peter's Hospital where I spent a week shadowing nurses, followed by three days with an ophthalmologist. This taught me a great deal about patient care, especially the importance of maintaining privacy, dignity and confidentiality. I also recognised the communication and empathy skills displayed by the team.

Following this, a week-long 'Introduction to the NHS' course at the same hospital gave me a chance to appreciate and understand further the different roles of those working there and the extent to which they are interdependent. Senior doctors and young medics were aware of the frustrations of having limited time and resources for patients, but I was impressed by the ability of healthcare teams to continuously aim to improve their services. In fact, this is something I am still seeing in action in the gap year I am currently undertaking, working as a healthcare assistant on an orthopaedic ward at St Peter's Hospital.

Away from work, I volunteer at my old primary school, helping children with special needs. I work, in particular, with a seven-year-old girl who has dyslexia. Last summer, I gained my National Pool Lifeguard Qualification after learning how to swim within a year. I enjoy passing on the determination and perseverance I displayed at this time to children who face greater challenges with learning.

My leadership and teamwork skills have been further developed through my weekly volunteering at a local Brownie pack, which I have done for almost 18 months. While at school, I played netball for my school team and spent a month on an expedition to Northern Peru. Singing in my school choir, achieving a Grade 8 in LAMDA Public Speaking and playing the violin to Grade 5 gave me a chance to enjoy activities that contrasted with my school subjects. Currently, I enjoy running, swimming, reading and socialising in my spare time which has been a real feat of time management.

11.4 A level entry — 3700 characters

SECTION 1 [1068 characters]

My intellectual interest for the biological sciences and my desire to work directly with people are my main drive to pursue a medical career. Throughout my childhood and adolescence my family GP has left a lasting impression on me, showing a deep understanding of her patients' lives beyond their medical conditions.

Not only could she manage and treat her patients' clinical concerns, she was also able to understand and take account of psychosocial factors such as their mental health, their family dynamics, their support network and their personal beliefs, thus providing truly patient-centred care. I saw how her long-term relationships with patients helped her diagnose conditions early, offer tailored advice, and provide emotional support. This experience showed me that medicine is not just about treating diseases but about understanding individuals as whole people.

It inspired me to consider general practice as a career option, recognising the immense value of continuity of care and the doctor–patient relationship in improving long-term health outcomes.

SECTION 2 [803 characters]

I have several achievements which demonstrate my intellectual suitability for a career in medicine. I gained third place in Northern Ireland in GCSE English Literature, won a School prize for overall GCSE results, a two-year school Scholarship for Outstanding Achievement, and an academic prize in every school year.

I represented my school in a 'Paperclip Physics' competition as part of a small team. I am a Senior School Prefect and the Deputy Head Librarian in the Careers Library. I have gained certificates in first aid and the European Computer Driving Licence.

These academic and extracurricular achievements demonstrate my abilities and interests. For relaxation, I am interested in photography and art, and was awarded a prize for the best final art and design examination piece in the school.

SECTION 3 [1829 characters]

I gained insight into the work of a doctor through varied work experience opportunities at several hospitals. In a Neurology Department I shadowed a Neurological Consultant, and observed him discussing with patients the symptoms of conditions such as epilepsy and Alzheimer's disease. This experience reinforced for me that it is not always possible for a doctor to 'cure' a condition, but to help the patient learn to control and live with their disease. I was impressed with the way the Consultant treated each patient as an individual and not just as a person with a disease. I discovered I could communicate well with the patients I was given the opportunity to talk to – I was involved in discussions with patients who had brain injuries, heightening my awareness of the distinctive needs of different patients.

In a Cardiac Department, I observed and spoke with patients undergoing procedures, such as ultrasound and ECG. This showed me how information is gathered to aid the diagnosis and treatment. In a Brain Injury Unit I accompanied different members of a multidisciplinary team, giving me insight into the value of various professionals working together to meet the needs of patients and demonstrating the pivotal role of the doctor in the team. While accompanying a Resuscitation Officer, I gained knowledge of life-saving techniques by participating in a Basic Life Support course for newly qualified doctors.

In addition, I volunteer with children who have learning and physical disabilities under the auspices of Barnardo's. I have achieved Grade 5 in alto saxophone and am working towards Grade 7 in clarinet, and I play in the award-winning school orchestra, jazz band, and saxophone quartet. I have learnt how to operate as a member of a team and how to undertake organisational and leadership tasks efficiently.

11.5　A level entry　3980 characters

SECTION 1 [479 characters]

The complexity of the human body never fails to amaze me. Specifically in young children, understanding how the body functions poses a challenge in itself as they are still growing, much like our knowledge of human biology.

It is this intermingling of constant change and the multitudinous possibilities for advancement that I believe makes medicine, and paediatrics in particular, a stimulating field to be involved in and that's the reason I want to pursue a career in medicine.

SECTION 2 [1295 characters]

Being an active member of the school debate club has sharpened my critical thinking, communication, and teamworking skills. Preparing for debates has taught me to analyse complex topics, construct logical arguments, and consider multiple perspectives, all of which are skills that doctors require when diagnosing and solving medical problems. Speaking in front of an audience has enhanced my confidence and ability to articulate ideas clearly under pressure, while collaborative discussions have strengthened my ability to work effectively with others. These experiences have prepared me to engage thoughtfully and empathetically in the dynamic and multidisciplinary environment of medicine.

Serving as the Class Vice Chairperson in secondary school and currently as the Publicity Secretary of the students' committee, I have developed strong leadership, organisational, and communication skills. Organising successful school events with both committees has taught me how to collaborate effectively, manage responsibilities, and stay dedicated to achieving shared goals.

These roles have required creativity, attention to detail, and the ability to motivate and work alongside others. Balancing these leadership duties with my academic workload has also enhanced my time management and resilience.

SECTION 3 [2206 characters]

For work experience, I shadowed a paediatric surgeon at Singapore's National University Hospital. It taught me the importance of good bedside manners and the need to show empathy when reassuring young patients. While observing surgical procedures, I realised that surgeons had to be patient and possess mental and manual dexterity as one error of judgement could impair a life forever. A particular case which interested me was a liver transplant patient who suffered post-surgery tissue rejection, requiring immediate remedial intervention. This made me realise the uncertainties permeating medical procedures.

I also began to appreciate the value of making a personal connection with patients while volunteering at a hospital. A simple act of engaging the patients in entertaining conversations could distract them from their discomfort, which I found very fulfilling. In July, I was employed as a Patient Service Assistant at Raffles Hospital in Singapore, where I was required to interact with patients from diverse ethnic backgrounds. Overcoming language barriers to communicate effectively helped me develop my interpersonal skills and gain a deeper respect of cultural diversity and needs.

I also assisted in the hospital's Annual Scientific Symposium where specialists presented papers on medical advancements. I was especially impressed by technological developments such as the 64-slice CT scan, which are reducing the need for invasive diagnostic procedures, thereby increasing the comfort of patients and the ease of diagnosis. Last year, I participated in a Model United Nations Conference where I was commended with an award for best presentation. Regular meditation and jogging helps me relieve stress and keep fit mentally and physically. Through my extensive work experiences, I have a realistic idea of the challenges and rewards of studying medicine.

I believe the demands of this course require maturity, which academic rote learning alone cannot provide. Hence, I am deferring entry to university by a year, to volunteer in hospitals in Asia with the company Projects Abroad. Additionally, I hope to seek placements in biomedical research firms to gain insights into this developing field.

11.6 A level entry — 3897 characters

SECTION 1 [952 characters]

When I first discovered the solar system over a decade ago, I wanted to be an astronaut. As I matured, I considered nuclear or particle physics research before settling on industrial chemistry. Inspired by molecular interactions, I participated in a 'changing perceptions of industry' scheme, arranged work experience in a testing lab, and attended the Sutton Trust chemistry summer school at Oxford. These experiences heightened my interest in science and broadened my skills.

Despite my interest in chemistry, I felt a strong urge to help others. I no longer wanted to improve industrial processes for profits. I wanted to give back to my community, driven by my faith. So, I chose medicine. This career satisfies my love of science and my desire to help others. I believe I have the empathy, enthusiasm, and excellence needed to become a doctor. I am excited about the unique opportunities medicine offers to make a positive impact on people's lives.

SECTION 2 [1035 characters]

Setting up and volunteering at a school-run dyspraxia support group has helped me strengthen skills that are essential for medicine. By supporting young people with homework and providing guidance I have learnt patience, active listening, and empathy. I needed to balance the diverse needs of the group which has challenged me to create a positive environment, fostering trust and collaboration. These experiences reinforced the importance of tailored support and compassionate care – qualities I am committed to applying in medicine, where understanding and addressing individual patient needs are vital.

Studying Religious Studies at A level deepened my understanding of compassion, service, and integrity. As part of the studies, I needed to explore different ethical perspectives, which enhanced my critical thinking abilities and empathy. These experiences instilled in me a strong commitment to treating others with dignity and respect and strengthened my resilience and moral grounding, invaluable qualities for a medical career.

SECTION 3 [1910 characters]

In order to be sure that medicine is the right career choice for me, I attended a work experience programme at my local hospital, which gave me an insight into how an NHS hospital works. I was also given the chance to witness clinical skills, such as catheterisation and venepuncture. I spoke to consultants from different disciplines and, despite many negatives explained to me by staff, I am still keen to become a doctor. I also shadowed my GP, which allowed me to compare primary care to the specialist hospital services I had previously observed. Volunteering at a local care home has allowed me to see how long-term illnesses can affect not only patients, but their families too. Speaking to patients, getting to know them and developing a rapport with them and their families enhanced my communication and patient skills and I have become more empathetic as a result.

I assist in the SEN department of my school, helping with homework and providing advice, guidance and comfort to those who need it. Although I sometimes find it challenging to meet the needs of all the young people, I strive to be as helpful and as friendly as possible, being a supportive and playful companion. I currently participate in first aid and life support training with St John's Ambulance. This makes me one of the first contacts for medical assistance at many large events, improving both my patient care and decision-making skills.

My Catholic faith is a very prominent aspect of my life and I currently lead the children's liturgy at my local parish church. This has made me a more confident and outgoing person, yet also more considerate and caring. Outside of academia, I particularly enjoy classical music. I teach piano in a local primary school and sing bass in my school chamber choir. Music allows me to relax and get away from everything in daily life and it is something that will stay with me throughout my life.

11.7 A level entry — 3967 characters

SECTION 1 [994 characters]

Witnessing a friend's fight against cancer was a turning point in my life which has driven my determination to pursue a career in medicine. It is often observed that extreme circumstances bring out the best in people, and I enjoy facing the difficulties of a challenge as I work well, if not best, under pressure. I understand that as a doctor it is vital to uphold personal responsibilities as well as be an effective team member. It was the dedication of the team who treated this complex disease and the strength and perseverance of the doctor specifically which inspired me to follow a career in medicine. Competency in clinical expertise and emotional support are two different but essential aspects of becoming a doctor which I aspire to excel in.

It was through an exhibition on malaria at the Royal Society's Summer Exhibition that I discovered a specific interest in infectious diseases and immunology, which I had the opportunity to develop during a week's work experience in the NIMR.

SECTION 2 [1087 characters]

Throughout my years of schooling, the study of science has been continually fascinating to me. I enjoyed attending lectures and many exhibitions that allowed me to go beyond the curriculum and inspired my contribution to the school's Medical Newsletter. I completed a genetics course run by the Institute of Education. As part of that course, I developed further knowledge of laboratory techniques and broadened my mind through ethical discussions about genetic testing and doctor–patient confidentiality.

While my main interests lie in science, I have equally enjoyed studying English Literature and Spanish, as these have opened many doors to a diverse range of cultures. These pursuits have led to visits to the theatre, taking a Spanish course in Barcelona and doing a Spanish exchange. Being a member of the debating society and representing the school in public speaking competitions has greatly developed my fluency and articulacy, which has developed my ability to work under pressure. I feel all these skills will help me make a proactive, curious, empathic and resilient doctor.

SECTION 3 [1886 characters]

Having the opportunity to shadow a Senior Registrar in Obstetrics and Gynaecology in Hillingdon Hospital was very beneficial to me as I was able to explore a range of science and medical-based departments, from pathology and microscopy, to the gynaecology clinic, labour ward, and theatre. In the latter two, I witnessed the demands of working successfully within a team and under pressure, where the complications of birth led to an epidural, attempts at an assisted delivery and a caesarean section. My understanding of the daily running of a hospital was developed through work experience in Northwick Park Hospital where I realised the invaluable role of nurses, especially in caring for the elderly. Attending Medlink was a valuable experience as the lectures broadened my knowledge of specific aspects of medicine, and I gained a brief insight into student life which I look forward to experiencing fully.

Striving to raise over £3,000 for World Challenge for our expedition to Argentina last year has made it vital that I manage time effectively in order to balance my employment with academic pursuits. Walking 60km and raising over £1,500 for Breakthrough Breast Cancer research was challenging and incredibly rewarding. This has inspired a particular empathy for cancer sufferers which I have followed by volunteering in a hospice for the past two years.

Belly dancing and lambada dancing are hobbies which I do purely for enjoyment. Playing in the school lacrosse team for six years and regular training at the gym has developed my perseverance as I have realised every challenge is a matter of mental strength. Through my experiences, I believe I have gained a realistic insight into the challenges of both studying medicine and becoming a doctor, challenges which have reinforced my dedication to medicine, a career in which I could never tire of striving to achieve my best.

11.8 A level entry — 3477 characters

SECTION 1 [825 characters]

As a child, I aspired to become a footballer. I was agile, quick and, in my opinion, crafty with the ball. However, living in Sierra Leone, a developing country with one of the world's highest infant mortality rates, I witnessed first-hand the trauma that sick and vulnerable people faced. This is a country where a doctor's consultation exceeds the average monthly wage; people simply fell ill and died. It infuriated me that lives were valued according to the size of a person's wallet, and I knew from a very early age that I wanted to be part of a solution to resolve these injustices.

My ultimate ambition is to train in the UK and work as a consultant to gain clinical confidence, academic abilities and experience of service development in the hope that one day I can go back to Sierra Leone and make a difference there.

SECTION 2 [771 characters]

Moving to England at the age of 11 without speaking English was a pivotal experience that taught me resilience, adaptability, and determination. Through dedication and hard work, I developed strong communication skills, which I further honed as an active participant in school debates. These debates not only helped me articulate my ideas confidently but also taught me the value of listening to and understanding diverse perspectives.

My reliability, organisational skills, and confidence have been recognised through leadership roles, including being a prefect at Wilson's school in Sutton and Deputy Head Boy at my previous school. These experiences have shaped me into a motivated and resourceful individual, qualities that will serve me well in the field of medicine.

SECTION 3 [1881 characters]

On a recent visit to Lebanon, I was fortunate to shadow a doctor. This experience strengthened my already solid desire to become a doctor and left me longing for the day I would be able to deal with the stress and pressure they face daily. I learnt that good medicine takes a holistic approach and is not just about diagnosing and treating patients. I saw how the patients who were properly informed and invited to ask questions became less nervous about their ailment. Although no statistical data was collated, I felt this approach yielded the best outcome. I understood this in greater detail when I was the chair of a fundraising committee for a charity specialising in youth homelessness. I saw how welfare issues combined with social ones led to good or bad health. My experience with the voluntary sector made me realise that we are fortunate to have a welfare state. It also enabled me to reflect on the actions of doctors in Sierra Leone, who often seemed to turn their backs on the needy, who have no other option.

I also volunteer at a refugee day centre, where I am able to support people from various cultures and age groups. Being trilingual, fluent in both Krio and Arabic in addition to English, I help them overcome the language barrier. I do my best to achieve a work–life balance, combining my studies, voluntary work and household chores with activities that I find personally stimulating, such as tennis, swimming and cooking. For many people the commitment that medicine requires is overwhelming, whereas, for me, it is one that I cannot wait to make.

I feel that medicine offers me a career where I would get total job satisfaction and combine this with my deep-rooted drive to contribute and serve the community. My dedication and desire to be part of a field where new discoveries are constantly being made can only be met by a career as dynamic as medicine.

11.9   A level entry   3878 characters

SECTION 1 [787 characters]

My A level biology teacher had an enthusiasm that was contagious. Their ability to explain complex physiological processes with clarity and excitement ignited my curiosity about medicine. I was particularly drawn to their discussions on genetic disorders and neurobiology, which led me to pursue further research into how medicine can alleviate suffering. Their encouragement pushed me to challenge myself academically, explore scientific literature, and take part in medical debates. Beyond their knowledge, they also emphasised the ethical and humanistic side of healthcare, reinforcing my desire to become a doctor who balances scientific expertise with compassion. Their mentorship instilled in me a deep sense of curiosity and a determination to contribute to the field of medicine.

SECTION 2 [1218 characters]

My dedication to academic excellence was recognised when I received the only subject excellence certificates in both chemistry and biology at my school. These awards reflect not only my passion for the sciences but also my commitment to consistently achieving high standards in my studies. Excelling in these subjects has deepened my understanding of the fundamental principles that underpin medicine, while also fostering a disciplined work ethic and a drive to master challenging material. This recognition motivates me to continue striving for excellence and demonstrates my readiness to embrace the intellectual demands of a medical career.

As Head of Year 8, I led the team to set up a 'drop-in centre' that enables students to discuss personal or study-related problems. In addition, I also became a peer mentor in 'Drugs Squad'. As part of these roles I demonstrated a good ability to listen and empathise, discuss important matters in a non-judgemental way and help people without being coercive. Those jobs illustrated the importance of interpersonal communication skills and particularly the fact that, if you take the time to build rapport with people so they see you as trustworthy, they communicate more openly.

SECTION 3 [1853 characters]

At my local GP practice, I shadowed a practice nurse where I learned about the importance of the patient's right to confidentiality and how adopting a holistic approach allows better understanding and thus more effective treatment. At Alderney Hospital in Poole, I spoke with stroke patients. At times, this experience was upsetting, but seeing how their quality of life could be improved served to strengthen my desire to embark on a medical career. Ward rounds and home visits with other members of the healthcare team highlighted how patient care depends on many individuals and requires efficient communication. A placement observing General and Orthopaedic Surgery at Bournemouth Hospital showed how an intimate understanding of the structure of the human body, as well as precision and skill, can improve lives.

Through my work as a shop assistant, a team member in a theme park and currently as a cleaner, I have developed an ability to engage with a diverse range of people and demonstrated hard work, resilience and adaptability. Good time management skills have been necessary to balance study for my 5 AS levels with extracurricular activities including rowing, cycling and rock climbing. I am a qualified Explorer Scout Young Leader and for the past three years have helped lead a Beaver Scout group, which has required a sense of humour, patience and ability to think on my feet. I frequently meet with the youth group from my church and help to run a soup kitchen for the homeless. The people attending often have drug and alcohol addictions or mental health problems. Talking with them and reflecting on why people become homeless helped me work in a less judgemental and more empathic manner. Participating in French and New Zealand exchanges has further increased my social awareness and respect for individuals from various backgrounds.

11.10 A level entry — 3771 characters

SECTION 1 [1111 characters]

My uncle is an orthopaedic surgeon in Hong Kong. We used to visit him on holiday and from the age of thirteen I used to accompany him to work. This experience is what started my journey towards a medical career.

I was surprised to find he spent relatively little time in surgery but often spent large amounts of time in clinical work, talking with patients and discussing each case with other doctors and the patients themselves. I witnessed how the medical teams worked together in harmony for long hours in an attempt to help patients to overcome their illnesses. I was impressed by the diversity of my uncle's job, the constant personal development the job entailed, the teamwork involved and the way he was able to provide holistic care to his patients. Wanting the same varied and interesting career has been my main motivation in applying to medical school.

The large number of specialities and things to learn make it such a diverse area of study. I look forward to the many opportunities that life at medical school will offer and the chance to become a doctor, working in a team to serve the community.

SECTION 2 [860 characters]

As my school's head music officer, I had the privilege of leading the music department and organising a music tour, responsibilities that taught me valuable skills directly transferable to a career in medicine.

Coordinating the tour required meticulous planning, teamwork, and the ability to adapt quickly to unforeseen challenges, such as last-minute changes to schedules. I developed strong communication skills by liaising with staff, students, and external stakeholders, ensuring every detail ran smoothly. Managing the diverse needs of the group honed my ability to empathise with others and remain composed under pressure.

These experiences have prepared me for the collaborative nature of medicine, where effective leadership, adaptability, and communication are essential for delivering patient-centred care in dynamic and often demanding environments.

SECTION 3 [1800 characters]

In my spare time, I am a St John's Ambulance cadet. As well as enabling me to practise basic medical skills effectively, I have also learnt a wide range of skills such as leadership among panicked people and working in a pressurised environment. I also found that teamwork and communication were extremely important and I feel these experiences will put me in a strong position when I enter the medical field.

I spent one month of my summer in India, dividing my time between trekking in the Himalayas, sightseeing and helping with a community project at a local school in Baragram. At the school, for the children of that town and the surrounding area, I worked with my teammates to repaint the interior of the building and carry out some maintenance work. Many of the children there were keen to help, sanding down the walls and painting. The classrooms contained only rugs for the children to sit on, a blackboard and a desk for the teacher. This showed me the dedication that some of the children put into their education to make it into secondary school, working in classes of between 40 and 50 children. My share of the cost for this expedition was raised by giving music lessons in piano and as part of that I learnt a lot about time management, communication and teaching both children and adults.

I have also achieved grade 8 in both clarinet and piano and I am currently working towards grade 7 on the organ. My self-discipline has been tested by having to divide my time between work and the school orchestra, concert band and choir, with which I have taken part in several concert tours to Europe. I also play the organ at Sunday Mass in my parish church. And to top all that I am also currently training in a martial art called Wing Chun, which has helped me develop skills in discipline.

11.11   A level entry   3614 characters

SECTION 1 [796 characters]

When studying biology I was introduced to some of the different ways in which our bodies are protected against diseases and infections, for example our ability to produce antibodies and memory cells to help prevent the recurrence of an infection. I was intrigued by the body's defence mechanism but was equally struck by the vulnerability of the body to diseases such as cholera, malaria and HIV. It made me value life even more, and knowing that doctors worked to help improve such people's lives and dedicate a career to help people made me really appreciate their role in society.

It is precisely this which has inspired me to pursue a career in medicine; the potential satisfaction I could gain by making such positive differences in people's lives is something which no other job can provide.

SECTION 2 [1081 characters]

A level maths taught me to approach problems with precision and logical reasoning, skills that are fundamental to medicine. Whether solving complex equations or analysing data patterns, I learned to break down challenges systematically, a mindset that translates well to diagnosing medical conditions.

Medicine, like mathematics, requires not just theoretical knowledge but also the ability to apply concepts practically. Studying calculus and statistics highlighted the importance of accuracy, particularly in medical fields such as pharmacokinetics, where precise calculations determine drug dosages. My interest in problem-solving was further reinforced when I worked on a collaborative maths project, where we had to troubleshoot errors and refine our approach systematically.

This experience reminded me of how doctors must consider multiple variables when diagnosing patients and adjusting treatments. I am excited to apply this analytical mindset in medicine, using evidence-based reasoning to make informed clinical decisions and provide the best possible care to patients.

SECTION 3 [1737 characters]

Last year I spent two weeks at a school for physically disabled children where I learnt how to work with and communicate with vulnerable children. Following my GCSE exams I spent 2 days a week for 5 weeks in a community hospital in various departments including Minor Injuries and Pharmacy, and visiting patients with the District Nurse and Occupational Therapist. During this time, I learnt about different medical professions, how they work individually and the importance of working together to ensure the patient receives the best care possible.

Over the past year, I have also volunteered once a week on a surgical ward, talking to patients and providing them with drinks. This has broadened my knowledge of an acute hospital environment and has also taught me the importance of good communication with patients, and I have gained confidence in being able to talk and listen to patients.

Having passed Grade 7 with merit on the flute, I am currently working towards Grade 8; I have also passed Grade 5 Theory at distinction level. For the past 6 years I have been a member of the school orchestra, playing a key part in helping younger students to participate.

I have travelled to Belgium and Austria on tour with the orchestra and have also been a member of several Birmingham Schools' ensembles for 5 years, performing in concerts. Working towards my Gold Duke of Edinburgh award, I learnt about teamwork during the expedition section and how to cope in unfamiliar settings, under pressure, which I feel will stand me in good stead for a career in medicine.

For the past 6 years I have helped at our annual Church Holiday Club, increasingly taking on more responsibility, and have been a member of the Girls' Brigade for 13 years.

11.12   A level entry   3513 characters

SECTION 1 [1191 characters]

As a child I learnt to speak later than usual, as a consequence of continual illnesses, and even had a device invented specifically for me – the Bell-Herold device – as I had difficulties producing certain sounds. I think that my interest in medicine began with my curiosity into these difficulties, and I have always had a fascination with language, whether spoken, signed, or 'mentalese', the language of thought. I enjoy reading books about linguistics, in particular Steven Pinker's 'The Language Instinct'. I have also found that the degeneration of language is often discussed in articles considering major health issues of the future, such as Alzheimer's disease or strokes.

After spending significant time in medical environments I am convinced that I am suited to a medical career. I am attracted by the way in which doctors are always learning and constantly have to be alert, whilst making challenging moral decisions. I know that my interest will be sufficient to sustain me through what is unquestionably a demanding career with a lengthy qualification time. Music and sports will provide a balance to my academic life, and I am very excited by the prospect of studying medicine.

SECTION 2 [725 characters]

After attending a talk at my school by an individual with autism spectrum disorders, I was inspired to delve deeper into the subject and wrote an article on Rett syndrome (a rare disorder) in my school newsletter. This exploration not only broadened my understanding of neurological conditions but also deepened my appreciation for the complexities of rare diseases.

Additionally, I was awarded prizes for articles on progeria, an extremely rare growth disorder, and the possible causes of left- and right-handedness. These experiences have enhanced my research and analytical skills, as well as my ability to communicate complex medical concepts effectively – qualities I look forward to applying in my future medical career.

SECTION 3 [1597 characters]

I have spent three weeks in local hospitals, spending time on ward rounds, in meetings and in theatre. During ward rounds, I recognised the importance of clarity and the patience needed by the consultants. I was also attracted by the teamwork involved. In a video meeting, I saw the importance of good communication, not only within hospitals but also between them. I was also lucky enough to attend theatre, seeing both a hip replacement and cardiac catheterisation, which I found exciting and stimulating.

During my holidays I volunteer for the trolley service at my local hospital. Although I play a fairly minor role, it allows me an insight into the basic minute-by-minute workings of a hospital. After talking to patients I often see the importance of the idea of "continuation of care". This made me question the current practice of patients rarely seeing the same GP when they book an appointment, which removes this important one-to-one relationship.

I enjoy sports and play for the badminton 1st VIII and tennis 1st VI. I also play the piano and take music theory lessons, in which I am working towards diploma and grade 8 qualifications respectively. I find both of these allow me time to relax from the daily stresses of life. Last year, I was part of a group which won the national CIMA management award, and I was Finance Director of 'Divine Taste', a student-run catering company. These were both superb team-building experiences: the former was a tough academic challenge and the latter a big responsibility and great fun, with the occasional awkward customer keeping us on our toes.

11.13 A level entry — 3977 characters

SECTION 1 [1061 characters]

My parents were foster carers offering respite care for children with disabilities or additional needs, so I grew up meeting a variety of different children who had many challenges to cope with. Consequently I developed an interest in various illnesses and disorders. My siblings and I often helped out when we could. Although this might sound gruelling, there were many happy and lighter moments caring for someone less fortunate and I saw how I could make a difference to someone's life. It made me more responsible and taught me the importance of patience when caring for others.

As a child, whenever I could find the time, I visited science and natural history museums and watched documentaries on the subject. Developing a science interest whilst needing to provide care to others made medicine an obvious career choice for me. Medicine will give me an incredibly varied, intellectually challenging and rewarding career and will also develop my critical thinking as well as my social responsibility. I feel I can bring both rigour and compassion to the job.

SECTION 2 [1115 characters]

As an elected student representative to the College Board, I ensure that new students feel comfortable transitioning into college life. This position has taught me the value of effective communication, active listening, and leadership, as I act as a bridge between students and staff to advocate for meaningful changes. The experience has highlighted the importance of creating environments where everyone feels heard and valued – an ethos I hope to carry into my medical career in medicine.

I am also a member of the student curriculum review board. As part of that role, I have honed my ability to critically evaluate complex systems, collaborate with faculty and peers, and propose constructive changes to improve the curriculum. I have gained skills in analysing data, balancing diverse perspectives, and advocating for the needs of the student body – qualities essential for a career in medicine. As part of this role I have demonstrated adaptability and the ability to work within a team to address challenges – skills that are directly transferable to the dynamic and collaborative nature of medical practice.

SECTION 3 [1801 characters]

I did two placements at St Peter's Hospital. In the gastroenterology placement, I attended ward rounds and gained an understanding of how important a methodical approach to writing up notes and good team management are to correctly diagnosing patients. In the A&E placement, I experienced my first 'difficult' patient, a bodybuilder who had overdosed on opium and needed to be restrained. The calm yet authoritative approach followed by the team helped a lot in this situation. This showed me another aspect of working as a doctor, particularly that the job is not all about medical diagnoses but also about managing people, needs and emotions. In this instance, I also learnt a lot about how the team needed to pull together to protect their own safety.

The most moving encounter I had in A&E was when a patient brought by ambulance could not be resuscitated. Although this somewhat affected me, I could see that the team was just 'getting on with it'. I saw this as a true test of my resolve and motivation towards medicine and how a certain level of professional detachment is essential.

Outside college, I coach badminton to a large group of primary school children. Originally, many were shy and reluctant to participate through fear of failure, but I was able to build their confidence and engage them, to the point that some have now started teaching others. Recently, I was elected to run the badminton club at college. This taught me good organisational skills but also a need to carefully balance the needs and wants of everyone in the group.

Parallel to my studies and other commitments, I also worked at David Clulow Opticians last year to finance the running of my car for the upcoming school year. This has taught me the benefits of hard work and made the rewards that much more enjoyable.

11.14 A level entry — 3510 characters

SECTION 1 [967 characters]

When I was younger, I would regularly visit my elderly grandparents and continued to do so when they moved into a care home. It was here that I learned the true value of empathy, by listening to their stories and also providing them with companionship. It showed me how connecting with others, understanding emotions and offering support, especially during challenging times, were as important as the practical care that was given.

Looking back, I realise these experiences were laying the foundation of my desire to pursue medicine. I learned that empathy and compassion can have a profound effect on others and have as much of a place in medicine as developing new drugs and carrying out research. Although I was very disappointed that I did not confirm a place for medicine last year, I am more determined than ever to be successful this year. I believe I have the ability, dedication and stamina to cope successfully with the challenges of a degree in medicine.

SECTION 2 [895 characters]

Studying five A level and one AS level subjects in the past two years meant I had to work conscientiously, prioritise my time efficiently and manage it well. It also meant having to cope with a heavy workload. Through my A level biology and chemistry courses I have gained exposure to cutting-edge medical technologies.

Last year, I particularly enjoyed attending a Medicine and Biological Sciences Masterclass at Imperial College. I also participated in many lectures and practical investigations, the highlight of my time being the visit to the Pathology Museum at Charing Cross Hospital, where I was able to see how disease actually affects particular organs of the body. I attended a Hammersmith Hospitals NHS Trust Open Day, where I had the opportunity to perform an angioplasty on a prosthetic model and attend a conference, during which I gained a lot of exposure to many ethical dilemmas.

SECTION 3 [1648 characters]

I enjoyed my work experience at Ealing Hospital in the Urology and X-ray departments, which allowed me to take a closer look at the doctor–patient relationship and gain an understanding of the implications of being a doctor. I felt particularly privileged to be allowed into the operating theatre to watch cystoscopies and the removal of kidney stones using an ureteroscope and in one case, due to the location and size of the stone, using percutaneous nephrolithotomy. Being able to then watch the progress and recovery of these patients during daily ward rounds allowed me to gain an insight into how important a doctor's role is in post-operative care.

Being bilingual in English and Polish and speaking French to a high level, I am now currently learning Spanish in order to prepare for my gap year placement in Peru (two months). I think it is important to be able to communicate with a degree of competency with speakers of other languages, especially in a medical setting. I also worked in the Ealing Polish Saturday School, supervising four to seven-year-old pupils. This helped increase my maturity and allowed me to gain valuable communication and organisation skills.

Performing with the Polish dancing group 'Mazury' for seven years has helped me keep in touch with my Polish roots and instil self-confidence. Volunteer work at a local hospice, Meadow House, has given me a very different type of experience. Here, providing help for the terminally ill has reinforced my strong desire to study medicine. I believe that, in caring for those awaiting death, I have above all learnt the true meaning of empathy and concern for the suffering.

11.15   A level entry   3952 characters

SECTION 1 [890 characters]

My interest in human biology over the past few years has steered me towards a career in medicine. I have an inquisitive mind and I enjoy reading and learning about all sorts of topics. For example I recently spent time reading many articles and journals on CRISPR-Cas9 Gene Editing and also the impact of AI on radiology. There is a satisfying degree of detective work involved in medicine, and where it's possible to solve a problem, and make a difference to someone with whom you have built up a relationship, it is even more gratifying.

Helping out at the local primary school for the past three years and at a home for the elderly has confirmed my belief that I would like to work with a variety of people, and being able to apply medical knowledge to do this would be fantastic. Talking both to children and to the elderly has taught me valuable communication skills vital for medicine.

SECTION 2 [1281 characters]

In my current biology course, I am enjoying the section on the brain. I had the opportunity to meet Prof. Steven Rose when he gave a lecture at our school. I did some background research on Prof. Rose, which showed that he had been a critic of genetic determinism and evolutionary psychology. I researched other arguments on the matter, cross-referencing with work published by other authors such as Darwin and Dawkins, and put together a presentation for the class. I was praised for demonstrating a forensic analysis of information and ideas, a strong ability to remain objective and the clarity of my presentation in view of the complexity of the arguments presented.

As a writer and editor for my school's science magazine, I have enhanced my communication and critical thinking skills while fostering a passion for sharing scientific knowledge. Writing articles has taught me how to simplify complex concepts and present them in an engaging way, while editing ensures that content is clear, accurate, and well structured. Managing submissions and deadlines has strengthened my organisational abilities and attention to detail. I had the opportunity to write a monthly medical column, which allowed me to expand my knowledge of medical conditions while honing my writing skills.

SECTION 3 [1781 characters]

To learn more about medicine, I attended a Medlink course, during which I felt inspired by doctors who talked honestly and enthusiastically about their work. This made me more aware of the pros and cons of a medical career, and I felt it consolidated my choice. I did a week's work experience in Rheumatology at the Royal Free Hospital and two weeks in Paediatric Surgery at Chelsea & Westminster Hospital. I discovered how the medical profession really operates, and the commitment one must have. Attending various clinics, I saw the less glamorous side of medicine and learnt skills that will enable me to deal with the social aspects of medicine, such as empathy and a good bedside manner. I also saw how vital clear communication is, not just between healthcare professionals but between doctor and patient, especially if the patient is young or has English as a second language. I was very impressed by one of the paediatric surgeons who was always at ease with people and had an amazing manner when working with children. I lived in Zambia for a couple of years so I experienced other cultures and some of the problems they face, such as the growing HIV/AIDS problem. I saw how this is not just a medical problem but also has wider social implications. This really showed me that medicine is not just about scientific knowledge but also about psychosocial factors.

For the past two years, I have enjoyed taking a course in metalwork and jewellery-making, in which I developed skills relating to precise hand–eye coordination, essential in surgical settings. I help run our Amnesty International group, setting up fundraising events for the sixth form, such as the annual Valentine's Ball. This has helped me deal with a variety of people and enhanced my organisational skills.

11.16 A level entry — 3740 characters

SECTION 1 [1032 characters]

My grandfather has PSP, a terminal disease. Our GP has been a huge support, full of authoritative advice, obvious concern and good humour. I know no other job that gives this opportunity to make use of scientific knowledge to help people deal with serious problems, or that could be so rewarding to someone doing it well. That is why I want to become a doctor.

While assisting in a university lab researching pre-eclampsia, I dissected a placenta, learned about medical research and observed mitosis under a microscope. This experience gave me a real feel of what studying medicine would be like and confirmed my desire to learn from a clinical point of view – for example, not just mitosis, but the process of uncontrolled cell division in cancer and the treatments available.

My ambition to study medicine is based on the belief that my interest in medical science, empathetic personality and capacity for work are well suited to life as a medic and will give me a chance to achieve the high standards I have witnessed in others.

SECTION 2 [846 characters]

I am naturally self-disciplined and this year found it easy to plan my own exam revision and complete it without last-minute dramas. As Deputy Head Librarian at my school, I developed organisational and leadership skills through managing the library's daily operations, mentoring younger students, and organising events to promote reading and learning. Assisting students in locating resources and collaborating with staff to improve efficiency enhanced my communication and teamwork abilities, while balancing these responsibilities alongside academic and extracurricular commitments strengthened my time management and resilience. These experiences have prepared me for the challenges of medical training, where effective communication, adaptability, and the ability to work under pressure are essential for providing high-quality patient care.

SECTION 3 [1862 characters]

All the medics I have met have enthused me with their dedication. In an ICU, I observed a team of 14 doctors and nurses helping a man survive a crisis. I felt strongly how good it would be to be part of this effort. I enjoy teamwork, and, for example, was a member of a first aid team which came second in the national St John's competition. A week in a GP surgery showed me the self-discipline which a GP needs to cope with a long list. My job was to sort the patient index cards, and it made me realise how patient care depends on good administration. A busy anaesthetist, whom I shadowed for a week, made time to communicate effectively with his patients and reassure them. This impressed me, as I find it easy to empathise with people and am a good listener.

My voluntary work this year in a nursing home has helped me develop this side of my character: I help out with activities, such as bingo and quizzes, and chat with the residents. This has shown the importance of building a good rapport with clients. My experience of caring for terminally ill people in the St Frai Hospital in Lourdes this summer was most rewarding. I had never before been anywhere with such a good atmosphere, created by both carers and the sick, and it helped me appreciate the psychology of medical care.

By making up for my size through determination and pace, I made the school 2nd XV at rugby in my lower sixth year. The enjoyment of the team's successes, and sharing of the odd failure, is a highlight of my school life. In a Young Enterprise company I had to push one flagging project through by my own efforts. We won an award, and I learned what is achievable through commitment. I am a school prefect and head of the CCF RAF section. In these roles I have learned the importance of communicating the purpose of a task and a sense of shared responsibility for its success.

11.17 — A level entry — 3790 characters

SECTION 1 [1085 characters]

A documentary on a pioneering surgeon performing life-changing operations left a lasting impression on me. Seeing the precision, skill, and decision-making required in the operating room fascinated me, but what stood out most was the surgeon's deep empathy for their patients. They not only restored function and saved lives but also transformed patients' confidence and quality of life. Witnessing such a tangible impact on people's well-being made me eager to explore the field of medicine. Inspired by their dedication, I engaged in surgical workshops, shadowed doctors, and studied anatomy with a newfound appreciation for the human body's intricacy. This experience cemented my aspiration to become a doctor who, like them, can blend technical expertise with compassionate care to make a meaningful difference in patients' lives.

I understand that studying and practising medicine will be demanding. However, for me this is a profession in which I can make the most of my intellect, experience and personality while working with people to try to improve the quality of their lives.

SECTION 2 [802 characters]

During my biology course, I did a neuroscience project on reflex arcs. I needed to interact with a public who weren't always very knowledgeable about such topics and I really learnt how to explain information to people from all walks of life. I have also demonstrated and developed my teaching skills by being a maths and English assistant for the past six years and arranging revision sessions at school. In medicine this will be a key skill to possess to engage fully with patients.

I was a prefect in Year 12 and an active member of the Charity Committee, which allowed me to contribute positively to my school life. My multilingual skills will be valuable while communicating with French and Asian communities and by achieving the ECDL I will be well equipped to work on electronic patient records.

SECTION 3 [1903 characters]

Work experience in a hospital burns unit helped me understand the physical and emotional suffering patients endure and the role of the medical team to help and heal on both these fronts. Observing junior doctors and consultants talking to patients highlighted the importance of interpersonal communication skills. By shadowing a GP for a week I learned about the social influences on patients' health and saw a wide spectrum of illnesses present in the community. Witnessing the breaking of bad news revealed the importance of being a good listener and being able to communicate clearly and sensitively. At the surgery I completed a research project, which involved interviewing patients on their opinions about hospital doctors and GPs. I discovered that continuity of care matters most to patients, as they develop trust in their GP, but they also regard hospital specialists highly.

I have been a volunteer at the League of Friends' tea bar at Wythenshawe Hospital. This has given me experience in communicating with a range of people, including patients and visitors. I have enjoyed helping and listening to the residents at a local nursing home for the past six months. This experience taught me the importance of empathy, and gave me the chance to build relationships and gain trust. For the past year, every Sunday, I have assisted disabled children and adults to swim at a local club. I am able to support them, as well as help develop their confidence and it is encouraging to see them improve.

I enjoy working with people and have developed my teamwork and leadership skills through my involvement in the Duke of Edinburgh Award Scheme. I attended a first aid course in preparation for the Gold expedition, which helped me to deal with a panic attack experienced by a team member. I also took a lead role in organising route plans and spreadsheets and delegated responsibilities to team members.

11.18   A level entry   3673 characters

SECTION 1 [1174 characters]

What makes a seventeen-year-old decide that he wants to do medicine? Is it just because his school says he is a high achiever and that he should choose a career that needs hard work and consciousness? In my case, there has never been any doubt about my career choice. Since I was small, I have been fascinated by what things really are and how they work, and that includes the most complex of all: the human body. I used to draw people from the inside out, showing their lungs, their brain, their stomach. I would draw these in place of the usual 'stick men' and loved looking things up in 'The way the body works' books that I accumulated. I marvelled at how all these complex structures fit together perfectly to function as one body. If my early fascination with the human body ignited it, then it is the last few years that have fuelled my determination to be a doctor.

I would feel honoured to be part of a profession that can use the scientific knowledge that I love so much, to help people in so many ways. I feel there is no better job satisfaction than this, and because every patient is an individual, every day will be different. That is why I want to be a doctor.

SECTION 2 [910 characters]

My innate sense of curiosity and thirst for knowledge has meant that I have always enjoyed school. I chose to take both maths and further maths at A level, so if I had cashed in the six maths modules I sat this summer, I would have achieved an A for A level maths. Studying maths has taught me the importance of making informed judgements about which concepts and methods to apply to solve complex problems. This skill has enhanced my ability to analyse situations critically, think logically, and adapt my approach when faced with challenges. These qualities are highly transferable and essential in medicine, where diagnosing and treating patients often requires selecting the most appropriate solutions from a range of possibilities. The discipline and precision I have developed through maths will support my ability to approach medical problems systematically while remaining open to innovative solutions.

SECTION 3 [1589 characters]

Work experience in several different areas of the NHS revealed how difficult it can be to find and treat a problem effectively, despite medical advances. While shadowing a district nurse, I observed how important it is to improve a patient's quality of life. Most of the cases I saw were either chronic conditions, such as rheumatoid arthritis or terminal cases such as gastric cancer. I noticed how the district nurse was not there to simply cure, but to counsel and offer palliative care. I have also found it useful to spend a day with a foundation year 1 doctor during a week at Pinderfields Hospital, as it showed me the less glamorous aspects of being a doctor; medicine is not always action-packed. However, I witnessed several endoscopies and an arthroscopic subacromial decompression, which I found deeply fascinating.

Every Friday night I am a volunteer at a nursing home. My work includes exercises to stimulate the residents' memories, encouraging conversation and discussion. I enjoy the work immensely and get great satisfaction out of making a small difference to their lives. I have been working with St John's Ambulance for over a year now and have learnt how to confidently put my first aid into practice. It has been a valuable lesson in teamwork, helping in big events such as the Humber Bridge marathon and Hull Fair. Being a mentor to inner-city primary school children contrasted with being a Form Prefect in our junior school. This has given me practical experience in dealing with people from all walks and stages of life, supporting them with patience and respect.

11.19 A level entry — 3794 characters

SECTION 1 [1013 characters]

Since an early age I have been fascinated by the complexities of the human body. I have always wanted to know how things worked in life and an inquisitive nature led me to study the sciences in more depth at A level. When studying biology I was introduced to some of the different ways in which our bodies are protected against diseases and infections, for example our ability to produce antibodies and memory cells to help prevent the recurrence of an infection. I was intrigued by the body's defence mechanism but was equally struck by the vulnerability of the body to diseases such as cholera, malaria and HIV. It made me value life even more, and knowing that doctors worked to help improve such people's lives and dedicate a career to help people made me really appreciate their role in society. It is precisely this which has inspired me to pursue a career in medicine; the potential satisfaction I could gain by making such positive differences in people's lives is something which no other job can provide.

SECTION 2 [1246 characters]

Ever since I determined that medicine was to be my career, I have been single-minded in my focus towards this goal. I have a thirst for knowledge, ability to interact and empathise with people as well as a capability of working under pressure, all of which I hope to exercise as a medical student. I am dedicated in my studies, evident by my achievement in getting one of the top 5 marks in the country for GCSE maths.

Learning about microscopy and cells in A level biology and helping younger students understand these concepts has significantly developed my ability to communicate scientific information effectively, which is essential in medicine. I gained a deep understanding of the structure and function of cells, including how they relate to health and disease, and I had the opportunity to present this knowledge to others. By guiding younger students through the process of using microscopes and understanding cell biology, I honed my ability to explain complex topics in an accessible and engaging way. The ability to educate and support others in understanding medical concepts is an essential part of patient care and teamwork in clinical settings, and this experience has equipped me to do so effectively in my future medical career.

SECTION 3 [1535 characters]

I volunteered at my local nursing home for five weeks where I gained invaluable experience in interacting with people, talking to them and developing my communication skills. This also allowed me to build my interpersonal skills. I further developed these skills while shadowing an SHO at Wexham Park Hospital. Seeing doctors work in their occupational environment taught me a lot about the nature of their job. I came to appreciate that being a good doctor does not depend solely on academic excellence; rather a whole range of attributes are required, including the ability to work as a team, interact with people, effective time management and the capability of working under pressure.

Attendance at the 'Medsim' workshop conference at Nottingham University provided me with invaluable hands-on clinical experience and as team leader of the rescue operation I was able to develop my leadership skills, make practical and pragmatic decisions, whilst remaining calm and composed at all times when under immense pressure. Aside from my academic interests, I also enjoy designing and programming websites, something which I self-taught. At 16 I started my own design and print business and, since establishing it, I now have over 15 contracts with companies who regularly come back to me. Meeting clients and being able to gain their trust is, by far, the most rewarding aspect of my business, even more than earning the money, and this has helped me with my self-confidence and being able to interact with people from all walks of life.

11.20   A level entry   3994 characters

SECTION 1 [1193 characters]

During a hospital visit, I observed a paediatrician interact with a young patient who was visibly anxious about their check-up. With remarkable ease, they turned the medical examination into a game, using humour and simple language to explain each step. The child, who had initially clung to their parent in fear, soon began to giggle and engage with the doctor. Witnessing this transformation left a deep impression on me. It showed me that medicine is not just about diagnosing and treating illnesses but also about building trust, particularly with vulnerable patients. The ability to communicate complex medical concepts in a child-friendly manner and provide reassurance through warmth and empathy is a skill I deeply admire. This experience inspired me to explore paediatrics further, leading me to volunteer with children in healthcare settings and study child development.

Through these experiences, I gained insight into the importance of early intervention and compassionate care. I aspire to follow this paediatrician's example, becoming a doctor who not only heals but also makes each patient feel safe and valued, helping to shape positive healthcare experiences from an early age.

SECTION 2 [817 characters]

As part of A level drama, I led a drama performance that was performed in front of an audience of more than 300. This has significantly challenged and enhanced my leadership and communication skills. As director, I was responsible for coordinating rehearsals, motivating the cast, and ensuring everyone worked together, a difficult task when everyone has their own idea of what should be done and occasionally challenged my approach. This role required me to think critically under pressure, make quick decisions, and maintain focus, whilst maintaining good relationships. Working closely with others and navigating different personalities and perspectives also helped me develop a strong sense of empathy and understanding. All those qualities will serve me well in providing patient-centred care as a future doctor.

SECTION 3 [1984 characters]

My extensive work experience has shown me that there is even more to the field of medicine than I originally thought. A doctor not only needs to provide medical expertise but must also be an effective communicator with compassion for their patients. During my two weeks in Haematology at UHW, I attended daily ward rounds and outpatient clinics. I shadowed a radiologist undertaking routine X-rays and ultrasounds. During my work experience at a GP practice, I discovered the differences in the relationship between a GP and their patient compared with a hospital doctor and their patient. Most recently, I spent a week with a maxillofacial consultant, shadowing him in A&E and on his research projects. I have gained a good insight into many aspects of being a doctor, for example the importance of working with other health professionals as part of a team. On all occasions, doctors talked me through procedures and made me aware of the importance of trust and confidentiality in the doctor–patient relationship.

I enjoy charity work and am involved in the Childline in Partnership with Schools scheme, where I advise younger pupils on problems that they may have. This gives me a position of responsibility and I have learned to communicate more effectively. For pleasure and relaxation, I enjoy modern dance and regularly perform in shows. I take part in drama lessons, which have helped to increase my confidence. I also have a passion for music and am a committed member of school choirs performing in many concerts. I was Operations Director of a successful Young Enterprise company that held a fashion show and reached the Welsh Final. I also organised our Year 11 School Ball. These successes have led me to being appointed Events Prefect.

I believe that the experiences I have gained both inside and outside school make me an ideal candidate for medicine. I have the dedication, motivation and ability to succeed. I look forward to meeting all the future demands of medicine.

11.21 A level entry — 3990 characters

SECTION 1 [785 characters]

My decision to pursue medicine was profoundly influenced by the care a doctor provided to a family member during a critical illness. Watching them navigate complex medical decisions with both confidence and kindness was inspiring. They took the time to explain treatment options, reassured my family during moments of uncertainty, and treated my loved one with genuine empathy. Their ability to combine medical knowledge with emotional support showed me the true essence of being a doctor and made me appreciate the transformative role of healthcare professionals in patients' lives.

I enjoy working with people as I can easily empathise with their problems, and by pursuing a career in medicine I hope to make a genuine contribution to people's lives in a scientific and rewarding way.

SECTION 2 [1255 characters]

While studying biology at A level I was fascinated to learn about the workings of the human body – from the dissection of a mammalian heart to the cutting-edge science of stem cell research – all of which has reaffirmed my desire to discover more about the use of biological knowledge for diagnosis.

Presenting a neurodegenerative disease in a school assembly helped me develop essential communication and presentation skills that are critical for a career in medicine. In preparing for the presentation, I conducted in-depth research into the disease's causes, progression, symptoms, and potential treatments, which gave me a comprehensive understanding of neurodegenerative disorders. This experience taught me how to communicate complex medical information to a diverse audience, making it accessible and engaging for people with varying levels of knowledge. Effective communication is a key skill in medicine, as it is vital for educating patients, collaborating with healthcare teams, and explaining diagnoses and treatment options. This opportunity also strengthened my confidence in presenting under pressure and in a public setting, skills that will be valuable when interacting with patients, colleagues, and in professional medical environments.

SECTION 3 [1950 characters]

I gained insight into the medical profession through various voluntary roles. As a Ward Volunteer at North London Hospice, I learned the importance of a compassionate approach to patients and gained experience working in a team. I also provide first aid at public events with the Red Cross, which has boosted my confidence and enhanced my communication skills. Additionally, as a Voluntary Befriender, I visited an elderly man with cognitive difficulties, emphasising the significance of clear communication, eye contact, and reassurance.

One of the most impactful experiences was with the Red Cross in Mexico, where I worked alongside medical professionals. By day, I assisted with basic procedures like stitches and injections, while at night, I joined ambulance staff on emergency callouts. This role gave me exposure to long hours and high-pressure situations.

Currently, I am taking a gap year. I work as a support worker, helping young people with special needs achieve their potential in performance. I am also training to use the EMIS system as a medical notes summariser at a health centre, which has deepened my understanding of the NHS. I plan to volunteer at Barretstown in Ireland to gain experience in paediatrics while contributing to a good cause. Additionally, I will continue offering first aid at public events and attend courses like 'Providing Emotional Support' and 'Child Protection.'

I also volunteer at a day care centre for individuals with dementia, further exploring different areas of healthcare. While academics are important to me, I recognise the need for a work–life balance. I stay active in sports and pursue interests in graphics design, photography, and music. I designed advertising for a fundraising cabaret for Lighthouse Ministries International this year.

I hope my diverse experiences demonstrate my genuine commitment to Medicine, and I look forward to the challenges and learning opportunities that lie ahead.

11.22 A level entry — 3448 characters

SECTION 1 [720 characters]

I like the idea of not knowing everything. I see medicine as a continuum of information, learning and experience and am not content with being happy to know only what is required. Reading the 'Scientific American' and Matt Ridley's 'Genome' has sparked my interest in the frontline of cancer treatment and the profound implications both physical and mental upon the patient. For example, a friend recently undertook the BRCA1/2 genetic testing to determine her susceptibility to cancer. This raised issues of surgical intervention, possible inheritance and all-round stress. Her case made me consider whether such sensitive information is necessarily a good thing but has also really made me want to be part the journey.

SECTION 2 [913 characters]

I have developed my attention to detail whilst studying A level maths, particularly during a group project where precision was critical to ensure the accuracy of our work. In this project, I carefully reviewed calculations, checked for errors, and contributed to refining our solutions to meet the task requirements. Collaborating with my team required clear communication and a shared commitment to maintaining high standards, teaching me the importance of accountability and mutual support in achieving a common goal.

These skills are vital for a career in medicine, where meticulous attention to detail is essential for diagnosing conditions, prescribing treatments, and performing procedures. The ability to collaborate effectively with colleagues ensures the best outcomes for patients, while a thorough approach minimises the risk of errors, reinforcing my readiness for the challenges of becoming a doctor.

SECTION 3 [1815 characters]

During a work experience programme at a hospital, I observed surgery, orthopaedic consultations, and A&E. I was intrigued by the role of the anaesthetist and fascinated by the collaboration between disciplines. Conversations with doctors about the challenges of their work gave me a more realistic view of medicine. I also observed the important role of doctors as educators and see myself fitting into this role. I believe teaching is crucial, as I've learned that true understanding comes from explaining complex concepts to others.

I have volunteered at Chase Hospice as Father Christmas, a dishwasher, and decorator, and led music and furniture restoration workshops at the Meath Epilepsy Trust. I also volunteer weekly at Cancer Research, sorting clothes and working the till, while also working at Waitrose on the meat and fish counter. Balancing these roles with my studies and social life has improved my time management and confidence in communicating with diverse people. Waitrose, in particular, has taught me the value of teamwork in meeting strict standards.

I play bass in a band, which was selected to perform at GuilFest. I organised ticket sales, press releases, and liaised with the festival organisers, sharpening my leadership and teamwork skills. Playing bass is a creative outlet and stress-reliever. I also enjoy trading recipes at Waitrose and trying them out. Completing my Bronze Duke of Edinburgh award encouraged me to pursue the Silver award, which I will finish in October. The award has helped me practice decision-making under pressure, a skill I'll need in my medical career.

This year has been both challenging and rewarding, reinforcing my commitment to medicine. My recent work experience has confirmed my desire to contribute to the field, and I'm eager to pursue a medical degree.

11.23 A level entry — 3810 characters

SECTION 1 [1037 characters]

Reading medical autobiographies like 'This is going to hurt' and 'Being mortal' gave me an unfiltered look into the realities of medicine. These books moved beyond textbook knowledge, revealing the emotional, ethical, and personal challenges that doctors face. Being Mortal deepened my understanding of palliative care and the delicate balance between prolonging life and ensuring quality of life. 'This is going to hurt' highlighted the pressures of working in the NHS, showing the immense responsibility and resilience required in medicine. These stories made me reflect on what it truly means to be a doctor – the sacrifices, the patient relationships, and the ethical dilemmas. They also reinforced the importance of compassion in healthcare.

Seeing medicine through the lens of personal experiences, rather than just science, strengthened my commitment to a career where both knowledge and humanity are equally vital. These books did not just inform me; they inspired me to pursue a profession where I can make a tangible difference.

SECTION 2 [849 characters]

Participating in my school's Young Enterprise scheme was a transformative experience that provided me with valuable insights into business management and teamwork. Collaborating with ten of my peers, I honed critical skills such as leadership, effective communication and financial planning. I learned the importance of taking responsibility and maintaining a commitment to quality and organisation, which were pivotal in guiding our team toward success. This experience not only enhanced my ability to work collaboratively but also taught me to adapt under pressure and make decisions with precision – skills that are equally essential in medicine.

The lessons I gained from balancing the demands of planning, execution, and financial control have strengthened my resolve to approach future challenges with the same dedication and strategic mindset.

SECTION 3 [1924 characters]

I undertook work experience in the West Wales General Hospital last year, where I spent time in various departments, clinics and theatre. I observed doctors diagnose and treat patients and learnt that confidentiality, honesty and trust between patient and doctor are of great importance, and that teamwork is also vital in order to achieve the correct diagnosis. I have also undertaken work experience in The Optic Shop in 2005, which also involved clinical observation. Here I observed the opticians diagnose several patients with various eye conditions and refer them appropriately.

I am currently a volunteer at a Red Cross charity shop where I help receive donations, organise the donated items and work as a cashier, which has developed my communication skills further. I participated in my school's Young Enterprise scheme working with 10 pupils. This has given me an insight into business management skills. It was through this highly enriching experience that I have developed further skills in teamwork, leadership, taking responsibility, and the need for commitment to quality, planning, financial control and communication. All these skills have helped my classmates and me to lead our business to success. I currently attend regular first aid training classes with St John Ambulance, gaining further knowledge of life support skills, as well as assessing and responding immediately in an emergency situation. In my spare time I read the 'New Scientist' magazine and newspapers to gain knowledge about current affairs in politics, science and healthcare. I attend the gym in order to improve my physical and mental fitness. I enjoy regularly playing chess, taking part in karate, badminton and critical thinking classes, and listening to music. I am also intending to go to Bangladesh over Christmas to do voluntary work at rural clinics, help the poor and those that have been affected by severe floods and cyclones.

11.24 A level entry — 3927 characters

SECTION 1 [918 characters]

Personal experiences from a young age, strong academic interests in the sciences and the prospect of a challenging and fulfilling career have led to a passion to read medicine. I am fully aware that this will offer immense challenges not only in clinical settings but also in terms of keeping abreast of current medical research and technological advancements. I see medicine as a unique and evolving profession and I believe that I have the commitment, enthusiasm and personality required to become a successful doctor.

Due to my own recent medical problems, I have visited several consultants specialising in different branches of medicine, giving me an insight into the various career paths available in the profession and the teamwork and communication required between these specialists and other departments. Both the courses and my experiences have confirmed that I have the dedication required to study medicine.

SECTION 2 [775 characters]

Studying A level art has been a rewarding journey that has nurtured my creativity, attention to detail, and ability to think critically – skills integral to a career in medicine. Participating in photography and showcasing my work at school art exhibitions taught me patience, observational skills, and an appreciation for diverse perspectives, enabling me to approach problems with precision and empathy. Organising these exhibitions developed my planning and communication skills, as I engaged with peers and teachers to present ideas effectively.

These experiences have strengthened my ability to balance creativity with analytical thinking, qualities that will support me in diagnosing and addressing complex medical challenges while connecting meaningfully with patients.

SECTION 3 [2234 characters]

Last summer, I volunteered in Zambia for a month, working as a medical and community assistant. I helped in local clinics with vital signs, inoculations, and baby weighing, and provided palliative and preventative care to people in their homes. This experience highlighted the stark differences between healthcare in a developing country and the UK, as resources were limited. I also contributed to creating an educational programme on HIV/AIDS for local adults.

Over the past year I have undertaken work experience at two contrasting hospitals. At a small post-operative geriatric hospital I spent time talking to patients on wards and in clinics, learnt about the many illnesses associated with the elderly, such as COPD, and witnessed the effects of the lack of funding facing CCGs. Whilst at UCH I was able to experience live theatre. It was particularly interesting to watch the extraction of a large facial tumour requiring extensive surgery. The consultant I shadowed is a leading expert on photodynamic therapy, a new form of non-invasive cancer treatment. I have since researched this and other cancer treatments to draw comparisons. Work experience has made me aware that medicine involves long, unsociable hours and high levels of stress and also that individuals have different needs and values that must be respected at all times.

My extracurricular activities are diverse. As a young leader for a local Cubs pack, I've improved my leadership and teamwork skills. I communicate well with both adults and children, a skill I further developed through an Acorn listening course.

I am also a music scholar at school, studying trombone at the Junior Guildhall School of Music and Drama, and working towards Grade 8. I've performed with the Guildhall Brass Band and Symphony Orchestra at venues like the Edinburgh Fringe and Symphony Hall in Birmingham. I've been a member of the National Children's Orchestra for three years. Additionally, I play hockey for my school's 1st X1 team, enjoy squash and badminton, and hold an advanced PADI Scuba Diving qualification. As an active member of the MUN team, I participated in an international conference at UNESCO in Paris, improving my confidence, teamwork, and communication skills.

11.25   A level entry   3905 characters

SECTION 1 [1139 characters]

'The man who mistook his wife for a hat' by Oliver Sacks opened my eyes to the intricacies of the human brain and the diagnostic challenges in neurology. Each case study illustrated how brain disorders can alter a person's perception, memory, and sense of self, showing me that medicine is not just about treating symptoms but understanding the profound ways in which diseases affect individuals. The book fascinated me because it blurred the lines between science and storytelling, illustrating that each patient is unique and requires a tailored approach to care. One case that intrigued me was that of a man who could not recognise faces but could identify people through their voices. This highlighted how adaptable the human brain is and how much we still have to learn about it. Sacks' compassionate approach to his patients inspired me to explore neuroscience further and read more on neurodegenerative conditions like Alzheimer's. His writing reinforced my belief that medicine is not just about solving biological puzzles but about understanding and improving lives. It's a challenge I will relish to adopt and strive to excel at.

SECTION 2 [1826 characters]

My studies of biology and chemistry have given me a better understanding of scientific theories. These two subjects complement each other perfectly: biochemistry added a new dimension to my knowledge of human physiology, explaining the metabolic processes that generate the energy needed by organisms. Further reading taught me about the biochemical mechanisms used by humans to survive in conditions to which they are not accustomed. These concepts are described in 'Life at the Extremes' by Frances Ashcroft, which conveys the vulnerability of the human body to disease.

I also channelled my passion for science into my role as vice-chair of Science Society, a position that requires both teamwork and efficiency to organise activities for science club each week for the younger years and arrange speakers who appeal to older students. Last year I founded and became editor of the school science newsletter. Producing an edition each month requires energy and creativity, characteristics which I think will prove invaluable while studying medicine.

This summer I was awarded a Nuffield bursary to work in the division of Molecular Immunology at the National Institute for Medical Research, hence I read 'Biomedicine and the Human Condition' by Michael Sargent to familiarise myself with terms such as histocompatibility, cell apoptosis and autoimmunity. During my four weeks at NIMR, I studied the T-lymphocytes of mouse mutants. Using techniques such as fluorescence-activated cell sorting and enzyme-linked immuno-sorbent assay highlighted the importance of molecular immunology in medicine, as both of these techniques can be used to test for HIV in patients. After spending a month investigating disease and the human body's reaction to infection, I would now like to study its counterpart, the cure for disease: medicine.

SECTION 3 [940 characters]

I volunteer weekly at 'Kids Can Achieve', a centre for children with autism, ADHD and schizophrenia. This allows me to interact with disadvantaged members of the community and help them to develop social skills and has helped me learn patience and empathy. The variety of ages, temperaments and personalities means having to adjust to suit the needs of each individual child. This is sometimes difficult and challenging work so requires a calm temperament and listening to the advice of senior professional members of the team. After completing work experience in both a GP surgery and a hospital I was able to understand the commitment involved in the medical profession. From operating on a sick child, to working continuously for a twenty-four-hour shift, the practice of medicine is both strenuous and demanding and I learnt the importance of time management and having a degree of professional detachment while still caring for people.

11.26 A level entry 3985 characters

SECTION 1 [1410 characters]

In my family, traditional remedies and modern medicine were often used side by side to address health concerns. Herbal teas, homeopathic treatments, and dietary changes were commonly turned to for minor ailments, while prescribed medications played a crucial role in treating more serious conditions. This coexistence of different healing approaches sparked my curiosity about how traditional practices could complement modern medical treatments rather than stand in opposition to them. I began to question how cultural and historical knowledge of medicine, often passed down through generations, could provide valuable insights that enhance patient care. This experience led me to explore the intersection between these two approaches and how they can work together to optimise health outcomes. I became particularly fascinated by how some traditional methods, such as plant-based treatments or mindfulness practices, have gained scientific validation and are now integrated into modern medical care.

The idea that healthcare can be both evidence-based and culturally sensitive resonates with me, reinforcing my interest in a holistic approach that respects diverse traditions while embracing scientific advancements. This perspective has deepened my desire to study medicine, where I can explore how different medical systems can complement one another to provide more personalised, well-rounded patient care.

SECTION 2 [1285 characters]

I am currently studying science-based subjects: biology, mixed with chemistry, obviously provides stimulating information on the human body and the world around us. It has taught me the process of research and has prompted me to think critically. I subscribe to 'Chemistry Review' and 'Biological Sciences Review' magazines and also try to read up on current research to stimulate my brain. My interest in medicine pressed me into reading a special report in 'Scientific American' called 'The Future of Stem Cells' and the book 'The Rise and Fall of Modern Medicine' by James Le Fanu. I enjoy the process of trying to understand some of the most complex mechanisms. Maths has allowed me to develop problem-solving techniques that are vital in the field of medicine and economics has taught me to be analytical and careful when considering the outcome of different possibilities.

As a result of my commitment to my school, I was chosen as a senior school prefect, a role that includes the daily running of the school in many areas. It is important to be able to communicate between the prefect body and the younger students to ensure the smooth running of the school. Furthermore, I was made my House's charities officer, teaching me leadership in organising a fundraising charity event.

SECTION 3 [1290 characters]

This summer I gained work experience in Pakistan at The Tabba Heart Institute, a private hospital, and The Sindh Institute of Urology and Transplantation, a caritative hospital providing free care. I observed a triple heart bypass surgery and a kidney transplant from within the operating theatre. It was interesting to see how the doctors worked with people who felt entitled to care and those who were simply grateful for any treatment. I also shadowed top consultants and learned about procedures such as lithotripsy. Shadowing consultants helped me to understand the demands of working at such a high level and also the importance of working as a team and having good relationships with other medical professionals.

I play for the school cricket 1st XI and have played for Stanmore Cricket Club up to under-17 level. In addition I have represented the school in rugby and basketball. I feel that the tense situations that can arise in sports can teach you to operate under pressure, which would stand me in good stead in a medical career. Being a member of Amnesty International and the Iraqi fundraising trust within school has also taught me the concept of teamwork. I have passed LAMDA public speaking awards up to a Gold level, further improving my ability to communicate confidently.

11.27　A level entry　3981 characters

SECTION 1 [879 characters]

Growing up attending Sunday school, I was deeply influenced by the Christian values of compassion and service, particularly the parable of the Good Samaritan. In this story, a Samaritan helps a wounded man, demonstrating selfless care despite their differences. This act of mercy resonated with me, as it highlighted the importance of offering help to those in need, especially the sick and suffering. Witnessing medical professionals embody this compassion in their work further fuelled my desire to study medicine. Just like the Good Samaritan, doctors and healthcare workers provide care to individuals in vulnerable moments, offering both physical treatment and emotional support.

I am inspired by the idea of dedicating myself to a profession where I can follow this principle – healing not only the body but also addressing the psychological and emotional needs of patients.

SECTION 2 [1157 characters]

I use every opportunity to delve deeper into the subjects that I study at school. My love of science led me to read 'Human Instinct' by Robert Winston, which investigates the influence of instincts on our actions. Studying medical ethics in R.E. has made me aware of the problems facing the NHS such as the allocation of resources: should they be focused on research or the alleviation of suffering at a more commonly experienced level? It has also helped me become more understanding and compassionate.

Last year, I had the opportunity to carry out research for my extended essay in school, where I tested the antibacterial properties of five different herbs. This experience not only strengthened my research skills but also deepened my interest in complementary medicine and the role of nutrition in maintaining health. Writing the essay allowed me to explore the scientific basis behind natural remedies and consider their potential benefits as part of a holistic approach to healthcare. This has further inspired my desire to pursue a career in medicine, where I can integrate scientific knowledge with a compassionate, patient-centred approach to care.

SECTION 3 [1945 characters]

During a placement at Durham Hospital, I practised skills such as taking blood and suturing a dummy and observed procedures such as nerve testing for carpal tunnel syndrome, ultrasounds and endoscopies. I met an inspiring man who had survived bowel and lung cancer and saw how vital family support was in battling against his disease. In contrast, I saw a woman who was told there was no cure for her condition: witnessing her tears was difficult but an important experience for me, helping me to understand that even less serious medical problems may still affect a patient's life.

Spending a week in a GP surgery allowed me to see a variety of medical problems and showed the value of each team member in maintaining a successful surgery. As a volunteer in a nursing home, painting patients' nails and listening to their stories, I learnt it only takes a little time to keep someone company but it is something that is greatly appreciated. I also helped children with dyslexia, which was extremely rewarding and provided me with the chance to communicate with people of all age groups.

As a member of Amnesty International, I often take part in activities to show support for those suffering from the breach of human rights. Participating in a Young Enterprise company helped me develop my teamwork ability but also concentrate on time and money management skills. Involvement in a debating society has helped me to argue my own opinion but to also consider the views of others. Having a part-time job has enabled me to manage my own money and deal with difficult situations using my own judgement, making me more confident and independent.

I enjoy playing a variety of sport such as rowing and tennis. I play netball and rounders for the school, having captained the netball team, and I help to umpire younger girls. My sporting abilities will allow me to relax and keep a healthy balance, leaving the stressful demands of being a doctor behind.

11.28   A level entry   3891 characters

SECTION 1 [1170 characters]

Throughout my life, I have been determined to succeed in every challenge that I face and the strong sense of vocation I feel towards helping people is what drives my ambition to become a doctor. Reading Lance Armstrong's autobiography, 'It's Not About The Bike', touched me emotionally and intrigued me academically, prompting me to investigate testicular cancer and advances in its treatment. His emotive account confirmed my desire to strive for success in medicine and to use that expertise to care for people with compassion and professionalism.

My experiences and discussions with medical professionals have allowed me to grasp the highs and lows of medicine and appreciate the vast amount of teamwork and communication involved in such an interpersonal career, cementing my ambition to become a doctor. Medical professionals are held in high regard, with trust and all-round appreciation for the difference they make to people's lives.

The prospect of contributing to society in this invaluable way along with involvement in an ever advancing and most gratifying field fills me with immense excitement. I would relish the opportunity to be part of this profession.

SECTION 2 [1347 characters]

My passion for the sciences has deepened throughout my school years, with chemistry standing out as the subject I find most captivating. This interest was further fuelled by my participation in my school's Extreme Hydrogen Challenge team, where I explored the potential of hydrogen as a renewable energy source. The experience honed my investigative and problem-solving skills while reinforcing my enthusiasm for applying scientific principles to real-world challenges. Studying chemistry at Advanced Higher has allowed me to delve deeper into the subject, satisfying my thirst for knowledge and strengthening my analytical abilities. These academic pursuits reflect my drive to excel and my determination to approach challenges with focus and resilience – qualities I believe are essential for a career in medicine.

As Deputy Head Boy of my school, my commitments are shared between my drive to succeed academically and leading my school by example. It has taught me self-discipline and requires strong organisational and people skills. I have competed annually in the Scottish Mathematical Challenge, gaining four gold awards, and each year I have been awarded Overall Academic Excellence for my achievements in school. This is the culmination of sheer determination, a lot of hard work, strong resilience, and an ability to push myself to excel.

SECTION 3 [1374 characters]

I shadowed a GP at Meeks Road General Practice in Falkirk, and an FY2 doctor at Stirling Royal Infirmary. I arranged another inspiring placement in the ENT department in Leeds General Infirmary, where I attended outpatient clinics and operating theatres. My experiences and discussions with medical professionals have allowed me to grasp the highs and lows of medicine and appreciate the vast amount of teamwork and communication involved in such an interpersonal career, cementing my ambition to become a doctor.

I am a fan of all sports and enjoy their competitive nature. I play golf regularly in the junior medal and have reduced my handicap from 36 to 22 over the last three years. Tennis, being one of my strongest sports, has seen me selected for the Central Scotland Squad. This along with competing for my school's rugby and football teams for the last two years has strengthened my skills in teamwork and has allowed me to appreciate the rewarding results obtained from a hardworking unit. This year, as part of a Sports Leader course, I am organising and delivering coaching to younger pupils in various sporting activities.

For the past two years I have been working part-time in a small accountancy firm where I am responsible for the accurate recording of financial data. This has shown me the importance of good record-keeping and being on top of the paperwork.

11.29 A level entry   3888 characters

SECTION 1 [898 characters]

Medicine has always been at the forefront of my mind but I was particularly inspired by a book called 'The Emperor of All Maladies: A Biography of Cancer' by Siddhartha Mukherjee. This compelling narrative not only explores the history of cancer but also delves into the science, human struggles and medical advancements involved in treating the disease. What struck me most was how Mukherjee intertwined the personal stories of patients with the scientific evolution of cancer treatment. It made me realise the intricate relationship between biology, medicine and patient care.

The book inspired me to pursue a career where I could be at the intersection of science and compassion, working to understand complex diseases and improving the lives of those affected by them. I am a hardworking, reliable, and caring person who has the dedication, enthusiasm and commitment needed to be a good doctor.

SECTION 2 [1438 characters]

Working on a group project about optical isomerism and enantiomers in A level chemistry enhanced my understanding of the intricate relationship between chemistry and medicine, particularly in drug development. Collaborating with peers to explore how enantiomers, despite having the same molecular formula, can have vastly different effects on the body, emphasised the critical importance of precision in pharmaceutical science. For example, examining the role of chirality in drugs like thalidomide highlighted the need for rigorous testing and quality control in medicine production. This project not only deepened my understanding of how chemical principles underpin pharmacology but also developed my teamwork and problem-solving skills. These experiences have prepared me to approach medicine with a keen attention to detail, a collaborative mindset, and a strong scientific foundation.

As part of A level biology, I set up a neuroscience project in partnership with Manchester Museum, where I prepared a series of posters on the 'sense of hearing'. Having to summarise a vast and potentially complex topic to the general public was very challenging and I am proud of the positive feedback it received.

I love challenges and have participated in the Mock Trial Competition, the European Maths Challenge, and the Paperclip Physics Competition. These opportunities have improved my ability to prioritise and solve problems under pressure.

SECTION 3 [1552 characters]

A week's work experience in a cardiac ward gave me insight into the challenges faced by doctors: time pressure, heavy workload, and difficult patients. Observing a pre-op clinic and daily ward activities highlighted the importance of communication, prioritisation, and building trust with patients. I was also struck by the dedication of medical and nursing staff. Shadowing a GP for a week showed the variety of roles they fulfil as clinicians, managers and team leaders. I appreciated how social factors and prevention can influence health. I saw doctors handle sensitive issues with empathy, such as transferring an elderly patient to a residential home. It was informative to attend a CCG meeting on child vaccinations and the challenges of meeting targets.

Over the past year, I've supported and listened to elderly residents at a local care home, building strong relationships. Volunteering at the League of Friends tea bar improved my communication through interacting with staff and visitors. I earned the Millennium Volunteer Award after 200+ hours with charities like Oxfam. Every Sunday for the past year, I've helped disabled adults become more confident swimmers.

In my part-time job over 5 years, I've helped young children overcome maths difficulties and run science revision classes at school. For relaxation, I play keyboard and enjoy craftwork. Practising tae kwon do for 8 years has taught me self-control and self-reliance while keeping me fit. I'm now working towards my black belt. These activities help me manage my time effectively.

11.30 A level entry — 3884 characters

SECTION 1 [814 characters]

I have a strong interest in a wide range of scientific topics and have developed a particular focus on genetics. As a result of this, I joined a small genetic research project attempting to determine the function of two genes located within the plant 'Arabidopsis Thaliana'. Working as part of this team over the past 14 months, I have developed many skills invaluable to a doctor: teamwork, problem-solving, stamina and dedication. The success of our project thus far was recognised by an invitation to address a national conference, Showcase Science. I enjoyed the challenge of presenting and defending original research to a large and knowledgeable audience. I would like to study medicine in order to get further involved in research and find ways in which it can be applied to making a difference to patients.

SECTION 2 [1546 characters]

As President of the School's Medical Society, I have the responsibility of organising and introducing talks from medical experts. The research work involved in this task and the logistics of making it work are very rewarding. I have a tenacious attitude to my academic work and am very proud to have received a number of School prizes and awards in recognition of my achievements.

Studying amino acids and DNA in chemistry, alongside completing an Extended Project Qualification (EPQ) on a related topic, has provided me with a solid understanding of the molecular processes that sustain life – a critical foundation for studying medicine. Through my EPQ, I conducted in-depth research into DNA replication and protein synthesis, which enhanced my appreciation of how genetic information orchestrates cellular functions and how errors in these processes can lead to disease. This independent project honed my research, time management, and critical thinking skills as I analysed complex information and presented my findings coherently. Exploring the role of amino acids in enzyme activity and metabolic pathways further deepened my understanding of how the body maintains homeostasis and adapts to challenges. These studies fostered a keen interest in the clinical applications of molecular biology, such as genetic therapies and diagnostics. By combining research and practical learning, I have developed both the knowledge and transferable skills needed to navigate the intricate scientific concepts essential in medical education and practice.

SECTION 3 [1524 characters]

I shadowed a variety of specialist consultants on ward rounds at Worcestershire General Hospital for four days, where I observed the delicate and precise work of surgeons, spent a day in A&E and worked with nursing staff. This made me realise the importance of teamwork in the medical profession, the pressures of working in busy units and the extremely understated, yet valuable, work of nurses. I also spent one week at Eli Lilly Clinical Trials Singapore and one week at the National University Hospital in Singapore. During this time, I learnt that certain diseases such as diabetes are more prolific in certain ethnic groups.

Helping in homes and day care centres for the aged developed my ability to empathise and communicate with the elderly. I also spent one week on a Mencap holiday working in a voluntary capacity helping a group of children with a variety of learning and physical disabilities. These experiences have taught me the importance of patience, compassion and maintaining the dignity of the patient. Although at times my work experience was challenging, it has vastly reaffirmed my desire to pursue a career in medicine.

I am a committed member of the Combined Cadet Force and, as an NCO Platoon Commander, I am responsible for leading and tutoring cadets: a challenge that I find both rewarding and exciting. I am a keen, if somewhat modest, sportsman, and I also enjoy drama and music. Balancing these activities with the demands of my curriculum has required commitment and effective time management.

11.31   A level entry   3978 characters

SECTION 1 [1247 characters]

Medicine appeals to me as a career choice because of my past experiences, the academic and personal challenges it offers, and the way it uses ever-developing science and technology to improve people's lives. My mum was diagnosed with multiple sclerosis and suffers acute depression. Through my teenage years, I had to assist her physically on a daily basis, due to fatigue, mobility problems and occasional limb paralysis. I regularly attended consultations and constantly discuss progress and treatment options. Recently she was prescribed a disease-modifying drug requiring daily injection, which I was trained to administer by a specialist MS nurse. I learnt tact and patience in dealing with her depression so as not to aggravate situations and have seen the positive and negative impact drug regimens can have. My grandmother has vascular dementia and I assisted her as she deteriorated. I also witnessed the development of Alzheimer's and emphysema in my uncle, who regrettably passed away as a result.

Through those tough times, I never gave up and in fact thrived at the idea of being able to make a difference. I am determined to continue my successful education via a medical degree and, as a doctor, make a difference to people's lives.

SECTION 2 [869 characters]

Studying A level chemistry provided me with a solid foundation in biochemistry and pharmacology, deepening my understanding of the molecular processes that underpin human health and disease. Writing a school essay on this topic, which explored how chemical principles inform drug design and treatment strategies, was a particularly rewarding experience. Winning a prize for this essay validated my ability to connect theoretical concepts to real-world applications, such as the development of new medications. This experience highlighted the intricate interplay between chemistry and biology in understanding the human body and the importance of targeted treatments in modern medicine. It solidified my commitment to studying medicine, where I aspire to apply these principles to improve patient care through a combination of scientific knowledge and clinical practice.

SECTION 3 [1862 characters]

Last summer I volunteered on the stroke care unit of my local hospital, spending time with patients and assisting with their rehabilitation. I observed how all healthcare professionals interacted with both patients and each other to provide patient-centred care. Subsequently I organised fundraising events for the MS Society and met many MS sufferers with differing levels of disability. This highlighted the fact that some diseases have varying levels of severity and therefore the need for healthcare solutions to be structured around the individual.

Last year the opportunity arose to be the Young Person's Patient Champion Governor for the Basingstoke and North Hampshire Hospital NHS Foundation Trust. I attend quarterly meetings regarding the governance of the hospital, where we discuss management issues. In addition to this, members of staff give presentations on current issues within the hospital, the latest of which was infection control. I am finding this experience a valuable insight into the organisation of the NHS.

I have been a member of Wessex Christian Fellowship for two years. Last year, I joined the technical team, which manages the computer-based audio-visual system, and is integral to the running of the church. Recently I have taken over as director, where my role is to ensure the effective delivery of this resource. I facilitate communication between team members and provide leadership. In this role I have learnt to understand where my boundary of knowledge lies and when to call on the support of others.

Earlier this year I became the youth leader of a newly created youth group for 11- to 14-year-olds. This has helped me develop mentoring skills and empathy towards people from difficult backgrounds. With all of these activities and my academic studies, I have learnt to manage my time effectively and to balance priorities.

11.32　A level entry　3862 characters

SECTION 1 [844 characters]

Scientific knowledge, complex skills, creativity and personal relationships are all aspects of medicine. For me they are also essential aspects of my education and personal outlook. Medicine's daily challenge will be academically stimulating and I hope that my intellectual ability and warm-hearted, compassionate nature will make me a stable and dependable doctor. I have been inspired by many people with whom I have worked and I noticed that the ability to make even the smallest difference to a life is precious. The range of specialities makes the career path exciting and unpredictable.

From a young age I have questioned everything to do with medicine, keen to learn as much as possible. The opportunities I have had so far have increased my curiosity and desire to study medicine and I relish the challenge of a demanding medical career.

SECTION 2 [1236 characters]

Studying A level French provided me with a deeper understanding of language and culture, while organising a French Day at sixth form allowed me to apply these skills in a practical context. Leading a team to plan and execute the event required effective communication, delegation, and organisational skills. From coordinating activities to ensuring everything ran smoothly, I learned to manage multiple responsibilities while motivating others to achieve a shared goal. This experience also enhanced my cultural awareness and adaptability – key attributes in a globalised world where understanding diverse perspectives is increasingly important. These skills are directly relevant to studying medicine, where teamwork, effective communication, and cultural sensitivity are essential for providing patient-centred care. Organising French Day reinforced my ability to lead, collaborate, and adapt under pressure, qualities I am eager to bring to my medical training and future career.

At school, I am a year 8 mentor, maths mentor and Junior Sports Leader and am currently senior prefect and music prefect. This means I have responsibility for younger pupils, developing skills such as organisation that will be useful in a medical career.

SECTION 3 [1782 characters]

This summer, I worked for two weeks on a research study in Boston, USA, investigating the effects of nutrition and drug abuse on people with HIV within the Hispanic community. I worked on determining causes of death of participants and analysing this data. Surprisingly, liver disease and violence were as common as AIDS as a cause of death. This has resulted in my interest in medical research and epidemiology.

I shadowed doctors in several departments at my local hospital, including observing an aneurysm operation, which resulted in a splenectomy due to complications. Whilst working in a GP surgery in London, I learned the importance of teamwork, communication and leadership. The diversity of the work interested me, as I saw that patients varied from having minor injuries to being recovering drug addicts.

Coaching young children in tennis for the last three years has enabled me to develop my teaching skills, using initiative and improvisation. I teach violin and find that perseverance, creativity and determination are crucial to maintaining attention. I have passed my grade 8 violin and I also play the oboe and piano to grade 7 standards. This requires devotion, commitment and reliability. I am a member of the Wirral Youth Orchestra, Liverpool Philharmonic Youth Orchestra, and two string quartets. Music and medicine require teamwork and integration of mind with body, intellect with emotion and communication ability with commitment. I hope that I can use these skills learned from music in medicine. In addition to my music I play tennis regularly for my local club and became junior captain. I am a keen kayaker and have competed regularly for many years for my trampolining club. These sports require trusting others and teamwork, skills important in medicine.

11.33 A level entry — 3996 characters

SECTION 1 [662 characters]

Since early childhood, I was surrounded by doctors both in the family and in hospital, where I spent much time as a patient. Having had many opportunities for observing doctors' work, I witnessed their professionalism, knowledge and efficiency in caring for what I deem the most precious possession: health. This made me aim for the vocation of a doctor, which I began seeing as my mission in life. On a less emotional level, medicine seems to me to be the ideal discipline as it combines my passion for science with my love of social contact. It also promises to quench my thirst for learning new things as medicine is ever developing, requiring lifelong study.

SECTION 2 [1760 characters]

Over the past five years, I have been a scholarship student at my current school, compelling me to maintain high standards in and outside the classroom. I believe my learning to cope with pressure will be useful both at university and in my chosen career, where critical situations are common. My logic and critical thinking enable me to achieve high standards in mathematics and science. I chose to explore the latter beyond the curriculum, chiefly in the medical field, by subscribing to the Medscape medical newsletter, which keeps me up to date with events in the medical circles, and also by deciding to write my extended essay on biochemistry, focusing on the effects of paracetamol and aspirin on living organisms. Through this I demonstrated many skills relevant to a career in medicine, including critical thinking and problem-solving, as the essay involved analysing complex biochemical processes. I also developed research skills, including data collection, analysis, and interpretation of scientific literature. Additionally, the essay honed my ability to communicate complex scientific concepts clearly, a crucial skill in medicine for explaining conditions and treatments to patients and colleagues. I enjoy taking up responsibilities and working with people to make things happen. Last year, I was elected to represent my class in the Student Council, comprising elected representatives of all classes between Years 7 and 13, aiming to improve the school for the students. This year I became Vice President of the Grammar School, making me responsible for the Student Council. I also enjoy debating and was picked for the school Senior Debate, where I defended the winning motion that children under 15 should be monitored while on the internet.

SECTION 3 [1574 characters]

I volunteer at a ward for terminally ill people in a local hospital. The insights I gain from weekly contact with these, mainly elderly, people enable me to see how people cope with illness. These conversations develop my listening skills, which I deem vital for a future doctor because, without listening to and understanding the patient, it is impossible to identify their needs and help them get better. Listening belongs to the sphere of communication skills, which I have been able to develop greatly throughout my life, where I had to change school five times due to my family's moving house, twice abroad. I was required to learn English, French and some German besides my native Czech and to socialise with people of different backgrounds, nationalities and religions, increasing my adaptability. Perhaps because of this, I enjoy working with people and learning from my experiences, which has led me to participate as a counsellor at a camp for mentally disabled people, helping to raise my awareness of mental disorders. I consider this important for a future doctor as it is common that mental problems accompany physical ones and vice versa.

In my free time, I engage in many other activities. For several years, I have been learning to play the flute, which allowed me to participate at last year's Maribor Spring Festival, where we explored the theme 'Diversity in Unity' with students from all over Europe through the media of music, dance and art. To keep fit I do cross-country running, and this year for the second time ran the 5km race for women in Prague.

11.34   A level entry   3802 characters

SECTION 1 [951 characters]

Doctors play a central role in society; they have the opportunity to improve people's welfare and contribute to their well-being. I realised this early, having been raised in medical campuses in various countries. I was an intensely curious child, querying the simple relationships between structure and function underpinning science, and I was immediately fascinated by the diverse aspects of medicine and its application in those varied countries. This early exposure allowed me to understand shifts in focuses of medicine over the years; it was also the foundation for my current dream. Medicine will be an incredibly varied, challenging and rewarding career, as it will allow me to apply theoretical knowledge, ethics and life events to improve health. It is hope, along with commitment and stamina, that has brought me to where I am. I believe medicine to be the path that leads to a better tomorrow, and I look forward to walking down that path.

SECTION 2 [1464 characters]

I've had many obstacles to overcome. I was in the gifted and talented stream of my comprehensive, yet I felt I was not challenged enough, so I applied to those sixth forms which could offer greater opportunities for development. My motivation won me scholarships to all, and I took up the Newham scholarship to the most well-rounded school. As a Secondary School Prefect, I had to assert myself over my peers, motivate and make quick and effective decisions. Studying evolution in A level biology has given me a deeper understanding of human development and the ways in which our bodies have adapted over time, which is fundamental to medicine. By exploring how evolutionary principles influence human physiology, I gained insights into the biological processes that shape health and disease. For example, understanding how certain genetic traits may provide advantages or disadvantages in survival and reproduction has enhanced my awareness of how genetic factors can affect health outcomes. This knowledge is crucial in fields such as genetics, epidemiology, and personalised medicine. Studying evolution has also strengthened my critical thinking skills, as I learned to assess how historical biological processes impact current medical challenges. The ability to analyse and interpret complex biological systems will be invaluable in medicine, where understanding the body's functions and how they evolve is key to diagnosing and treating diseases effectively.

SECTION 3 [1387 characters]

To gain hands-on experience, I worked at Plaistow Hospital for two weeks, providing companionship, and learning that patience, compassion, and sensitivity are as crucial as scientific skills. I also received wheelchair training. Volunteering for four years, I created language materials for refugees and asylum seekers, leveraging my multilingual skills to present basic lessons effectively. I developed interpersonal skills and earned a Millennium Award for 200 hours of voluntary work.

To broaden my experience, I worked at a school for the disabled, where I provided therapy through everyday activities, making them easy and functional. My ongoing voluntary work at a nursing home taught me that improving quality of life is sometimes all we can do. A pivotal experience was a paediatric placement at Lewisham, where I learned the physics behind instruments and the stress of ICU. Talking to patients and staff gave me a holistic view of medicine, teaching me empathy, humility, and multitasking.

I created a charity to raise awareness of climate issues and participate in various activities, from competitive shooting to flying, for which I hold an RAF proficiency certificate. I am passionate about history, sci-fi novels, and writing, with one of my poems winning an Islington libraries competition and airing on BBC. I also produce music, currently negotiating with a record company.

11.35 A level entry — 3866 characters

SECTION 1 [756 characters]

I have always been intrigued by the trust that patients place in their doctor and I appreciate the responsibility involved in medicine, where a doctor's input can significantly influence people's lives and well-being. It is the combination of science and human interaction that I find stimulating about medicine, along with the prospect of lifelong learning. I am aware that life as a doctor can be both physically and emotionally demanding. Knowing, however, that I will be able to use my strengths in science for the benefit of others will be the greatest reward.

I feel that, by managing demanding academic and extracurricular commitments successfully so far, I have proved that I have the ability to handle the significant pressures of a medical career.

SECTION 2 [1329 characters]

Further to my academic pursuits, I am a Year 7 form prefect and have also been a mentor to a child from a disadvantaged background for a year. This commitment, alongside mentoring a younger girl in German, has improved my interpersonal skills and helped me to develop patience. In school, I created and managed GreenSoc, an environmental society formed to raise awareness and sell recycled stationery. This taught me how to motivate others and the importance of teamwork. I was also the editor of the school newspaper, which taught me how to manage a team and work to strict deadlines.

Participating in the 'Young Analyst' chemistry competition was a rewarding experience that highlighted the importance of effective teamwork in achieving success. Collaborating with my teammates, we combined our analytical and problem-solving skills to secure fifth place out of twenty-eight schools, and our commitment to precision and organisation earned us the 'Good Lab Practice' award. This experience taught me how to work efficiently under pressure, communicate clearly, and approach challenges methodically – skills that are essential in the field of medicine. It reinforced my ability to contribute meaningfully to a team while striving for excellence, preparing me for the collaborative and detail-oriented nature of medical practice.

SECTION 3 [1781 characters]

During my four-week shadowing experience at Manchester Royal Infirmary, I enjoyed conversing with acutely and chronically unwell patients and observed the importance of attentive listening. Encountering psychological illness and dementia sparked my interest in mental health. I recognised the need to offer the same care to patients with psychiatric conditions as to those with physical ailments, while understanding the challenges in diagnosing mental health issues. The ward rounds highlighted the importance of teamwork and communication among doctors, nurses, physiotherapists, and pharmacists to develop effective treatment plans.

As a chapel volunteer at Christie Hospital, I witness the emotional distress of patients and families, learning the challenges of offering comfort. I also participate in a health professions group where we discuss ethical issues. Leading a discussion on the use of cannabis for multiple sclerosis required research into the ethical considerations of this topic. Volunteering at a nursing home has enhanced my communication skills, particularly in listening to the concerns of residents and their families.

Through my work with St John Ambulance, I have gained experience in healthcare, becoming first aid certified and providing support at events like pop concerts and football matches. I am proud of my Indian heritage and I hold a Kathak dance certificate, earned after two years of dedicated practice. Both dance and sports help me manage academic pressure. I've also been part of a Hindu youth group for four years, preserving my cultural roots through prayer and activities. As a part-time worker at a personal injury call centre, I have learned about the responsibilities of working life and decision-making based on basic medical knowledge.

11.36   A level entry   3930 characters

SECTION 1 [994 characters]

Growing up, I noticed stark differences in healthcare access across communities. In underprivileged areas, I saw patients struggle to afford medications, wait months for appointments, or rely on overburdened hospitals with limited resources. These experiences made me aware of the barriers preventing people from receiving timely, quality care. Witnessing patients who were unable to seek treatment until their conditions worsened reinforced the importance of preventive medicine and health education.

I became interested in the systemic issues affecting healthcare, from funding gaps to the role of public health initiatives. This drove me to research policies aimed at improving access and to consider how doctors can bridge the gap by advocating for their patients. The idea that healthcare should not be a privilege but a right has fuelled my motivation to pursue medicine, ensuring that all patients receive the compassionate, high-quality care they deserve, regardless of their background.

SECTION 2 [742 characters]

Studying biology, chemistry and mathematics A level has enabled me to develop my analytical skills, imperative to medicine. My enthusiasm for these disciplines is reflected in my academic aptitude; I won the Lower 6 chemistry prize and I am a scholarship boy and holder of an academic bursary.

Biology has always been my favourite subject because of its broad scope, ranging from cellular investigation to whole organisms. I would now like to learn the aetiology of diseases, understand why patients are ill and formulate methods of treatment. The study of chemistry, the composition of substances and their properties and reactions, came to life for me in the operating theatre when witnessing the immediate effect of anaesthesia on patients.

SECTION 3 [2194 characters]

Observing an emergency caesarean section was intensely emotional; just fifteen minutes earlier I had been in the intensive care unit where an elderly lady was dying. My experience of these two extremes whilst shadowing a consultant anaesthetist last year illustrated to me the demands of being a doctor. An additional week with the anaesthetist this summer gave me further insight into life in the operating theatre. I was particularly impressed by the surgeon's dexterity with hip and knee replacements and laparoscopic surgery. Comparing the controlled drama of the operating theatre with the stillness of the intensive care unit highlighted the diversity of the medical profession. These contrasts and challenges attract me.

Time spent in a fracture clinic with a consultant orthopaedic surgeon and accompanying a GP on home visits accentuated the importance of trust and confidentiality between doctor and patient. For over a year I have been visiting a nursing home on a weekly basis. Talking to the patients has been a humbling and rewarding experience; it has improved my communication skills and taught me to be an empathetic listener.

I play county squash for Hampshire at under-19 level and I am the under-19 Channel Islands champion. As captain of the Guernsey junior squad I developed my leadership skills; I looked after the juniors at national tournaments and adopted a pastoral role during their time away from home. Over the past two years I have acquired a professional level II coaching qualification, enabling me to work as a squash coach. I now run the weekly junior league matches for up to forty children, enhancing my organisational and interpersonal skills. In my role as referee at county and national squash matches, making decisions quickly and with authority is essential. For my Sports Leadership award, I am teaching basketball to underprivileged children and am now confident in child management. Playing in the school cricket and football first XIs and in the Guernsey under-19 cricket team has highlighted to me the value of teamwork. This seems relevant to medicine, as I witnessed the collective participation of the surgeon and nurses in the operating theatre.

11.37 A level entry — 3971 characters

SECTION 1 [879 characters]

Having encountered the rites of birth, death and disease at first-hand, I know the care and compassion needed as a doctor is second to none. Three years ago, I was asked by a friend to be her birthing partner. This was a daunting prospect that I fully embraced and made me realise how vital it is for doctors to respect the beliefs of the mother, her preferences for treatment and her need for encouragement and explanation. Reflecting on my past few years in the NHS, I have seen that people's experience of health and illness is uniquely personal and influenced by the medical intervention they receive.

With this in mind, I am committed to entering a vocation where I will be able to make a positive impact on others' quality of life. It is this challenge, coupled with enthusiasm to understand how disease affects the body, which has made me determined to succeed in medicine.

SECTION 2 [1211 characters]

Achieving highly in the Access to Medicine course and continuing on to biomedicine provides an excellent academic basis from which to approach a pure medical course that offers both science and humanity. As part of my course I analysed case studies on disorders such as schizophrenia and depression, which refined my analytical thinking and deepened my understanding of the complexities involved in diagnosing and treating mental health conditions. Exploring the multifaceted causes of these disorders – spanning genetic, biochemical and environmental factors – highlighted the importance of adopting a holistic approach to patient care. I was particularly inspired by how advancements in neuroscience, such as neuroimaging and targeted pharmacological treatments, are transforming our understanding and management of these conditions.

These studies also underscore the necessity of empathy and effective communication when supporting patients facing mental health challenges. This experience has not only enhanced my problem-solving abilities but also reinforced my passion for integrating scientific innovation with compassionate care, preparing me for the diverse and demanding nature of a career in medicine.

SECTION 3 [1881 characters]

Working with the UK Health and Learning Disabilities Network in Lancaster, my goal was to empower the clients to integrate with the community. Being ultimately responsible for clients in crises honed my ability to listen, give reassurance and lend emotional support in times of distress. I developed techniques in interpersonal communication whilst gaining the trust of the clients and the multidisciplinary team. Making decisions to benefit the client was an evolving skill which required autonomy and delicate reasoning, and could often expose ethical dilemmas.

Whilst studying for the Access course, I worked part-time as an auxiliary nurse. Nursing allowed me to talk closely with patients about their feelings and experiences of illness and I saw the difference that both a good and poor bedside manner can make. I recognised the need to quickly prioritise tasks, often in pressured circumstances, and learnt that it is vital to function as a team and manage time effectively.

Recently I provided respite care for my grandfather who had Parkinson's disease. I hold no illusions of how devastating and debilitating chronic disease can be for both patient and family. I recognise the importance of the doctor's role in diagnosing and treating Grandpa's condition, helping him to live independently and with dignity.

Having taught myself to play several musical instruments, I have led 3 major bands and produced 6 recordings, one of which was on sale commercially. Between playing ultimate frisbee and cycling, I captain the BioMed football team, organising matches twice a week, and take pleasure in the competitive edge it brings. Being captain makes me feel proud and I am able to conduct the players with confidence. I have volunteered for Homeless Action and over the last year for St John Ambulance, developing skills in first aid and helping at community and sporting events.

11.38 — A level entry — 3830 characters

SECTION 1 [629 characters]

When my uncle was diagnosed with bowel cancer, I was forced to realise the full effects of cancer upon both the sufferer and their relatives and how important a role the state of mind plays in helping to influence the outcome of a disease. As I accompanied him to his chemotherapy appointments, I saw how different cancer patients had different attitudes to their diagnoses and prognoses. Some were in denial, some were fearful and some faced their disease with determined optimism. The professionalism of the staff in dealing and sympathising with these differing attitudes reinforced my decision to choose medicine as a career.

SECTION 2 [1421 characters]

Last July I won a school prize for 'Scholarship and Initiative' and I am a Senior Prefect, a position that caused me to learn a lot about being proactive at troubleshooting, planning, managing expectation and supporting others.

I read the 'Biological Science Review' and medical reports in the daily newspapers to help increase my understanding and provide information on topics that complement my biology course. Last year, I wrote an extended biology essay on the effects of smoking on the body and investigated the synthesis and analysis of aspirin, which taught me about the structure of the drug. I also presented a congenital disease in a biology lesson. This required researching the genetic causes, symptoms, and treatment options for the condition, from which I gained a deeper understanding of congenital diseases and their impact on patients.

These experiences helped me develop the ability to explain complex medical concepts in a clear and structured manner, an essential skill for communicating with patients, families, and healthcare teams. Being able to convey scientific information in an understandable way is vital in medical practice, where clear communication can significantly affect patient care. This presentation also strengthened my ability to critically assess medical information and present it in a professional setting, preparing me for the communication challenges I will encounter in medicine.

SECTION 3 [1780 characters]

I spent a week at a GP practice, performing simple procedures and attending house visits, where I learned the importance of bedside manner. I have also spent a day at the Douglas Macmillan Hospice as a listener. For five months, I listened weekly to primary school children reading and my time at the two primary schools helped to improve my ability to communicate with children. I shadowed senior psychiatrists at Harplands Hospital last August, which increased my understanding of mental illnesses.

My travels to Cambodia and Laos exposed me to the challenges faced by people in developing countries. I aspire to work with organisations like Médecins Sans Frontières to apply my medical knowledge in such environments. Having studied French at AS level, I plan to incorporate this interest into my medical career.

I have played hockey for school, am part of the 1st XI, and coach younger players to develop teamwork. I participate in the school orchestra, wind band, and flute group, and help with drama productions. This year, I judged Junior House Music. I hold Full Colours in Music and Half Colours in Hockey and have been in the CCF for four years. My Young Enterprise Group won the Local Finals and three County Finals prizes. I am self-motivated, determined to succeed, and committed to excellence.

Outside school, I am Head Chorister at my church, where I lead the Junior Choir and occasionally play the organ during services. I take piano, flute, and organ lessons, holding Grade 7 on piano and flute, with plans to take the Grade 8 flute exam in July 2009. I have also achieved Grade 3 on the violin. I enjoy reading, listening to music of all genres, watching films about different cultures, travelling and spending time with friends. All these are good means to escape.

11.39 A level entry 3966 characters

SECTION 1 [817 characters]

Medicine appeals to me as I have a strong interest and aptitude for sciences and I get a great deal of satisfaction when helping people. I am interested in the practical application of knowledge and am particularly excited by the prospect of applying ongoing genetic research to helping people with a wide range of illnesses.

My enthusiasm for medicine has been confirmed and heightened by my work experience and conversations with practising doctors. Work experience and talking with doctors has given me real insight and a commitment to the medical profession. I am eager to learn, have good personal skills, am responsible and hardworking and have a strong desire to help people. I am ambitious, have a strong record of commitment and success and am confident I have the capabilities to be a capable, caring doctor.

SECTION 2 [1008 characters]

Writing an essay about genetic mutations and disorders in A level biology and winning a prize for it has deepened my understanding of the role genetics plays in medicine. In the essay, I explored how specific genetic mutations can lead to various disorders, such as Huntington's disease and Down syndrome, and the importance of genetic testing in diagnosis and treatment. This experience not only enhanced my knowledge of genetic disorders but also strengthened my ability to research, analyse, and communicate complex scientific concepts clearly and concisely. These transferable skills – critical thinking, research, and communication – are essential in medicine, where the ability to understand complex medical conditions and effectively explain them to patients and colleagues is crucial.

Winning the prize reinforced my passion for genetics and its application in medicine, further motivating me to pursue a career where I can contribute to advancements in genetic research and personalised patient care.

SECTION 3 [2141 characters]

I attended the 'Hospex' course at Derby Hospital and shadowed a variety of medical staff, where I noted the doctors' excellent communication skills even with non-English-speaking patients. In surgery, I witnessed an appendectomy and keyhole surgery for gall bladder removal. The teamwork was impressive and allowed the procedures to run smoothly. I accompanied consultants on ward rounds and the many conversations I had have given me great insight into the importance of time management, with a busy schedule to keep around the hospital.

I volunteer four hours a week as a carer at a nursing home. Communication in the home can be a challenge as many of the staff have limited English and some patients are physically unable to speak. I am learning a lot about patient care and respect and find that working as part of a team has many benefits; I can ask members of the team for support when I lack experience of the task in hand.

I have an RLSS lifeguard qualification with first aid training and work as a lifeguard at my local pool several hours a week. The role requires me to be alert whilst observing the pool and identifying weak swimmers and hazards; I enjoy the feeling of responsibility. My shifts vary each week so I must manage my time well to keep this, my other interests, and schoolwork in the right balance.

In year 12 I was part of a team of Millennium Volunteers; we designed and produced a charity calendar. Teamwork was important to ensure a successful outcome. I also helped in a year 7 maths class once a fortnight. I especially enjoyed helping two boys who were struggling most; I got satisfaction from passing on some of my maths skills and it helped me to make complex ideas easily understandable to the younger students.

I have taken weekly lessons in trumpet and piano since I was 5, passed grade 6 in both and play in both school bands. I attend tennis coaching weekly and enjoy football, snooker and cycling. I organise summertime canoe/camping trips in the Norfolk Broads with my friends which have made me more independent and built my confidence. I also like reading books, especially autobiographies and novels.

11.40   A level entry   3744 characters

SECTION 1 [835 characters]

It wasn't just in a single spark of inspiration that I decided I would like to pursue medicine as a career. Rather, it was my enthusiasm for science from an early age, which nurtured and instilled my love for human biology, with all its complexities and intricacies. My interest in medicine was fuelled too by weekly visits to a local residential home for the partially blind over the last three years. I learnt how to empathise with a diverse group of people while playing board games, organising competitions and reading to them. Not only has this improved my communication skills and given me a sense of responsibility, but I have since developed an interest in the functioning of the human eye and read about the causes and preventative measures of blindness, thus causing me to contemplate a possible career as an ophthalmologist.

SECTION 2 [739 characters]

Participating in my school's debating society has been an enriching experience that has allowed me to engage deeply with complex ethical issues, including euthanasia. Through structured discussions and rigorous analysis, I have developed critical thinking skills and the ability to consider multiple perspectives before forming balanced and informed opinions. Debating such topics has strengthened my communication skills, taught me to articulate ideas clearly, and fostered my ability to navigate sensitive and nuanced conversations.

These experiences have not only enhanced my understanding of the ethical dimensions of healthcare but have also prepared me to approach challenging discussions in medicine with empathy and professionalism.

SECTION 3 [2170 characters]

Work placements at two university hospitals allowed me to comprehend the demands of a medical career. I witnessed the importance of teamwork skills and the understanding between the surgeon, anaesthetist and nursing staff during a cardiac bypass operation. Observing the workings of an orthopaedic clinic, ward rounds and the ICU gave me an insight into the breadth of healthcare provided by the NHS. I then arranged a week's placement in the department of radiology at Coventry where the importance of the Breast Screening Service in diagnosing early cancer was highlighted. Here I watched as one of the doctors broke bad news of cancer to an elderly patient, showing care and compassion. This emphasised the significance of the holistic approach that doctors take when caring for their patients.

I had the opportunity to compare the health service in this country with India when I completed a project on amputees at a regional limb centre in Lucknow. I noticed that the success of proper rehabilitation of amputees is directly related to the type of accident, injury, the creation of stump and the selection of prosthesis which suited the lifestyle of the amputee. It was the 'Mukti' limb prosthesis which was the most economical and best suited for the Indian conditions.

At lunchtimes, I listen to Year 3 children read at a local primary school, helping them improve their skills. This has made me aware of the different approaches required when interacting with the young and the use of encouragement whilst correcting their mistakes.

I am well aware that the ability to cope with pressures of student life is essential and so I enjoy playing badminton on a weekly basis and train in Indian classical dance, both of which help me to relax and keep fit. Through this I am also able to maintain my multilingual skills as the 'Kathak' dance is primarily taught in Hindi. I have also enjoyed learning the Spanish composition 'Mi Palomita Blanca' while working towards my Grade 5 singing.

My experiences have affirmed that medicine is a career path I would like to follow, and the demands of lifelong learning and dedication have only deepened my desire to become a doctor.

11.41　A level entry　　3950 characters

SECTION 1 [673 characters]

Volunteering at a homelessness charity exposed me to the healthcare challenges faced by vulnerable populations. Many of the people I interacted with had untreated medical conditions, often worsened by poor living conditions and limited access to healthcare. I helped distribute essential supplies, assisted with outreach programmes, and engaged with individuals to better understand their needs.

This experience deepened my awareness of social determinants of health and the role doctors play beyond the clinic. It strengthened my commitment to becoming a doctor who advocates for equitable healthcare and ensures that vulnerable patients receive the treatment they deserve.

SECTION 2 [1189 characters]

Arguably, medicine is both an art and a science and the IB has enabled me to pursue both disciplines. I have the sound scientific base required for medicine, balanced by the arts skills of logic, analysis of evidence and communication – all vital for a medical career. My interest in biology was deepened by my IB extended essay on the feeding behaviour of barnacles – excellent preparation for the independent research of an undergraduate degree. The problem-solving and analytical aspects of chemistry are ones I especially enjoy. I have expanded my intellectual curiosity through the IB Theory of Knowledge, and my essay on the relationship between knowledge gained from science and the arts was particularly thought-provoking. Reading the 'New Scientist' and contemporary science literature has deepened my awareness of critical issues.

I am a calm and committed individual and these qualities, together with my excellent communication skills, have been recognised by my school. Chosen to be a Prefect, I was also selected as a Classroom Assistant on their summer science course for gifted and talented primary school children. I immensely enjoyed contributing to this stimulating week.

SECTION 3 [2088 characters]

Pursuing my interest, a week with a urological consultant at King's College Hospital offered an insight into the evolving field of laparoscopic surgery, the dedication and skills of surgeons and the impact of doctor–patient communication. Time on a geriatric ward at Kent & Sussex Hospital highlighted the complex clinical and social needs of our increasingly elderly population, in particular the interdisciplinary coordination between diverse services such as physiotherapy, occupational therapy and social services. Shadowing an FY1 doctor revealed the sheer hard work and dedication that medicine requires. My commitment to helping weekly at a school for the disabled has been a most rewarding experience. The pleasure of building a rapport with the children has been especially fulfilling and developed my communication skills with vulnerable patients.

One of my passions is drama. Both acting and supporting backstage have developed my commitment and teamwork, both of which were tested on a tour of Germany with a school production of 'Oedipus' and 'Antigone'. I am an avid theatregoer and value the camaraderie of singing with school and local choirs. I keep fit with swimming and badminton, relish the thrills of skiing, and have taken great satisfaction from mastering the technicalities of ballroom dancing. I am keen to continue these activities at university, as opportunities for reinforcing my perseverance, coordination and stamina.

Having lived abroad, I enjoy travelling and the challenge of new destinations. A recent biology expedition to Ecuador and the Galapagos was physically demanding but rewarding, teaching me that I am adaptable, resourceful and resilient. My determination to participate in this project tested my ingenuity as I funded the trip myself through organising fundraising activities and working as a waitress at a local NT property.

A caring and focused individual with an independence of mind and a lively intelligence, I am confident and excited to face the demands, challenges and intellectual stimulus that a vocational career in medicine offers.

11.42 A level entry 3988 characters

SECTION 1 [939 characters]

As a child, I always insisted on visiting my grandparents so that I could look after them. I enjoyed helping with their bandages, reminding them to take their pills and also helping them understand their conditions by looking things up on the net and discussing that information with them. As a 16-year-old, I decided to take this a step further and work as a volunteer on a female geriatric ward in the local hospital, which I have now been doing weekly for the past two years. Although it was initially distressing to see confused elderly patients, I enjoyed getting to know individual patients and have gained an appreciation of some of the problems of long-term care for the elderly. I sensed that simply talking to some of these patients had a positive impact on their quality of life.

Being adept at all things scientific and equipped with a strong sense of altruism, I want to take this even further by embarking on a medical career.

SECTION 2 [1028 characters]

As a school science mentor during A level chemistry, I had the opportunity to support younger students in their studies, helping them grasp complex concepts and develop their practical skills. One significant moment was delivering a presentation on chemical safety to a younger school, where I emphasised the importance of handling chemicals responsibly and the real-world implications of safety protocols.

This experience sharpened my communication and teaching skills, as I had to convey technical information in an engaging and accessible way. It also strengthened my leadership abilities, as I took responsibility for guiding students and fostering their confidence in science. These skills are directly relevant to studying medicine, where educating patients, promoting safety, and working collaboratively with diverse groups are crucial. This role also highlighted the importance of empathy and adaptability – qualities I aim to bring to my medical training as I work towards delivering safe and effective care to patients.

SECTION 3 [2024 characters]

Two years ago, I did a week's work experience in the John Radcliffe Hospital, Oxford. I spent time in radiology, surgery and pathology. I spent one day with a surgical manager and a morning with the UNISON representative. This gave me an insight into managerial issues and some health service employment problems. I also spent a week shadowing a local GP. This included a day with a drug rehabilitation clinic. This experience illustrated the importance of continuity of care and good communication skills.

Last year, I organised work experience in the genetics department. I was given several examples of ethical and clinical dilemmas related to genetic diseases. This stimulated my interest in both ethics and genetics. I have subsequently read several books on these topics, such as 'Introduction to Medical Ethics' by A. Hope and 'The Language of Genes' by S. Jones. Since then, I have been working for a medical research company, Colonix. The project involves taking samples of mucus from the inside of the lower bowel with a balloon. The DNA content of the mucus is measured. I have observed and progressively assisted in the processing of samples in the laboratory. This has already improved my understanding of the scientific basis of modern medical practice.

In October this year, I am going to spend a month as an observer in a hospital in Manali in Northern India. Having never been to India before, I am both excited and anxious about the vast differences in culture that I will experience. I am looking forward to seeing how healthcare is delivered in a very different environment to the UK.

I was a member of my school 1st XI Hockey team together with representing the school in tennis and athletics. I was also a sports leader. This involved taking sports lessons and organising sporting events for younger pupils. At school I was also a founder member of a film club. With three friends, we acted in, directed and produced two films. This required teamwork, good communication skills and lots of problem-solving.

11.43 A level entry — 3978 characters

SECTION 1 [689 characters]

Having always enjoyed and been fascinated by science, my interest in studying medicine properly began three years ago when I experienced life as a patient first-hand. Whilst I was in hospital with a broken arm I became intrigued by the diagnostic and curative process of medicine and the care, sensitivity and understanding shown to me by hospital staff made a significant impression on me. I began to realise that the attributes of a doctor necessitate not only a scientific and intelligent mind but encompass qualities such as logical thinking, compassion and effective communication – traits I believe I possess and could develop further during my medical studies and subsequent career.

SECTION 2 [1169 characters]

My A level subjects reflect my passion for science and have taught me to look at the world with a thoughtful and analytical approach. I have enjoyed reading around and beyond the subjects we have studied at school and I have become an avid reader of various scientific journals. I have also been introduced to the 'Student BMJ', which has given me an insight into life as a medical student and some of the issues they face on a daily basis. I have found the accounts of student's electives particularly stimulating.

As a member of the sixth form year council, I engage in weekly discussions about school events, contributing to the development of ideas and reaching conclusions as part of a collaborative team. This experience has strengthened my ability to listen actively, think critically, and work towards a common goal. For the past four years, I have also served as a guide for parents and students transitioning to my school, offering support, answering questions, and providing guidance. These roles have honed my communication skills and ability to connect with others, both of which are essential in building rapport and providing compassionate care in medicine.

SECTION 3 [2120 characters]

I organised placements in a variety of areas from radiology to elderly medicine, but I particularly enjoyed the time I spent in the Accident and Emergency department. I was able to observe the efficient interactions of the multidisciplinary team in achieving effective patient care in often pressured and demanding situations. This, I am sure, is a challenge that I would relish being part of in the future. I also witnessed the various healthcare professionals working well as a team, although sometimes poor communication led to problems among the staff. Some doctors had better interpersonal skills than others and it was obvious that calm and kind explanations were most effective for patients during a time of distress.

In addition to my academic studies I have taken on various extracurricular activities in school. I was recently selected as Captain of my School House, a role that has allowed me to develop my communication, organisational and leadership skills. I have also been involved in the pastoral care of younger pupils, an undertaking that I have not only found rewarding but one that encourages unity and cohesiveness in school life.

I have always recognised the importance of having interests and hobbies outside academia, to provide both a balance to and outlet from the pressures of studying. I am an enthusiastic sportsman and have represented my school in athletics, water polo and fives – a sport in which I reached the National Championship semi-finals.

During the last two years I have worked regularly as a babysitter for a family friend with a young child. In the school holidays I play an important part in the care of my younger brother as my mother is in full-time employment. I feel that these active caring roles have contributed greatly to my character-building.

I believe that the attributes I have mentioned previously and the enjoyment I receive from meeting new people and finding out more about them make me an ideal candidate. Should I be given the opportunity to study, I believe my determination and enthusiasm will allow me to succeed in the challenge that is a career in medicine.

11.44   A level entry   3944 characters

SECTION 1 [992 characters]

My desire to pursue a career in medicine started when I was 12, when my aunt gave birth to a 24-week baby girl. I was awestruck as I watched the paediatric team miraculously nurture a tiny speck of life, no bigger than my hand, with such care and capability. My aspiration was refuelled when I was confined to hospital earlier this year following a road traffic accident. I witnessed and absorbed first-hand a very full range of hospital experiences: staff anxiety about my injuries; the application of a wide range of medical practices and expertise; the extreme demands on medical staff time and the satisfaction gained by the hospital team as they led me to a full recovery.

Coming from a family of people with medical backgrounds, it is clear that the depth of medical understanding has increased enormously over the years and continues to grow. I desire intensely to be at the forefront of this dynamic and challenging career which promises even further exciting innovations and advances.

SECTION 2 [1014 characters]

My A level in chemistry demonstrated the interdisciplinary nature of science, bridging fields such as biology and physics to provide a deeper understanding of the world around us. As a peer tutor, I had the opportunity to share this perspective with students, helping them grasp complex concepts and see the connections between chemistry and other topics. I needed to adapt my explanations to different learning styles, simplifying intricate ideas while maintaining their accuracy.

This role developed my communication and problem-solving skills, as I needed to identify where students struggled and guide them toward understanding. It also emphasised the importance of patience and empathy in creating a supportive learning environment. These skills are directly transferable to medicine, where educating patients, collaborating across disciplines, and solving complex problems are essential. Peer tutoring strengthened my ability to think critically, work collaboratively, and explain scientific concepts clearly.

SECTION 3 [1938 characters]

I undertook work experience on the Rheumatology Ward at Northwick Park Hospital, where I was intrigued by maggot therapy. I shadowed the junior doctor who cared for me during my stay at St Mark's Hospital. This was a unique experience that allowed me to observe a range of procedures including colonoscopies. It gave me a sound overview of the responsibilities and dedication required by a medical team towards the recovery of their patients.

I enjoyed doing weekly voluntary work on the HIV/AIDS ward at UCLH last year as it has enabled me to help people from many walks of life. Similarly, entertaining the elderly and disabled at John Grooms Home and assisting in the care of Reception Class at school has taught me to adapt to the needs of different age groups and varying backgrounds. I have spent considerable time nursing at my father's dental surgery and this has confirmed my passion for interacting with people.

The value of diplomatic leadership and rewarding teamwork were apparent to me while holding the post of Marketing Director of a highly successful Young Enterprise company that won numerous awards. I am a member of the publicity team of an active science society, responsible for producing a fortnightly newsletter and I am thoroughly enjoying the research and exploration involved in this project. In addition, being appointed Secretary of the Asian Society has taught me to be self-reliant and cultivate my organisational and time management skills.

I play the piano to Grade 8 and the guitar to Grade 7. This has increased my manual dexterity and has required high levels of discipline and perseverance. I enjoy playing badminton, have represented the school in lacrosse and hold a Bronze Medallion in Lifesaving.

Given my personal and work experiences, I believe I am aptly suited to the combination of application of scientific knowledge, dedication and enthusiasm needed to pursue a medical profession successfully.

11.45 A level entry — 3973 characters

SECTION 1 [931 characters]

Growing up, I was inspired by my aunt, a dedicated obstetrician whose unwavering commitment to patient care shaped my perspective on medicine. I admired her ability to remain calm under pressure, problem-solve in critical situations, and treat each patient with compassion. Observing her late-night shifts and hearing stories of lives she had impacted made me appreciate the sacrifices and responsibilities that come with being a doctor. Her passion for continuous learning and patient advocacy resonated deeply with me, motivating me to explore medicine further. Through shadowing and volunteering, I began to see first-hand the blend of science, empathy, and resilience required in this field. Her journey has shown me that medicine is more than a career – it is a lifelong commitment to serving others, and I am eager to embark on this path. My empathy and concern for other people has especially contributed to this aspiration.

SECTION 2 [1097 characters]

My A level subjects were an easy choice for me. They are the subjects I find most rewarding and feel I am good at. Biology taught me about various aspects of the human body. I found a logic in the way all the systems interact. Maths offers its own rewards through the use of logic too but feels more like a jigsaw puzzle where you have to piece things together to find the solution to a problem, a process not dissimilar to diagnosing. In chemistry I enjoy experimental work where you can apply knowledge learnt in a more practical way. By studying German, I have enhanced my critical thinking, communication, and cultural competence, all skills essential in medicine. Understanding the complex language structures associated with German sharpened my analytical abilities.

Alongside my A levels, I am taking an Open University course in 'Human Genetics and Health Issues', broadening my knowledge in a more specific and often controversial field. The course provides greater insight into many issues in the A level syllabus and the media, whilst also developing important independent study skills.

SECTION 3 [1945 characters]

Shadowing members of staff on a short-stay surgical ward at my local hospital, I experienced many aspects of hospital work. Interacting with current medical students reinforced my enthusiasm for the subject. Recently I helped at the hospital as a weekly volunteer, chatting with patients on the ward and making sure they had everything they needed. Gaining the patient perspective was eye-opening.

I have worked as a volunteer with a swimming club for disabled children for the past 5 years. I help with structured lessons for children of all ages and disabilities. I now know many of the children well and it is extremely rewarding to see them steadily improve while enjoying themselves. During the holidays I was asked to work with a disabled child in a wheelchair on a one-to-one basis as part of a play scheme. Although this requires much patience and is often challenging, I enjoy the work. Last year, I completed the 'National Pool Lifeguard Qualification' and now work at a local pool – dealing with the public, administering first aid and ensuring pool safety. Teamwork is essential, and I have gained much through working with colleagues and the general public.

I swim with my city swimming club. Having previously competed at county level, I now swim three times a week for fitness. Since completing two exchange visits to Germany, including a week working in a primary school, my confidence in speaking German has grown. Socially, I enjoy travel, music, meeting friends and the occasional salsa class.

I believe myself to be a committed student with the vocation, determination and ability to succeed in a career in medicine. My AS results have placed me on track to achieve the necessary academic standard. Through my work and experience I have developed excellent communication skills and the sensitivity to deal with people in varied situations. I feel strongly that I would meet the challenges and value the rewards of being a doctor.

11.46   A level entry   3919 characters

SECTION 1 [858 characters]

My desire to enter the medical profession is based upon a fascination with the workings of the human body, both physically and psychologically. Although I may not be able to 'cure' every patient, I believe I am a passionate person who would always strive to ensure patients receive the best quality of life possible. I appreciate that a medical degree can be emotionally, physically and academically challenging; however, I consider myself to have the determination and ambition to complete the course and continue using the knowledge I acquire. I hope my positive attitude to my studies and life provides a stimulus for my peers, which I wish to maintain throughout my professional working life. I am an enthusiastic, self-motivated individual who is committed to continual learning and personal development for a rewarding and fulfilling career in medicine.

SECTION 2 [1320 characters]

A level chemistry and biology have increased my scientific knowledge and I particularly enjoy lab-based work and the application of theory to practical situations. After dissecting a heart, I was able to perceive the variation that exists between textbook and specimen. My hard work was acknowledged when I received the only subject excellence certificate in both chemistry and biology from my school. In maths I have learnt to make judgements about which knowledge to best apply to different problems, a valuable and transferable skill.

As a member of the sixth form year council, I participate in weekly discussions concerning school events. This has involved me listening to ideas, developing them and reaching a final conclusion as part of a group. For the past four years I have acted as a guide for parents and students transferring to my school, which involves answering questions and giving opinions. I was given the responsibility of being a 'buddy' for a class of year 9 students; this required me to organise team-building activities during their induction day. I also conducted informal discussions with the students to ensure they were settled in their new school environment. All of these responsibilities have taught me to be responsible, show initiative, be supportive and focussed on the needs of others.

SECTION 3 [1741 characters]

During my work experience in a cardiology outpatient unit at Bedford Hospital, I had the opportunity to observe the roles of a variety of staff within the department. I was able to watch the doctor collate the available information about a patient and use his knowledge to make a diagnosis. I learnt how important it is for a doctor to be able to communicate with a multidisciplinary team who continued the care of the patient. In order to increase my knowledge of hospital life I am volunteering at a local hospital and I am currently placed on an orthopaedic ward. My duties include serving meals to patients, reception and paperwork tasks. I have built up a professional working relationship with patients, their families and staff; this allows me to improve my communication skills through working with a diverse range of people.

I have been employed part-time for the past two years in a busy high street fashion store working closely and constantly with the general public. My experience on customer services has shown the variety of approaches that different members of society use and I now appreciate that it is very important to listen, confirm and resolve any issue as calmly as possible. The demands of a vibrant retail environment have required me to be flexible and adaptable and not to expect to leave work on time!

Since completing a GCSE in textiles, I have continued to use my skills for my own pleasure and satisfaction and I am currently working on an evening dress. I read a wide variety of books, including 'Bedside Confessions of a Junior Doctor' and 'Bodies', both written by junior doctors. Both books highlighted the demand on a doctor's time and patience; however, neither deterred me from wanting to study medicine!

11.47 A level entry — 3985 characters

SECTION 1 [765 characters]

From having ileal atresia at birth to abdominal adhesions at seventeen, medicine has been a strong factor in my life. Growing up, I spent a great deal of time at Great Ormond Street Hospital, allowing me to observe and appreciate the role of doctors in our society, and aspire to become one myself. I also spent many hours researching the conditions that affected me and gained an appetite for connecting the dots and balancing various treatment options.

The obscure mechanics of the heart intrigue me and I believe that my diverse interests, both academic and extracurricular, have enhanced the skills I need to pursue a career in medicine. I am eager to study this fascinating subject at university and reinforce my skills to make me a worthy doctor in the future.

SECTION 2 [836 characters]

Biology has deepened my understanding of conditions such as atherosclerosis, and how it leads to myocardial infarction or peripheral arterial disease. From an article in a medical journal, I discovered how they can be reduced using anticoagulants or antiplatelet agents. Chemistry increases my practical skills and allows me to understand everyday phenomena on a molecular level. Latin and Greek indirectly provide me with skills to read medicine. I formed a logical approach doing translations: elucidating the sentence structure and carefully assembling it. Literature produces many heated class discussions; we construct arguments, working as a team to come to a consensus when composing translations. Mathematics has improved my problem-solving and time-keeping skills, as I persevered through challenges despite the volume of work.

SECTION 3 [2384 characters]

Working on a diabetes ward shows me the importance of communication: a patient's anxiety is often due to a fear of the unknown. My fluency in Gujarati allowed me to help a patient who did not speak English; conveying their concerns to the healthcare team was very rewarding. I explore interests that I develop there: I discovered that dual-action insulin can influence the patient in a positive manner, providing more stable blood glucose levels over the day. Volunteering here shows me the unglamorous side of medicine but convinces me that this is where my future lies.

I spent a week shadowing doctors at Lister Hospital. Endoscopy interested me, having undergone similar procedures myself. Seeing it from the doctor's point of view was powerful as I appreciated the intricacy involved. I was fortunate enough to spend time in Cardiology watching ECGs of stroke patients as well as observing joint replacements and a fasciectomy. I realised how demanding the life of a doctor is, but conversely, when witnessing a patient being told her IVF treatment was successful, I perceived the career satisfaction.

Volunteering for Mencap enables me to work with fine role models with learning disabilities like Down's syndrome. Attending two training courses has improved my knowledge on this topic and developed my interactive skills. I play an active role in the community by volunteering at the Garden House Hospice shop four hours a week and by working closely with children and their eager parents at the Kumon Centre. The past three years here have been fulfilling and have heightened my responsibilities. Volunteering at a GP's practice has shown me the value of the administrative staff and has increased my management and organisational skills.

In school, I am a Senior Prefect and a member of the Classics Society, demonstrating my dependability and self-confidence. I am entrusted with mentoring a Year 10 student: preparing suitable materials, building her confidence, as well as gaining her trust.

In my spare time, I play the violin and piano, the latter of which I have played for ten years, and I am about to take my Grade 8 examination. I also sing in the school choir, Vox Humana. Completing the Bronze Duke of Edinburgh was an achievement as it honed my teamwork skills, requiring cooperation and leadership. In addition, I play sports such as badminton and tennis every week.

11.48 A level entry — 3944 characters

SECTION 1 [984 characters]

I volunteered for a national charity, raising awareness about vaccinations and hygiene. Educating communities about disease prevention made me realise that medicine isn't just about treating illnesses – it's about stopping them before they start. I saw first-hand how misinformation and fear could prevent people from accessing life-saving interventions, reinforcing the importance of clear, science-based communication. I also gained an appreciation for the challenges of implementing large-scale health initiatives, from logistical barriers to cultural differences. This experience confirmed my desire to become a doctor who not only treats patients but also works to prevent illnesses at a broader level, ensuring better health outcomes for entire communities.

As the first person in my immediate and extended family to go to university, I would embrace this opportunity fully and, as someone who thrives on academic and physical challenge, I am eager to pursue medicine as a career.

SECTION 2 [636 characters]

As Deputy Head Girl, I have taken on a range of responsibilities that have strengthened my leadership and organisational skills. I initiated an academic mentoring system, pairing older students with younger pupils to support their studies, and helped peers understand their learning styles to improve academic performance.

I also speak regularly at school events, liaise between students and staff to ensure effective communication, and assist with organising and running various school functions. This role has deepened my sense of responsibility and taught me how to manage time effectively, work collaboratively, and take initiative.

SECTION 3 [2324 characters]

I did two weeks of work experience at a medical centre in Ghana. Two incidents stand out as examples of extremes to be found in a medical career. The accidental death of our guide and the realisation that I could do nothing to save him made me acutely aware that doctors regularly face situations in which the saving or extending of life is beyond the realm of medical skill. Conversely, the excitement of sitting in on a consultation with a patient presenting with the rare diabetes insipidus, a condition the doctor had not seen in 10 years' practice, was incredible. I was also privileged to stand in theatre and watch a hysterectomy and appendectomy, take and record blood pressure, weigh and check babies and advise mothers on basic baby care. It was an unbeatable experience which has given me a perspective on medicine I would not otherwise have had.

Shadowing medical staff at Wexham Park Hospital showed me that effective patient care is as much teamwork as individual responsibility. I was shown the CT scan of a cancerous tumour and could see the trauma caused to the patient by the tumour pushing aside the rest of the organs in his abdomen. I saw patients on the road to recovery but also the dead body of a man I had spoken to earlier that day and this made me aware of the conscientiousness, yet necessary objectivity, exercised by staff in the care of terminal patients.

At Hillingdon Hospital, a consultant radiologist explained to me how to interpret simple MRI and CT scans and how to detect tumours and calcification of blood vessels. I watched on screen as he injected painkiller into the spine of a patient to discover which vertebra was causing chronic pain. This enabled me to appreciate the radiologist's skill, the intricacy of the human body, the interconnectivity between systems and the genius of MRI and CT machines as diagnostic tools.

I competed nationally in gymnastics and cross-country, at county level in athletics and at interschool level in netball, rounders and swimming. I coach children in gymnastics, have achieved grade 5 drama and my enjoyment of chemistry motivated me to tutor a pupil for GCSE. These activities, together with waitressing and shop work, have equipped me with the teamwork skills, time management, patience, diplomacy, determination and endurance vital in medicine.

11.49   A level entry   3637 characters

SECTION 1 [748 characters]

My interest in medicine developed at an early age when I lost my grandfather to lung cancer and I did not understand why. In my quest to find out about the disease I soon found myself fascinated by the human body and how it works and, more recently, the way in which illnesses can be cured and prevented. It took me little time to realise that this was my passion and was what I wanted to study and pursue as a lifelong career due to the variety and dynamic nature of the subject.

With my work experience and varied interaction with people at all levels, I have learnt a lot about the challenging and demanding yet fulfilling nature of medicine and am looking forward to making a positive contribution and enjoying medicine as a lifelong profession.

SECTION 2 [1135 characters]

By studying biology at A level I have discovered that human physiology is my strength, attaining 98% in the first year. With biology and chemistry I feel that not only have I developed my intellectual skills but I have also learnt to analyse data and research topics effectively, while further maths has enhanced my ability to solve problems in a logical manner. By studying ethics at A level, my curiosity for the subject has only grown and I intend to look further into it outside of my studies. I find that it is extremely relevant in the world of medicine today, where advances in science are forever pushing the boundaries of what seems to be morally acceptable. It is only by keeping an open mind that these issues can be resolved.

Being both a mentor and prefect has provided me with great responsibility. However, I enjoy the opportunity to reassure and give sound advice, especially to new students who may feel out of place in an unfamiliar environment. As form representative for the school council, I liaise between staff and students and this has conveyed to me the importance of an open mind when searching for compromise.

SECTION 3 [1754 characters]

To reinforce my belief that medicine is the career for me, I spent three weeks at Ashford and St Peter's hospitals both shadowing doctors and helping nurses on the wards. This taught me a great deal about how the wards are run, the administering of drugs and what being a doctor involves on a day-to-day basis, from communicating with patients to teamwork and interacting with a range of health professionals. I observed the pace of the work, the rigour, skills and level of competence required whilst forging confidence and trust and the responsibility placed on the doctors. After witnessing two abdominal aneurisms, both associated with smoking, I appreciate the role of preventative medicine and the NHS campaigns to deter people from the habit. Additionally, for the past three years, I have been volunteering at a local nursing home where I help with the meals and enjoy communicating with the residents, from whom I learn a vast amount, not only of their chronic debilitating illnesses such as arthritis, but also of their invaluable life experiences.

In my free time I am an avid badminton player, playing regularly with my family and at school, as I find that keeping fit is an important part of achieving success in the long run. In the summer I relish the opportunity and challenge of playing cricket for the school's 3rd XI. It is our teamwork and determination which has led to the great success of the team and such qualities are equally important in the medical field.

In addition to responsibilities at school, having a part-time job for over a year has challenged my time management and organisational skills, whilst working in a public environment has taught me much about working under pressure and communicating with people of all ages.

11.50 A level entry — 3972 characters

SECTION 1 [1052 characters]

For me, a career in medicine is the perfect opportunity to stimulate my mind in a fascinating field in which I am highly motivated to succeed. I eagerly anticipate the opportunity to be able to combine my caring personality with the practical aspects of the subject and so have a major impact on people's lives. The prospect of lifelong learning in a subject for which I have such an affinity excites me. More inspiration to choose medicine came from participating in the Access to Medicine Course at King's College London and attending lectures given by top practitioners. A lecture on cardiac diseases was particularly relevant as my father suffers from angina and this prompted me to do further research into the subject.

Essentially, I feel I have gained a realistic appreciation of the challenges, both emotional and physical, involved in pursuing a career in medicine, but believe that my experiences have given me the motivation and commitment to withstand such trials and enable me to succeed as a valuable member of the developing medical field.

SECTION 2 [1248 characters]

I thoroughly enjoy studying A level biology and chemistry and my intellectual curiosity ensures I stay well ahead of the syllabus. For example, I was recently intrigued by an article on developments in cancer treatment, discussing how antibodies can be engineered to bind to specific antigens on the surface of cancer cells, allowing attached drugs to be delivered directly to tumours, and was inspired to do further research. As Science Representative, I organised a science exhibition for younger students, an experience that strengthened my leadership, communication, and organisational skills. Coordinating the event required careful planning, from selecting topics to creating engaging displays, ensuring the content was accessible and inspiring for the students. I worked collaboratively with teachers and peers, enhancing my teamwork skills and my ability to delegate tasks effectively. Presenting the exhibits allowed me to explain complex scientific concepts in a clear and engaging way, fostering my ability to communicate effectively with different audiences. These skills are essential for a career in medicine, where clear communication, teamwork, and the ability to explain complex ideas are crucial for providing patient-centred care.

SECTION 3 [1672 characters]

My commitment to studying medicine was solidified during a work placement at Princess Royal University Hospital in Orpington. Shadowing doctors in A&E, across minors, majors, and resuscitation, I gained first-hand experience of both junior and senior doctors' roles. The experience revealed the immense emotional and physical pressures doctors face daily, yet also highlighted the deep rewards of positively impacting patients' lives. Observing consultations taught me the significance of a compassionate bedside manner, empathy, and strong communication with both patients and staff.

Volunteering at my local church, I assist elderly members at social gatherings, finding great fulfilment in helping them enjoy their time. Additionally, as a member of the 'Welcome Team', I hone my communication and teamwork skills, ensuring guests feel welcomed and the meetings run smoothly.

The residential science summer school at Imperial College was a transformative experience, where I led a project team. This role required planning, decision-making, and organising to meet deadlines. Our 'Green Power' project earned a Silver B.A. Crest award, and I was honoured to receive the 'Most Likely to be a Mentor Award.'

Living and studying in India for three years at Hebron School broadened my worldview and fostered independence. Returning to the UK mid-Year 10 was challenging, but hard work and perseverance allowed me to achieve strong GCSE results and be elected prefect.

I'm also an avid table tennis player, organising clubs for my school and coaching beginners. I captained football and hockey teams at Hebron for two years, strengthening my leadership and organisational skills.

11.51 A level entry — 3886 characters

SECTION 1 [642 characters]

In A level psychology, studying OCD and depression revealed the intricate relationship between mental health and brain physiology. Learning how neurotransmitter imbalances contribute to these conditions fascinated me, particularly the role of serotonin in OCD and how cognitive behavioural therapy can alter brain function.

Beyond the science, I was struck by the profound impact these disorders have on daily life, from compulsive behaviours to persistent negative thought patterns. This sparked my interest in medicine, as I wanted to understand how medical interventions, combined with psychological therapies, can improve patient outcomes.

SECTION 2 [1433 characters]

As Head Boy and Dux of my school, I play an active part in all aspects of the school, such as organising events, representing the school at functions and communicating the views of my peers. I have completed my bronze and silver Duke of Edinburgh Awards and am now working towards gold. I thoroughly enjoy the responsibility of undertaking these awards and being part of a team in the expeditions. I also represent my school at the Stirling Student Forum and the area at the Forth Valley Young People's Conference. In fifth year, I joined the paired reading scheme which helps younger children who find reading difficult.

Winning the Arichi Prize for Science and representing my school in chemistry and physics competitions have been pivotal experiences in my academic development. These opportunities allowed me to apply my scientific knowledge while working closely with teammates to solve complex problems. The competitions taught me how to think critically under pressure, collaborate effectively, and draw on each team member's strengths to achieve our goals. These experiences have not only strengthened my academic skills but also enhanced my ability to work as part of a team, a crucial aspect of pursuing a career in medicine. I attended a week-long Salter's chemistry camp in St Andrews University. Having been awarded several gold awards in the UK maths challenge, I was then selected for the European mathematical Olympiad.

SECTION 3 [1811 characters]

To broaden my knowledge of the medical profession, I spent time at Stirling and Falkirk Royal Infirmaries, rotating through Cardiology, ENT, and Pathology. This gave me a unique opportunity to experience the everyday life of a busy hospital. In A&E, the wide range of patients and the department's fast pace showed me the diversity and satisfaction medicine offers. I was fortunate to attend surgeries, including an endoscopic sinus procedure for sinusitis and nasal polyps, where I saw the importance of teamwork in patient care. Engaging with consultants, junior doctors, and staff inspired me with their dedication and positive views on their profession.

After my hospital placements, I shadowed a GP, gaining insight into the community-based aspect of medicine and the crucial role of doctors outside the hospital setting. I currently volunteer with NHC Action for Children in Alloa, supporting vulnerable homeless young people, and work at Kumon Education Centre, helping children with their education. Both roles allow me to contribute to others' development, fulfilling my desire to work with people. I also completed a 3-month St Andrews Ambulance first aid course, where I learned essential skills for handling accidents and medical situations.

Sport plays an important role in my life, teaching me time management alongside my school commitments. I represent my school in rugby (as captain of the sevens team), football, golf, and badminton. I also play tennis at the national level, having represented Scotland in internationals and reaching a ranking of 3 in the country. To give back to the tennis community, I became a qualified coach and regularly assist the Scottish national coach with junior squads. The satisfaction I gain from helping others develop motivates me to pursue a career in medicine.

11.52 A level entry — 3839 characters

SECTION 1 [687 characters]

Throughout my school life I have been fascinated by science, and my ambition now is to embark on a career that will contribute to medical knowledge. This is a challenging and competitive field, but I believe I have the dedication and academic ability to achieve great success. I enjoy working with people and would like a career that combines medical research and clinical practice.

A degree in medicine will provide me with a wide and varied range of opportunities as a career and I would hope to make breakthroughs into new drugs and medical techniques. I want to work on diseases such as HIV/AIDS and tuberculosis, which have such a devastating effect on people in developing countries.

SECTION 2 [776 characters]

In my A levels, I have particularly enjoyed course elements relevant to medicine. For example, the biology course made me want to learn more about haematology and the complex role of blood, and drug production pathways was an enjoyable part of the chemistry syllabus. As a member of the college medical and chemistry societies, I have attended many lectures, including one talk about rotary motion in mitochondrial enzymes. I was fascinated by the subject, and biochemistry is an area I would like to pursue further. Studying further mathematics has been challenging but has improved my problem-solving abilities, and statistics is useful for medicine. Physics is essential for medicine, and studying economics is useful in a healthcare system that has many financial worries.

SECTION 3 [2376 characters]

My career choice follows work experience in both pure and applied scientific fields. I worked for one week at Addenbrooke's Hospital in the Plastic and Oral Surgery ward where interacting with staff and patients helped to improve my communication skills, and I learnt basic clinical techniques such as how to take the blood pressure and temperature of a patient. I also attended the medical induction course Medlink, which I enjoyed because I was introduced to areas of medicine such as paediatrics, psychiatry and neurology. In terms of research, I learnt a lot during a fortnight at the Cambridge Department of Plant Sciences. My role was to set up and take part in students' experiments, during which I became competent at using scientific equipment and enjoyed the discipline of research work. It helped me to achieve distinction in the Analytical Measurement Proficiency Competition.

During weekends I have volunteered at a care home, organising games and entertainment to keep residents active. I have met some wonderful personalities and enjoyed helping them with creative tasks and activities. Talking with elderly people who are suffering from long-term physical and mental illness has helped me to empathise with them and appreciate their needs. I also pursue a range of sporting, musical, outdoor and social activities. I am a committee member for the village tennis club and am responsible for managing the website and junior matches. I play cricket and football for the village and cycle into college, all of which helps to keep me fit. With my family I have had many active holidays in Britain and abroad and have visited all the large National Parks in the UK. I have completed the Duke of Edinburgh Bronze and Silver Awards and will soon complete Gold. The expeditions were a fantastic opportunity to lead my group maturely and successfully to the finish.

I play piano and will soon finish Grade 5. I have taught myself bass guitar and formed a rock band. We have successfully built our own website, recorded a CD, and performed at many clubs and festivals. Playing to audiences of up to 300 has given me confidence and my public speaking has also been enhanced through reaching the semi-final in the Youth Debating Competition and the final of the Young Consumer of the Year Competition. For both events I worked with my team to think quickly and present ideas.

11.53 A level entry — 3824 characters

SECTION 1 [1265 characters]

Medicine, as a cocktail of hard science, social interaction and pragmatic thinking, suits me more than any other discipline. The precision with which medicine explains the complex human body thrills me. Meanwhile, the ever-dynamic nature of the subject, its constant progression, appeals to me greatly since it makes a medical career one of lifelong learning. Honestly, I haven't met a doctor who has not experienced great pressure intellectually, emotionally and physically in his/her professional life. But somehow, I regard the challenging nature of the occupation to be a merit, something which adds to the job satisfaction. Studying medicine creates the possibility to have an intellectual and rewarding career working with people of high expertise and thus would allow me to fulfil many of my goals for the future.

The last two years of living away from home have taught me a great deal about independence. Faced with myriad opportunities opened by the UWC movement, I have really had to evaluate my goals, from which subject to study to the country in which to do so. The fact that I am still applying to medicine is a testament to my dedication to the career. Moreover, I genuinely believe that I would contribute successfully through the medical profession.

SECTION 2 [945 characters]

In college, I have been involved in mediation and peer listening, the principles of which have helped me enhance my interpersonal skills. And in my holidays, I was involved in a summer scheme for refugee children in South London. I particularly enjoy voluntary work which involves my own interests, therefore this term I've taken up training athletes for the Special Olympics. At 15, I won a place at the newly founded United World College Costa Rica. Seeing communication as vital, my decision was swayed by a desire to learn a new language. Being involved in building such an international community has been an invaluable experience.

I have learnt how to overcome cultural differences which, in the increasingly multicultural setting of the UK, would come in useful in a medical career. Through living with people of 75 different nationalities I have also developed a high level of conscientiousness, which is another key quality for a doctor.

SECTION 3 [1614 characters]

I have spent three years as an after-school receptionist at Tollgate Surgery, which have rendered me at ease with the medical setting and patients. Observing consultants in ophthalmology and family planning, I have experienced theatre settings and seen the rewards of specialisation. Sitting in with GPs has shown me the importance of a good patient–doctor rapport. It also highlighted that sensitivity to a patient's mental and social conditions, as well as physical, is integral to providing care. Volunteering in Northern India with a group of doctors and medical students to offer health camps for nomads also gave me insight into primary healthcare delivery in rural, underdeveloped areas. Encountering patients sceptical about modern diagnosis and treatments, and learning about the traditional Amchi practices, made me appreciate the effect cultural setting can have on care delivery. More than anything, my time there showed me that working with and learning from a team of able, driven individuals is hugely stimulating.

From a young age, I have enjoyed contributing to my community and, last year, I received the Princess Diana Memorial Award and was nominated as Colchester Volunteer of the Year. These experiences have shown me that working effectively as part of a team leads to efficient progress towards the end result. More recently, since last October I've spent an afternoon each week in an underprivileged community helping children with homework and teaching them English, which has given me an insight into the health problems experienced by vulnerable people and those from different cultures.

11.54 A level entry 3655 characters

SECTION 1 [830 characters]

I was deeply inspired by a doctor I read about who worked in war-torn regions, providing medical aid to those in desperate need. Their courage and selflessness in facing extreme conditions, from natural disasters to refugee camps, demonstrated the profound impact doctors can have beyond traditional hospital settings. Their commitment to treating patients despite limited resources and overwhelming challenges resonated with my passion for global health and equitable healthcare. Learning about their work motivated me to explore volunteering opportunities where I could contribute to underserved communities, reinforcing my desire to pursue medicine as a means of social impact. I aspire to follow their example by not only treating illnesses but also advocating for vulnerable populations who lack access to quality healthcare.

SECTION 2 [843 characters]

Studying optical isomerism and enantiomers in A level chemistry, along with giving a talk to younger students on the topic, has enhanced my analytical thinking and precision – skills essential in both chemistry and medicine. Preparing and delivering the talk allowed me to break down complex concepts – such as how enantiomers, though identical in molecular formula, can have dramatically different effects in the body – into an accessible format. This experience improved my ability to communicate scientific ideas effectively and engage an audience. This experience developed my public speaking and teaching skills and instilled a disciplined approach to problem-solving. These skills will be invaluable as I navigate the complexities of medical practice and patient care, where precision, communication, and critical thinking are paramount.

SECTION 3 [1982 characters]

I spent a week at a GP clinic, gaining insight into the role of the GP as one of the 'front lines' of the NHS. I realised the need for an approachable figure in whom people can confide, and the array of interpersonal skills needed to establish a good rapport with the patient. A week at the A&E department at the Hillingdon Hospital taught me about how doctors deal with pressure, such as their ability to communicate effectively with their team in emergencies and to prioritise cases according to clinical need. I also arranged a three-week placement at hospitals in Sri Lanka and India, where I was touched by the doctors' sensitivity to complex social issues, such as patients' socio-economic status, when deciding on the treatment. Whilst studying ECGs with a cardiologist I learnt about the analytical skills required to process data before arriving at a sound diagnosis.

Since June 2008, I have volunteered at the Three Wings Trust, supervising children with disabilities in after-school play sessions. This involves my taking the initiative in resolving distressing situations involving difficult behaviour; I remained patient and empathetic towards the children and their parents alike. I have also been volunteering weekly at a local nursing home and have learnt to adapt my approach according to their individual needs and personalities. Working as part of a healthcare team has impressed on me how important flexibility and upholding morale are in teamwork when delivering care to the patient.

I regularly play cricket for my local team, which has developed my teamwork skills under pressure and has also taught me the value of perseverance in achieving my goals. As the co-founder of the school's Amnesty International group, I have developed proficient leadership skills. I have led and supported my fellow members as I organised logistically demanding events, such as sponsored walks and assemblies. Through delegation, I have brought out the strengths of my colleagues.

11.55 A level entry — 3877 characters

SECTION 1 [1066 characters]

I have been inspired to embark on a career in medicine through the excitement of scientific endeavour and by the people I have known who have struggled against disability and cancer. Their unfailing personal strength and belief in the medical profession have cemented my resolve to pursue a life in medicine. My aunt, who was diagnosed with multiple sclerosis in her early twenties, has been a great inspiration to me. Watching her treatment and her daily struggle with the disease serves to show how it is not only doctors who give hope to patients, but patients who give hope and inspiration to doctors.

During my preparation for this application I have felt a powerful sense of fulfilment and purpose in my work in the medical field. I have recently been accepted on to a work experience placement at Salisbury NHS Foundation Trust where I hope to widen my patient contact experience. I am a hardworking, dedicated and enthusiastic individual and I believe that there is no better way to apply my skills than in the pursuit of excellence in the medical profession.

SECTION 2 [903 characters]

Learning about neural plasticity and neurotransmitter systems has further illuminated the relationship between biological and psychological factors in mental health and neurological disorders. This exploration deepened my understanding of how interconnected these areas are, highlighting the complexities of both fields. In addition to broadening my knowledge of medicine's vast scope, it reinforced my commitment to studying mental health and brain function.

My EPQ allowed me to conduct independent research on these topics, enhancing my ability to critically analyse information, manage projects, and present findings clearly. These skills, developed through both my A level studies and EPQ, have equipped me to approach medical education with a strong analytical mindset, a passion for understanding the intersection of mind and body, and a commitment to furthering research in these essential areas.

SECTION 3 [1908 characters]

Last July, I joined Albany House Dental Practice as Practice Manager. I was responsible for the daily running of the practice, including dealing with emergencies, Devon doctors and visiting hygienist appointments, so I have much experience dealing with a variety of patients. I was also responsible for the human resources of the practice: I wrote and implemented the health and safety policies and procedures, the company contracts and many recruitment initiatives, which has involved key skills of time management, working as a team and working independently in a professional capacity. My position at Albany House was an invaluable learning experience and I took an active interest in expanding my knowledge base for the role by attending advanced resuscitation training, and a course in dealing with emergencies in the dental surgery.

In August this year, I became a healthcare assistant at Hays House Nursing Home, where I am currently employed. Hays House is a very well-respected home with 43 residents with an emphasis on dementia and palliative care. My role includes delivering full personal care to all the residents. This is a highly responsible role involving being alone with vulnerable patients, many of whom cannot perform basic tasks of self-care. It is my job to closely observe the residents' health on a daily basis and formally report and log any changes to their condition in order to allow their care to be constantly adapted to their changing needs. This has been an unparalleled experience of intense patient contact and has cemented my desire to pursue a career in medicine. I am constantly looking for ways to improve the range of care which I can deliver and regularly attend training courses. I already feel I have much practical experience of dealing with patients/clients from the front line to more intimate aspects of care, which I have delivered with empathy and sensitivity.

11.56 A level entry — 3909 characters

SECTION 1 [888 characters]

My ambition to become a doctor stems from both a fascination with science and a desire to work with people. When I first investigated medicine as a career path, I was struck by the continuous scientific learning undertaken by even the most senior of the profession. This prospect excited me, as I enjoy encountering challenges in my everyday life, and it is definitely an aspect I look forward to in a medical degree and career.

I regularly search newspapers for medical articles and have a subscription to the 'Student BMJ'; these have provided me with more in-depth knowledge of life as a doctor and current issues in medicine. Medicine is a profession which requires a strong mental attitude, complex scientific knowledge and excellent social adaptability. I believe I am capable of combining these skills into a lifelong medical career and look forward to having the opportunity to do so.

SECTION 2 [1071 characters]

Studying psychological therapies has greatly enhanced my understanding of the holistic approach required in medicine, particularly in treating mental health conditions. Learning about interventions like cognitive behavioural therapy and their role in managing disorders such as anxiety and depression, alongside pharmacological treatments, highlighted the importance of addressing both biological and psychological aspects of health. Additionally, giving an assembly during Mental Health Week on the significance of mental health awareness allowed me to communicate these concepts to a wider audience, strengthening my public speaking and presentation skills. Analysing case studies further provided valuable insights into developing individualised treatment plans, emphasising the balance between medication efficacy and the long-term benefits of therapy.

This experience not only deepened my appreciation for multidisciplinary care but also honed my critical thinking skills and cultivated a patient-centred mindset, both of which are essential for a career in medicine.

SECTION 3 [1950 characters]

During a week's work experience in the orthopaedic department at my local hospital, I gained a first-hand understanding of the hospital environment, and of how a specialist works. I also visited the clinical trials unit attached to a surgery. While there, I spoke to senior nurses about their work and observed the monitoring of and, more fundamentally, communication with the patient. At both placements, it struck me how often more useful information was acquired through this method than through medical tests.

For several months I volunteered at a residential home for adults with severe learning disabilities. This allowed me a great insight into patient contact in a care environment. My duties involved waking the residents and serving them breakfast. I got to know several of the residents; this further improved my communication skills – particularly my listening ability. A strong mental attitude is an important quality for a doctor to have, so that he/she is able to remain calm even when under immense pressure.

I believe that participating in the Duke of Edinburgh Silver Award helped to develop empathy and communication skills. I had further opportunity to increase my leadership and mentoring skills by captaining my football team and also coaching a youth team. These roles require persistence, enthusiasm and a sense of humour, as such qualities are necessary to earn respect as a leader and a motivator. In my spare time I work in a local supermarket and am frequently tasked with a security role that also involves welcoming customers to the store; this requires both vigilance and an open, friendly manner.

While at secondary school I was managing director of a successful Young Enterprise company. As house captain I was responsible for the organisation of sports teams and for speaking in assemblies about competition results. Both these positions developed my organisational abilities and my ability to cope with responsibility.

11.57 A level entry — 3176 characters

SECTION 1 [1092 characters]

For me, medicine is the most exciting subject of all. It unites my interest in human biology with my love of pure science. It is constantly evolving and will challenge and stimulate me throughout my life – I will never stop learning. My enjoyment in studying cardiovascular disease in A level biology strengthened my attraction to medical studies. I have always been interested in medicine, but the ill health and demise of a close relative made me think of it as a vocation as well as a career. There is also a huge range of career opportunities within medicine, from community work and bedside care to academic research and laboratory work. The difficulty would be in choosing which path to follow!

Everything that I have read about medicine, discussed with medical professionals and experienced as a volunteer, has strengthened my determination to study this fascinating subject. I know that I will encounter challenges on a daily basis as a doctor, but I am certain that I will more than meet them and thoroughly enjoy doing so. I look forward with immense excitement to studying medicine.

SECTION 2 [674 characters]

During my school's recent biology expedition to South Africa, I gained valuable insights into the broader aspects of medicine through the camp doctor, who taught us about hygiene and basic emergency procedures. Observing the doctor's approach to healthcare in a remote setting deepened my interest in how medicine can be applied in diverse and challenging environments.

This experience highlighted the importance of preventative care and quick, effective decision-making in emergency situations. It strengthened my resolve to pursue medicine, as I saw first-hand the significant impact that medical knowledge and practical skills can have on both individuals and communities.

SECTION 3 [1410 characters]

I witnessed medical care in a busy teaching hospital in York and was impressed by the crucial role of every member of the team. While shadowing nurses, I admired their patience and compassion in delivering close patient care. I talked to several doctors, gaining an impression of the emotional aspects of working closely with ill people, from dealing with death to saving lives. I also gained some insight into the tiredness and stress that is part of the job. I learned that the role of a doctor is a demanding one that encompasses the science of diagnosis and the art of dealing with patients. It requires an ability to listen and communicate, and to explain technical terms and complicated problems simply. I believe that much of medical practice concerns the management of symptoms, as we don't have cures to as many diseases as is popularly believed.

Outside school, I am a keen actor and also sing in the Chamber Choir. I love sport and run a football activity for younger students. Currently, I am leading the development of a nature trail around the school grounds. My responsibility for these after-school activities involves talking to, and motivating, a wide range of people from the youngest students to members of staff. It has developed and stretched my organisational, communication and time management skills to the full and led me to become more confident working with a wide variety of people.

11.58   A level entry   3825 characters

SECTION 1 [1359 characters]

A tanker colliding with a motorbike; a poor man who couldn't afford shoes or medication; a sick grandmother's unconditional love; when I look back upon my life, these moments stand out, not only as life-changing experiences but ones that subconsciously fuelled my childhood desire for medicine. At a young age, I saw someone die in front of my eyes. Although a very traumatic experience, I learned to understand and respect the true fragility of life. I felt helpless and insignificant; I wanted to be in a position to make a difference. I didn't realise it then, but my aspirations for a career in medicine had just begun. Medicine offers the unique opportunity to integrate my dedication to science with my natural flair for interacting with people.

My voluntary experience has made me aware that medicine is a challenging profession, which is laborious, time-consuming and one that requires an extraordinary amount of dedication. However, when I get to see the look of fulfilment on a doctor's face when they have helped a patient in their time of need, I know that there can be no better feeling, and every part of me wishes to experience it for myself later on. I believe that my love for science along with my caring and empathetic nature coupled with a passionate drive to succeed and my strong communication skills make medicine the only career for me.

SECTION 2 [646 characters]

I have attended several leadership and problem-solving courses and have over twenty hours of flying experience with the armed forces. These activities have not only helped me hone my communication and organisation skills, but have also improved my physical and mental stamina. I undertook an Open University module in 'Molecules, Medicines and Drugs' to further expand my knowledge, whilst also conducting extra reading on cancer to supplement my observations during work experience. I am an avid reader of 'New Scientist' and 'Student BMJ', as these allow me to keep up to date with recent findings within the profession to which I truly aspire.

SECTION 3 [1820 characters]

As I matured, my yearning for medicine only grew stronger. I undertook a four-week placement shadowing a GP, which allowed me to become familiar with the full primary care cycle. I learned to empathise with patients about their illness in their time of need and saw the progression of their health, interacting with them throughout their visits.

I arranged for a placement at a district general hospital to experience the secondary care aspect of the NHS. It was a hectic week in which I observed many fascinating procedures. I was impressed by the efficiency and professional manner with which they were carried out. I was also given the opportunity to see an electron microscope and a mass spectrometer being utilised. This made me appreciate the necessity for a sound scientific basis as I saw the theory that I had learnt being applied in a hospital environment. During the week, my self-belief and interpersonal skills improved tremendously, especially whilst conversing with terminally ill patients and senior clinicians. On an acute ward round, I bore witness to two cancer patients being told that they had less than three months to live. This helped me realise that medicine consists of both curative and palliative elements.

I am fluent in English, Hindi, Urdu and Punjabi, which means I can effectively communicate with many people and I have excellent communication skills. I have achieved grade eight in both piano and electronic keyboard and my commitment towards such a time-consuming activity shows my intense dedication. I enjoy playing cricket and have played at a club level for many years which has taught me the importance of teamwork – similar to a challenging Duke of Edinburgh expedition on an extremely hot day, which proved that, with enough determination, teamwork can achieve inspiring results.

11.59 A level entry — 3962 characters

SECTION 1 [1090 characters]

I have always had a fascination with science. Listening to medical podcasts has sparked my curiosity about the future of healthcare. Engaging with discussions on cutting-edge advancements, from AI in diagnostics to breakthroughs in cancer treatment, has shown me how rapidly medicine evolves. I was fascinated by how CRISPR gene editing could revolutionise genetic disorders and how machine learning is improving early disease detection. These discussions made me realise that medicine is not just about applying existing knowledge – it's about constantly learning and adapting to new discoveries. Hearing real doctors discuss their experiences also gave me insight into the challenges of medical practice, from patient care to ethical dilemmas. Podcasts like 'The doctor's kitchen' also highlighted the role of nutrition in medicine, reinforcing the importance of a holistic approach to health. Exploring medicine through these conversations has strengthened my enthusiasm for a career where I can contribute to scientific progress while maintaining a deep commitment to patient well-being.

SECTION 2 [1282 characters]

I actively attend my school's medical ethics society, where we engage in discussions on thought-provoking topics such as organ donation. These debates have allowed me to explore the complex ethical dilemmas that healthcare professionals face and consider the moral implications of medical decisions. By examining various perspectives, I have developed a deeper understanding of the balance between scientific advancements and ethical responsibilities. This experience has strengthened my critical thinking skills and reinforced my interest in the ethical dimensions of medicine, preparing me to approach the challenges of medical practice with both compassion and integrity. I also enjoy painting and drawing, which is why I chose to do A level art. Art has helped me balance the intensive academic science subjects I have undertaken at A level with something more creative. As part of an art history study, I visited Paris to view a number of paintings such as Claude Monet's 'Series' paintings. I feel my art studies are helping me take a different perspective on problems and have added a more holistic approach to my way of looking at issues. Not everything is measurable and quantifiable, and sometimes it is those less measurable variables, like patient feelings, that matter.

SECTION 3 [1590 characters]

I recently attended a conference for medical applicants, which improved my understanding of the course and career. In particular, I have become more aware of the challenges of medicine, such as the need to undertake continued assessment beyond graduation. I undertook work experience at a GP surgery. I reviewed and filed incoming correspondence, which helped me to appreciate the range of medical problems dealt with by GPs. I also observed how GPs communicate with and treat patients, particularly taking histories of patient illnesses and making a diagnosis. This experience impressed upon me the need for strong communication and interpersonal skills when advising patients. It also made me appreciate that doctors can help patients even where there is no medical cure. Last summer, I completed work experience at both Selly Oak and Northwick Park hospitals. At Selly Oak hospital, I spent time in a liver outpatients clinic. In contrast to the GP surgery, this experience gave me exposure as to how specialist units operate and the focused knowledge of the doctors who work in this unit.

I am also involved in team events such as creating science news podcasts, available for download from our school website, which I undertook with several classmates. I acted as the team leader, organising meetings and being responsible for ensuring that team members completed their tasks. This role has greatly improved my leadership and organisational abilities. I am a school prefect and my duties include helping at the school's entrance exam and acting as a tour guide at the school's Open Day.

11.60 A level entry — 3946 characters

SECTION 1 [874 characters]

I have always had a strong interest in the sciences, especially chemistry, which first attracted me to a career in medicine. The teamwork, interacting with patients and having the opportunity to make a difference, along with my fascination with the sciences and the desire to keep learning, compel me to pursue a career in medicine. I know from personal experience that the impact a medic and their team can make on someone's life is huge, and I would like to have such a responsibility, doing something that I have a true interest in and passion for.

The four days I spent at Medlink also reinforced my interest in medicine and I particularly enjoyed the A&E role play session. In order to gain some understanding of the constant developments in medicine as well as in other areas of science, I have recently started reading the 'New Scientist' and visiting the BMJ website.

SECTION 2 [948 characters]

Organising a paired reading club for younger students who were not meeting their target has been an incredibly rewarding experience that has honed my ability to adapt and tailor my approach to meet individual needs – skills that are essential in medicine.

By working closely with students, I was able to identify their specific challenges and provide personalised support to help them build confidence and improve their reading skills. This required patience, empathy, and strong communication, as I ensured that each student felt understood and encouraged throughout the process. Managing the logistics of the club also developed my organisational abilities and time management, ensuring that each session ran smoothly. These experiences have deepened my understanding of the importance of personalised care, active listening, and adaptability, all of which I believe will help me excel in the patient-centred approach required in a medical career.

SECTION 3 [2124 characters]

To further my understanding of the medical profession I have undertaken several work experience placements over the past two years. I worked at a play centre for disabled children on a weekly basis for six months where I enjoyed interacting with the children and was also able to develop my communication skills. After half an hour, during one very rewarding session, I managed to get two girls with Down's syndrome, who fought frequently despite being friends, to understand that they should not throw sand at each other. I have been working at a children's hospice since January and through this have discovered another way in which doctors are involved in the community. In July I spent four days at the Royal Sussex County Hospital, where I was shown a variety of different aspects to medicine including ward rounds, laboratory work and clinics. One of the patients being cared for by the Infectious Diseases department where I was based had bacterial meningitis. I was shown her scans as well as her cerebrospinal fluid sample and, from the care of this patient, I was able to see the teamwork involved not only within the hospital but also with community organisations. For a week in August, I was based at Woking Community Hospital, where I was shown a variety of different departments and witnessed the removal of a sebaceous cyst, which I found fascinating.

Outside of school, I am part of a tae kwon do club and I also enjoy the physical challenge and outdoors nature of windsurfing. I have completed both my Bronze and Silver Duke of Edinburgh Awards and aim to finish my Gold in February. The team element of the expeditions has been a real highlight of all three awards, and in preparation for my Gold final I completed a wilderness first aid course. I also have a strong interest in music and have achieved Grade 5 piano as well as playing guitar. Within the school community I have assisted with weekly paired reading and contributed to sports day and RAG week along with prospective parent tours. On top of this, I have been working at WHSmith, which has given me the opportunity to interact with many people.

11.61 A level entry 3907 characters

SECTION 1 [1019 characters]

Growing up, I saw how a compassionate psychiatrist helped a close friend navigate severe anxiety, transforming their outlook on life. Their ability to listen without judgement, provide tailored treatment, and empower their patient with coping strategies was inspiring. I realised that medicine is not just about treating physical illnesses but also about addressing the mind and its complexities. It has always amazed me how the human organism can be reduced to a complex soup of biological molecules, yet displays emergent properties, like consciousness, so distinctly removed from the biochemical sum of its parts.

This experience awakened my interest in psychiatry and mental health, leading me to study psychology at A level and research the connection between cognition and emotional well-being. The psychiatrist's holistic approach reinforced my belief in patient-centred care, and I aspire to pursue medicine with the same empathy, ensuring that mental health receives the attention it deserves within healthcare.

SECTION 2 [1501 characters]

Neurological illnesses are so frightening because organic damage to the nervous system has a translational effect on our actions and behaviour, redefining the philosophical concept of who we are, as demonstrated by the characters in the works of Oliver Sacks. Exploring this interest in neuroscience, I independently researched and wrote an essay entitled 'There's only one way to make a brain. Discuss', which was highly commended for the Kelvin Science Essay Competition.

The development of antiretroviral drugs targeting Reverse Transcriptase was a topic I investigated with Pfizer researchers on Biology Project Week. I tested the potency of candidate compounds in inhibiting this enzyme and disrupting the mechanism of retroviral replication. This opportunity contextualised theoretical biology in a medical situation and gave me an appreciation of the pharmacological basis of medical treatment.

Writing articles on the social and ethical implications of science for the school's online science journal has sharpened my analytical and critical thinking skills, which are vital in the medical field. By examining complex issues and exploring the broader impacts of scientific advancements, I have learned to approach problems from multiple perspectives, weighing both the benefits and potential risks. This ability to analyse, question, and synthesise information will be invaluable when diagnosing conditions, evaluating treatment options, and considering the ethical implications of patient care.

SECTION 3 [1387 characters]

Shadowing a respiratory medicine team at NHS Kent & Canterbury Hospital, I witnessed the intellectual challenges of diagnosing disease. Each patient is a puzzle, with pieces ranging from scans and physical exams to symptoms and personal history. This process emphasised medicine's blend of problem-solving and humanistic care, especially when I saw a patient being informed of a lung cancer diagnosis, which taught me the emotional and intellectual aspects of the profession.

As a volunteer in a psychogeriatric day centre for five weeks, I designed activities for occupational therapy, aiding in the rehabilitation of mentally ill patients. Attending cognitive behavioural therapy sessions, I gained empathy for those struggling with depression and a deeper understanding of elderly behaviour, which sparked my interest in mental health and brain diseases.

I enjoy various sports, from table football to hurdling, and as an assistant stage manager for a Shakespeare adaptation, I coordinated backstage activities and designed props. Every Thursday afternoon during the past year, I've also helped supervise a pre-prep class, nurturing creativity and curiosity in children. This has strengthened my communication skills and affirmed my desire to pursue a medical career.

With dedication and a desire to understand humanity, I am ready to commit to the study of medicine and become a doctor.

11.62 — A level entry — 3847 characters

SECTION 1 [1356 characters]

A keen scientist from a young age, I have always been fascinated by human physiology. Whilst the structural framework of the human body is undoubtedly impressive, it is the complex array of systems, organs and cells which keep the body functioning through chemical processes that I find particularly awe-inspiring. Fusing a deep love for the sciences with my keen desire to help and care for others, medicine seems a logical career route for me.

My interests in the subject further developed after I attended an 'Exploring Healthcare' spring school and a recent Medsim conference. From lectures to laboratory work, and from clinical practice to participation in PBL, I found the course an invaluable learning experience. I especially enjoyed wearing surgical scrubs and putting my manual dexterity to the test whilst performing a simulation of keyhole surgery. Although I was initially apprehensive about being observed by practitioners during this procedure, this challenging clinical task gave me a sense of the pressures encountered by surgeons on a daily basis.

I am looking forward to a lifetime of learning and a long journey towards possessing the expertise necessary to be of valuable service to society. I have always pursued my studies and all other goals in my life with rigour and conviction and I will continue to do so at university and beyond.

SECTION 2 [841 characters]

My 200 hours of voluntary service for the Millennium Volunteers scheme, a school-led project, has been immensely rewarding and helped me develop vital skills for a career in medicine. I learned the importance of compassion, patience, and dedication while working with diverse groups, including those facing personal challenges. I developed a deeper understanding of the impact of support and care on individuals' lives, which is essential for building meaningful patient relationships. Volunteering also taught me time management, balancing responsibilities, and collaborating within teams. These skills will be invaluable in a medical career, where providing high-quality care, effective communication, and teamwork are essential. This experience reinforced my commitment to a career where I can make a positive difference in people's lives.

SECTION 3 [1650 characters]

My work experience at Barnet General and Edgware Community Hospitals solidified my career choice. Two moments stand out: shadowing an orthopaedic surgeon, I was moved by how he put a young girl at ease during a thorough but discreet examination, earning her trust. Despite her diagnosis of in-toeing gait, the strong rapport allowed the parents to cope better with the news. Later, in Barnet's busy A&E department, I witnessed the doctors' concern for an unconscious patient with abnormal vital signs. The tension was palpable as the consultants made difficult decisions with limited information to save the patient. Despite the long hours and administrative duties, I learned that doctors are compassionate professionals who combine biomedical knowledge with emotional intelligence, empathy, and clinical judgement.

Volunteering weekly at the Marie Foster Centre was initially overwhelming but ultimately rewarding. Caring for patients with multiple sclerosis deepened my understanding of the social and psychological aspects of patient care. I also mentored 12- and 13-year-old students in maths and science, improving my communication skills with children.

Outside school, my work in Waitrose enables me to engage with a variety of people and has taught me to handle stressful situations using effective communication skills combined with self-confidence. Playing badminton with my friends at the local sports centre has become a part of my weekly timetable, in addition to regular table tennis and swimming. My interaction with diverse people on a regular basis has encouraged me to travel annually, learning about various cultures and backgrounds.

11.63   A level entry   3985 characters

SECTION 1 [860 characters]

A day may come when our practice of medicine is so advanced that we no longer fear illness, and, to reach that ideal, students who are committed to giving their best to the subject are needed. I believe I am one of those students. A career in medicine will involve challenges and pressures but will ultimately be rewarding to society and personally fulfilling. I am enthused by the research and development of new and increasingly sophisticated treatments, medication and technology, but also with the caring aspects of the doctor–patient relationship, and I know this will involve a lifetime of learning and applying knowledge and skills. Medicine is not just a career; it is a challenging vocation and one in which I feel I can succeed using the skills and achievements that I have already acquired, and those that I will work hard to gain at Medical School.

SECTION 2 [1479 characters]

Competitively, I have captained my school's chemistry team to victory in this year's National RSC Top of the Bench competition. I feel that I was an effective leader for the team, as I was able to coordinate our efforts to complete the range of challenges as well as maintaining morale. These are important attributes of a doctor that apply directly to hospital life. Whilst chemistry has given me a solid basis for understanding areas of medicine, such as the mechanisms of drug action, physics and maths have helped me develop my logic and problem-solving abilities, which are indispensable in a diagnostic medical career. In physics, I achieved my school's highest ever Gold Award in the Physics Challenge, whilst in biology I scored 100% at AS level along with a 97% average module score in all subjects.

Last summer, after winning a scholarship, I attended the Medical Future Leaders Summit in Los Angeles as part of the prestigious International People-to-People Programme. This enabled me to investigate recent research into stem cells, to argue a real-life case study for a patient to receive a liver transplant and to develop my leadership skills. These have already helped me in my appointment as Head Boy at my school. I am continually growing as a confident public speaker and team leader, skills that will serve me well in the future so that one day I may become a top expert in a field of medicine and travel to many venues to give lectures and train future doctors.

SECTION 3 [1646 characters]

Recently, I arranged a three-week work experience placement in the Gastroenterology and Ophthalmology departments at the Royal Liverpool Hospital. After speaking to both junior doctors and consultants, I gained insights into their work, noted the importance of asking the right questions of a patient, of listening skills in searching for clues, and of making patients feel at ease. I also witnessed procedures including colonoscopies, the insertion of drains, vitrectomies and artificial lens insertions in theatre. I saw how doctors and patients forged bonds with each other, and this led me to join the Red Cross as a qualified First Aid Volunteer. I have since been on many duties where I have been thrilled to provide assistance to people in need. As a compassionate person, I have developed my listening skills and the ability to keep myself and others calm in a situation.

To experience medical research, I secured a four-week Nuffield bursary research placement where I studied why social attitudes have affected public perception of sex education and the sexual health of Britain's youth. My involvement with NAGTY summer schools has allowed me to attend many enriching courses (such as anthropology and robotics), which have helped develop my character.

I enjoy playing all manner of sports. I hold a black belt in the Korean martial art Kuk Sool and two years ago I won the coveted UK Junior Grand Champion Title. In addition, I have completed the Duke of Edinburgh Bronze Award, and represented my school in basketball, where we came fourth nationally, both of which required teamwork, cooperation, handling pressure and resourcefulness.

11.64 A level entry 3982 characters

SECTION 1 [878 characters]

My lifelong ambition to study medicine perfectly combines the people and problem-solving skills I am developing and my very keen interest in science. I also find the medical field exciting and dynamic, such as the recent article I have read about the use of aerosol sprays containing cultivated skin cells as an alternative to skin grafting. I also helped to film a teaching video, made by a local surgeon, showing a procedure for removing facial skin cancers using skin flaps. This was fascinating, and I was allowed to practise techniques on pig's skin.

But medicine is more than relating symptoms to treatments. I feel that I can make a positive impact on people's lives and have the ability to gain the patients' trust. I understand that the medical course is demanding, but I have the determination, positive attitude and sense of humour needed to become a dedicated doctor.

SECTION 2 [1021 characters]

Studying A level maths and competing in an interschool maths competition allowed me to develop advanced problem-solving and analytical thinking skills. The competition challenged me to apply mathematical principles to complex problems under time constraints, fostering perseverance and the ability to remain focused under pressure. Working collaboratively with my team also enhanced my communication and teamwork skills as we pooled our knowledge to devise innovative solutions.

These experiences are directly transferable to studying medicine, where diagnosing illnesses and determining treatment plans require critical thinking, evidence-based decision-making, and effective collaboration. As a future doctor, these skills will enable me to approach clinical challenges methodically, work seamlessly with multidisciplinary teams, and deliver high-quality patient care.

As Deputy Head Girl and Captain of the 1st XI Hockey team, I am learning leadership skills, enabling me to motivate and support others more effectively.

SECTION 3 [2083 characters]

Work experience at the Severn Hospice showed me the importance of the more emotionally demanding side of medicine – palliative care – so people with life-threatening illnesses can enjoy more dignified lives. Whilst helping to feed patients on my weekly visits to the Midlands Centre for Spinal Injuries, I have become a more sympathetic listener and interact better with patients. This led to my interest in the use of embryonic stem cells to grow back parts of the spinal cord as a possible treatment for paraplegics and quadriplegics.

Work experience in a GP surgery helped me understand primary care, a more holistic approach to medicine. I found the continuity that the GP has with the patients appealing as it enables the doctor–patient relationship to grow stronger. I witnessed secondary healthcare in the Royal Shrewsbury Hospital; spending time with consultants in endocrinology, radiology and paediatrics gave me a broad view of the hospital. I sat in on clinics including oncology, diabetes and vascular surgery. On the ward rounds I saw some interesting, rare cases such as Williams syndrome. I would relish opportunities for lifelong learning in a medical career.

Two years ago, as part of an Ecuadorian Highlands Reforestation Project, I provided local children with equipment to start up a school; interacting with children from a different culture was gratifying. Last year I spent time at a Romanian orphanage, helping the orphans, some of whom were blind, to learn English through activities and conversation. Teaching in an unfamiliar environment presented daily challenges, but the work was very rewarding. I feel this is similar to medicine, where not all patients are cooperative and grateful, but they are still worthy of our best efforts.

I have represented Shropshire for hockey and cross-country, and play for Shrewsbury Hockey Club and the school lacrosse team. I passed the English-Speaking Board examination at advanced level, giving a presentation about the use of stem cells in medicine. This improved my communication skills and confidence still further.

11.65 A level entry — 3889 characters

SECTION 1 [470 characters]

When I was five years old, I received a CD-ROM about the human body as a Christmas present. I spent hours viewing the structures integral in creating such a fascinating organism, although with very little understanding of their functions; I wanted to know more. It is this curiosity that attracts me to a constantly changing profession. The combination of scientific understanding and new advances in treatments and diagnosis creates a profession which I aspire to join.

SECTION 2 [1230 characters]

After first exploring the human body, I became particularly interested in the eye, a topic integrating concepts from my A level subjects. I enjoyed studying physics' role in diagnostics, from the Doppler effect in blood flow measurement to X-ray and ultrasound imaging. Biology fascinated me, with genetics and cell structure leading me to research diseases like retinoblastoma and BSE. Chemistry deepened my understanding of drug synthesis, and producing aspirin enhanced my precision and manual dexterity.

I have represented the school's first teams in chess and football, with both winning district competitions this season. Chess has been a passion and a skill-building pursuit. Starting a school chess club allowed me to foster strategic thinking and patience in others. Competing nationally sharpened my ability to think critically under pressure, anticipate outcomes, and adapt. Chess has taught me focus, resilience, and decision-making, qualities vital in medicine.

Whether diagnosing a case or devising a treatment plan, the analytical and strategic skills I've gained will help me tackle challenges with precision. Leading the club also strengthened my communication and leadership, which is key for teamwork in medicine.

SECTION 3 [2189 characters]

My early interest in bone structure was intensified by work experience at a local hospital, where analysing X-rays before and after surgery enabled me to evaluate the aim of surgery in each case. I was able to see how different techniques are used to analyse the cause and extent of specific ailments, essential in giving the most effective pathway of treatment. Witnessing the care provided after surgery showed me the importance of teamwork and the roles played by professionals in providing the best possible service to the patient.

A year of working in a pharmacy has given an insight into the treatment of certain ailments using over-the-counter medicines. I enrolled in a pharmacy assistant course, where I learned how the law controls the sale of certain drugs and the role of a pharmacist in protecting members of the community. These skills were essential when confronted by a patient with a codeine addiction. I referred the patient to the pharmacist, who convinced them to see a doctor, demonstrating the importance of good communication skills. In order to improve my understanding of medicine, I spent a week at a remote practice in Gt. Eccleston, where I witnessed how the doctors were able to gain the trust of patients. Establishing a comforting atmosphere is imperative in building a successful relationship, helping to provide an accurate diagnosis through extracting essential information.

Two years ago I began weightlifting; I hope to excel in the forthcoming British Junior championships, as my understanding of the science behind this sport has been supplemented by commitment and hard work. Over the summer, I conducted an experiment to see the effect of supplementation with creatine ethyl ether over a series of repetition ranges, aiming to compare the improvements within the glycolytic, phosphocreatine and aerobic stores of the muscle tissue.

It is impossible to predict exactly what new technological and scientific advances will be made within my lifetime; I want to be part of medicine as new treatments are discovered. After independent scientific reading and working amongst healthcare professionals, I believe that I can contribute to the future of medicine.

11.66   A level entry   3948 characters

SECTION 1 [797 characters]

I once witnessed a paramedic responding to a critical emergency with incredible composure and skill. Their ability to assess the situation quickly, provide life-saving treatment, and reassure the patient and their family in a moment of crisis left a lasting impression on me. I was struck by the way they combined medical expertise with emotional resilience, making split-second decisions that could mean the difference between life and death. Inspired by their work, I sought out opportunities to learn more about emergency medicine, including volunteering at health camps and shadowing healthcare professionals.

Their example showed me that medicine is not just about knowledge but also about the ability to stay calm, think critically, and provide reassurance in the most challenging situations.

SECTION 2 [1177 characters]

I am keen to follow a course with a strong scientific foundation, and, though not taking physics A level, I studied astronomy to GCSE and am taking up further maths next year to develop my knowledge of mechanics. Studying Latin has helped me to hone my analytical skills and learn to think with precision and clarity.

As head of my school's science society, I took the initiative to organise a series of lectures aimed at inspiring curiosity and engagement with scientific topics. Coordinating these events required strong organisational skills, effective communication, and the ability to collaborate with teachers and peers to secure speakers and manage logistics. Serving as head of house allowed me to lead a diverse group of students, fostering a sense of community and motivating them to excel in academics, sports, and extracurricular activities. These roles taught me the importance of leadership, teamwork, and adaptability, qualities that are crucial in medicine. Whether working in multidisciplinary healthcare teams or connecting with patients from diverse backgrounds, I am confident these experiences have prepared me to rise to the challenges of a medical career.

SECTION 3 [1974 characters]

During work experience at the LGI, I met children with various cancers, sparking my interest in oncology. I furthered this by gaining experience at the Haematology and Oncology Day Unit at Airedale NHS Trust, as part of a week covering Respiratory Medicine, A&E, and General Practice. I observed patients at different stages of their disease, some undergoing chemotherapy and one on the Liverpool Care Pathway. I also volunteer at a local hospice in the inpatient unit, assisting with feeding, which has exposed me to the emotional challenges of medicine. This role has allowed me to interact with patients and families, trying to meet their needs, and has been a rewarding experience.

I received a bursary from the Nuffield Foundation to research the role of the helicase hPif1 in cancer pathogenesis. I compared its sequence in cancer cell lines with that of a wild-type in non-cancerous cells during a month-long placement at the Institute of Cancer Research at Sheffield University. This involved lab work, extensive background reading, and writing a report, 'A Comparative Study of Human Pif1 Helicase cDNA Sequences in MRC5VA and HCT116 Cells'. Through this, I learned about research ethics, principles, and methodology.

During a cadet leadership course with the OTC last summer, I managed simulated combat injuries and learned the importance of triage, basic field medicine, and casualty evacuation, often under pressure. This complemented practical experience in anaesthesia and surgical asepsis from a week at a dental surgery. These experiences have prepared me for the demands of medical training. Additionally, I manage the new cadets' training programme, act as a form warden, organise lectures for the science society, and am currently head of house.

As a keen musician, I play percussion for the Leeds and Yorkshire Youth Orchestras and sing with the Leeds Youth Opera. I also work as a music tutor and served as managing director of a Young Enterprise company.

11.67 A level entry — 3981 characters

SECTION 1 [828 characters]

My motivation to be a doctor came from my father. Multiple infarcts in the brain have progressively reduced my grandmother from a vivacious and successful businesswoman to a patient with senile dementia, incapable of tending to her basic personal needs. One day at the dinner table, my father, who had been caring for my grandmother for years, told the family pensively that we should let him go if he ever became like that. That remark shook me to the core. It was then that I knew I wanted to study medicine, not only for my ageing parents, but also for patients who have to suffer personal indignities from these debilitating geriatric diseases. I am firmly committed to a career in medicine and prepared for the sacrifices and difficulties that lie ahead. Thus, I sincerely hope to obtain the opportunity to realise my dream.

SECTION 2 [1365 characters]

I find the rigour of scientific methods taught in biology and chemistry, and their explaining power, both stimulating and emotionally satisfying. Yet, apart from sciences, humanities such as history, German and Chinese also inspire me, as knowledge of these subjects can be useful when integrated into medicine, since doctors are required to strike a balance between people-oriented patient care as well as the rigorous application of scientific knowledge and techniques.

As a member of my school's debating team, I sharpened my ability to think critically, articulate complex ideas clearly, and engage in respectful discussions – skills that are essential for effective communication in medicine. Debating taught me to analyse issues from multiple perspectives, enhancing my problem-solving abilities and adaptability under pressure. Additionally, my involvement in the Energy Conservation team, which won the Student Environmental Protection Ambassador Award, allowed me to lead initiatives promoting environmental education. This experience required teamwork, creativity, and the ability to inspire others to embrace sustainable practices. Both roles reinforced the importance of collaboration, advocacy, and responsibility – qualities I aim to bring to a career in medicine, where clear communication, teamwork, and a commitment to improving lives are paramount.

SECTION 3 [1788 characters]

Last summer, I worked for two weeks at the integrative Community Health Centre managed by HK Polytechnic University's School of Nursing. The Centre offers health monitoring, advice and healthcare to those in public housing estates. The experience impressed upon me the importance of public education and the need for preventive medicine, especially for the socially disadvantaged.

I also shadowed a cardiologist for two weeks in his clinic. I observed first-hand the work and life of a medical professional. I fully appreciate the demand for discipline, commitment and sacrifices from a doctor and his family, especially when emergency situations arise during dinnertime and in the middle of the night. However, I too shared the same joyful sparkle in his eyes when a life had been saved. Yet, following the death of one of his patients, an elderly woman with a thoracic aortic aneurysm, I understand that medicine is not foolproof and the perfect treatment does not always exist. All a doctor can do is to work to one's best ability, and this I am willing to do.

Since the start of last school year, I have devoted each Saturday morning to voluntary services in a semi-government institution for the mentally handicapped, the Fu Hong Society. From this exposure, I have realised how lucky I am to be healthy and independent. This is my way of giving back to the community for my good fortune.

I am active in many extracurricular activities, acting as School Prefect and Captain of the school's Inline Hockey Team. Moreover, I have taken part in the Silver Hong Kong Award for Young People, am an active member of the school debating team as well as the Energy Conservation team, which won the Student Environmental Protection Ambassador Award for promoting environmental education in school.

11.68 — A level entry — 3760 characters

SECTION 1 [815 characters]

Reading about a scientist who developed a groundbreaking treatment for a previously untreatable disease sparked my fascination with the intersection of research and medicine. Their relentless pursuit of knowledge and commitment to improving patient outcomes showed me that medicine is not only about treating existing conditions but also about pushing the boundaries of what is possible. This realisation fuelled my interest in medical research, leading me to explore genetics, pharmacology, and the role of innovation in healthcare. I was particularly fascinated by how discoveries translated from the lab to real-world patient care. Inspired by their work, I aspire to contribute to medical advancements while maintaining a strong connection to patients, ensuring that research remains focused on improving lives.

SECTION 2 [1639 characters]

Studying A level religious studies has deepened my understanding of ethical reasoning, cultural diversity, and the role of spirituality in people's lives. Exploring complex moral dilemmas has sharpened my critical thinking and decision-making skills, qualities that are vital in medicine when addressing ethical challenges. I founded a Christian youth group in school to create a supportive space for students to explore faith, share experiences, and discuss values. Organising and leading the group taught me leadership, active listening, and the importance of fostering a compassionate and inclusive community. These experiences have enhanced my ability to empathise with diverse perspectives and provide holistic care, both of which are essential for a career in medicine.

Within my school community, my role as a Prefect has given me a great sense of responsibility via the running of the Eco-Committee and Fair-Trade stalls. I have received the School Overall Achievement Award in Years 8, 9, 10 and 11 and several Bronze and Silver Awards in Maths Challenges. Partaking in the chemistry Young Analysts' competition at Liverpool University was a great stimulus, introducing topics I was yet to cover and utilising my problem-solving skills.

Visiting residents in a nursing home for three years has given me an insight into the pressures placed on the NHS by an ageing population. It also led me to enjoy a range of books including 'The Man Who Mistook His Wife for a Hat' and 'The Invisible Enemy'. Through my chemistry course I have completed work on 'What's in a medicine' and I am looking forward to the 'Medicines by Design' module.

SECTION 3 [1306 characters]

In the wider community, my part-time job of three years in a local library has been immensely enjoyable due to interaction with the public. Via activities that have tested my teamwork skills and determination, such as the Duke of Edinburgh Awards, I found I enjoy both leading a group and trusting someone else to lead me. To date, I have completed the Bronze and Silver Awards and am near completion of the Gold Award. However, there is fun to be found in helping others to achieve. I have trained participants of the Duke of Edinburgh Award and accompanied leaders during expeditions and have organised maths and reading clubs. These experiences have taught me the importance of body language, empathy and patience.

I love playing the piano and have recently passed Grade 6. I have also passed Grade 3 flute. I play in an orchestra of all abilities which I find is a good outlet for my music. I play several sports including volleyball, kickboxing and running, and have broken the school record for 1,500m running. As a member of a Christian youth group, I am stimulated by the discussions and challenging issues raised, especially since, through my theology course, I have explored such issues as IVF, euthanasia and abortion. This has helped me appreciate various views held on medical ethical dilemmas.

11.69 — A level entry — 3907 characters

SECTION 1 [925 characters]

For several years I have been totally committed to training for, and ultimately pursuing, a career in medicine. As a child I watched a BBC1 series 'SuperDoctors' – I was inspired by Dr Steve Mannion's selfless work in Malawi. He has a remarkable impact on such a large number of people, and as such has inspired me to one day work where I can have the greatest impact. My aspirations for the future include doing voluntary work in a developing country, and perhaps working in a lively A&E department back in the UK. By these or other means, I hope that my training will not only be personally fulfilling, but hopefully also benefit others, and particularly help those whose needs are greatest.

My academic ability and drive, along with my personality, make me an ideal candidate to read medicine at university. I believe I am equipped to deal with the intellectual and mental challenges that this degree will undoubtedly pose.

SECTION 2 [1332 characters]

Science has been a long-standing fascination for me, but it has become increasingly clear that my academic interests and strengths lie in the medical field. I believe myself to be a confident and clear-thinking scientist who can work consistently and accurately. Studying health and disease in biology prompted me to consider some of the moral issues that have a bearing on the treatment of patients, and thus I explored Tony Hope's 'Medical Ethics'. The mental agility that I have developed from mathematics has particularly helped my learning in biology and chemistry, especially in tackling practical problems. Chemistry has proven to be a particularly enjoyable choice, and the understanding of more advanced chemical principles should prove crucial at degree level. I also chose A level French as a means of widening my horizons and, hopefully, of opening up opportunities for me later in life.

I like to get involved in school life and am an active member of the Medics Society and the football squad. I am also a form prefect and a maths buddy. These two jobs allow me to care for and act as a role model for the younger members of the school. I believe I am suited to my role as prefect, as I have good social skills, meaning I don't find talking to new people too much of a challenge, and I am able to empathise with others.

SECTION 3 [1650 characters]

Working with the scientists at GSK for four days was fascinating, and, whilst recognising the importance of their work in the medical field, I still found the hectic week's work I completed in the A&E department of Lewisham Hospital far more stimulating. Here I experienced many situations which required an ability to work effectively under pressure, which I feel is a quality of mine. In all, I remain certain that the medical profession is one which I shall find challenging, varied and rewarding. I'm also currently volunteering for the National Blood Service, by helping raise awareness of donor sessions, a cause for which I feel strongly.

This summer, my World Challenge expedition to Honduras presented me with an opportunity to work both as part of a team and to nurture my leadership qualities as team leader. Being completely immersed in another culture for over a month was a fantastic experience. However, it also opened my eyes to the conditions, and more specifically the medical conditions, that people in these regions are subjected to.

In my free time, I like to keep myself busy. I both teach and play guitar. I am also a member of a tennis club, and like to play at least once a week. Most Sundays I referee youth football, which has enabled me to be able to more efficiently and more effectively deal with difficult situations – of which there are inevitably many. Furthermore, I maintain a keen interest in film and music.

Despite my many interests, I have never had trouble juggling academic work with other activities, as displayed by my consistently outstanding performances in public examinations and my very high attendance.

11.70 A level entry — 3952 characters

SECTION 1 [841 characters]

He was shaking unceasingly on the floor, unable to control his body movements, unaware and non-responsive to the world around him; I was in a powerless and frightening position. I lacked the knowledge, skills and experience to be able to provide help for my cousin who was going through an epileptic seizure. Since that humbling day, I have discovered that there are different types of seizures and treatments used to control this debilitating condition. This experience has highlighted for me the importance of improving one's mind by reading, to facilitate the understanding of the world in us and around us.

Whilst being demanding and at times stressful, a medical career will give me the chance to fulfil my scientific aspirations and intellectual curiosity as well as my supreme desire to promote the health and welfare of human society.

SECTION 2 [994 characters]

Studying memory in A level psychology has deepened my understanding of cognitive function and its decline, which is highly relevant to a career in medicine. Exploring the processes of encoding, storing, and retrieving information, alongside theories of forgetting, provided valuable insights into the neurological mechanisms underlying conditions like Alzheimer's disease. I learned how ageing impacts memory systems, with brain regions such as the hippocampus playing critical roles in forming new memories and recalling information. A key aspect of this learning involved giving an oral school presentation on Alzheimer's disease, where I explored its effects on individuals and their families.

This experience enhanced my public speaking and research skills, while also emphasising the importance of early diagnosis, effective interventions, and empathetic care. It reinforced my dedication to delivering patient-centred care, particularly in supporting older adults facing cognitive decline.

SECTION 3 [2117 characters]

For the past two years, I have volunteered at the Royal Brompton Harefield Hospital heart and lung transplant ward. I help the medical staff and improve patient welfare by performing services such as changing bed covers, assisting in the use of diagnostic tools such as the ECG and talking to transplant patients. This year, I discovered some of the ambitions and thoughts of a mentally handicapped young man through house visits. These experiences have helped me to actively exercise patience and have taught me the importance of showing compassion when dealing with people.

Last year, I attended an ophthalmology clinic. I gained an understanding of some commonly used diagnostic procedures, such as the retinal laser scanner. My knowledge of medical imaging techniques such as the MRI, EEG and the novel MEG has grown considerably through a fascinating guided tour of the UCL Functional Imaging Lab. This summer I spent 8 weeks at an electrophysiology lab at UCL studying the effects of a new drug on the functioning of hippocampal CA1 Pyramidal neurons. This experience gave me valuable insight into the life of a scientist and equipped me with new skills, including dissection, microscopy and single-cell recording.

I love playing the cello and am a member of the Harrow Young Musicians Philharmonic Orchestra. I particularly enjoyed our orchestral performance in front of a full house at the Royal Albert Hall. My musical experiences have helped me to rise above my fear of performing in front of a large crowd and have helped me to build up my confidence. I also take pleasure in long-distance running. At the age of 19, I was the youngest person to finish the New Forest Marathon. The time I spent training and running the race taught me the importance of planning and perseverance, which are required for success.

I grew up in Hungary then, at the age of 12, moved to South Africa, before coming to live in the United Kingdom 5 years ago. This mobile lifestyle has granted me the special privilege to meet people from a wide variety of backgrounds, which I feel would be beneficial for a future career in medicine.

11.71   A level entry   3980 characters

SECTION 1 [705 characters]

I would like to study medicine because it combines an evolving base of knowledge with the need for logic and manual skill, all with the aim of helping a patient. My experience of life as a patient, however, has shaped and clarified my interest. After suffering an injury while playing rugby for my school, I developed a back condition which led to my seeing a large number and variety of healthcare professionals over the course of a year. During that time I saw first-hand how an aloof or distant bedside manner can have a negative impact, but equally how much difference the alternative can make, even when the news itself is disappointing. I also feel I better understand the limits of modern medicine.

SECTION 2 [1151 characters]

My A level subject choices have suited me well. Biology has intrigued me throughout the course, while chemistry and maths have allowed me to develop a more analytical way of thinking. Studying A level Spanish has expanded my linguistic abilities and cultural awareness, equipping me with the skills to communicate effectively with people from diverse backgrounds. The challenge of mastering a new language has taught me perseverance, attention to detail, and adaptability. Additionally, helping to edit my school's magazine allowed me to channel my creativity while honing my collaborative and organisational skills. Balancing the creative aspects of editing with meeting deadlines required effective time management and teamwork. These experiences have strengthened my ability to communicate clearly, think critically, and approach challenges with creativity.

As Senior Prefect, I have developed communication skills both with staff and junior pupils, and demonstrated reliability and leadership. I have made the most of my organisational skills as Operations Director of my Young Enterprise company, and as a member of the school's charity committee.

SECTION 3 [2124 characters]

A week of work experience in a hospital helped me identify the qualities a good doctor needs: the competence to solve problems; the compassion to look beyond the problems; the ability to deal with stress; and the ability to work in a team with other professionals. I also organised a volunteer stint on a geriatric ward for two hours a week for eight months. This opened my eyes to the realities of medicine, gave me experience of dealing with the vulnerable and confirmed my desire to study medicine. Furthermore, it showed me how rewarding that kind of work can be, and consequently in the current academic year I am working for a charity which helps children with learning disabilities. I am especially interested in neurology, as although the brain is the most powerful organ in the body, it seems relatively little is known about its function.

I have become a frequent reader of the 'Student BMJ', which has given me a good introduction into medical ethics and the important role they play. For example, one article criticised Richard Dawkins' view that consciousness can be explained by atom collision as overly simplistic, a view I agree with as, when applied to medicine, it emphasises the problem over the patient; and I believe in a holistic, patient-orientated approach.

I used to represent my school and club at rugby and, since being forced to stop, I have begun to referee matches as a way of staying in touch with the game. This has taught me about the value of staying committed to something that you love and has also improved my decision-making under pressure. As a way of relieving stress I have begun to teach myself to play the steel pan, which has been challenging but enjoyable. Above all I am a person who delights in helping a team to success as I tend to flourish in more team-based activities such as rugby, Young Enterprise and Duke of Edinburgh's Gold Award.

I look forward to the beginning of a career in medicine and feel it is one I am well suited to, through my academic qualities, my personal qualities, and the knowledge that even subtle actions can make a big difference to the life of a patient.

11.72 A level entry — 3998 characters

SECTION 1 [1236 characters]

At the age of ten, I was taken along to a first aid course at my sailing club. I started as an onlooker but ended the course as a certified first aider. My interest in medicine started there. I maintain my certification and find it remarkable how much a CPR method can change in three years, demonstrating the necessity of continued improvement in order to refine methods of treatment.

As a teenager, I did some charity work and was inspired by a doctor who dedicated their career to working in a rural village where access to healthcare was limited. Despite facing resource shortages and challenging conditions, they remained committed to their patients, often going above and beyond their clinical duties to advocate for better healthcare infrastructure. Their dedication to bridging healthcare disparities resonated with my own experiences witnessing unequal access to medical care in different communities. Inspired by their work, I became involved in outreach programmes, volunteering at health camps, and learning about public health initiatives. Their example reinforced my belief that medicine is not just about treating individual patients but also about working toward systemic change to ensure healthcare is accessible to all.

SECTION 2 [1258 characters]

My enthusiasm and enquiring mind encouraged me to study science at A level. I discovered the importance of technology in medicine during a project I undertook at Lancaster University. As a small group we researched the use of nanotechnology in medicine, discovering essential progressions made in diagnosis, cancer treatments and drug delivery. Further reading has led me to 'Biomedicine and the Human Condition' by Michael Sargent who cites Jacques Monod in describing the human genome: a 'tone-deaf conservatory where the noise is preserved along with the music'. Upon reading this, I wondered what the noise and the music represent but as I read on, the relation of noise interfering with music causing changes and evolution interfering with our DNA doing the same became clear. This type of project taught me a lot about the process of research, the spirit of teamwork and the importance of building good relationships with colleagues.

Within my school community, I have always taken an active role including my position as a prefect, being a tutor to two GCSE chemistry students and running a netball club. I recently represented the school in the Institute of Biology Quiz as part of a team of four; we finished first to win a microscope for our school.

SECTION 3 [1504 characters]

During continued voluntary work in a nursing home I have illustrated that my commitment to medicine will not be deterred by the most gruelling tasks or responsibilities, taking pride in all that I do. A three-day work experience in Westmorland General Hospital helped me to learn more about the routine care of the patients by assisting with the nurses' duties. I learnt a great deal about the hospital, watching people from all different areas of medicine coming together as a perfectly balanced team.

I have recently embarked on a World Challenge expedition to Madagascar during which we spent a week in an orphanage doing building work and improving ecological schemes. My eyes were opened to the consequences of poverty, especially concerning the lack of healthcare that we are so used to receiving in our Western lives. Being in an underdeveloped country meant leadership, teamwork and organisation were essential in order to function as a group. Throughout the expedition I grew in confidence, became more independent and am now more socially aware than I was previously.

I have also developed skills and found enjoyment in many activities such as playing the violin to Grade 5 and in the school orchestra, singing in my school's choir, horse riding for the past seven years and sailing for my county youth squad.

I know I have the ability and commitment to join this lifelong learning profession. I am eager to have the opportunity to direct all my energy into medicine as both a subject and a career.

11.73 A level entry — 3974 characters

SECTION 1 [1119 characters]

When my brother was diagnosed with HIV, it was a turning point that deepened my understanding of the realities faced by those living with the condition. Seeing first-hand the emotional and physical toll of the disease, as well as the challenges in navigating treatment and healthcare systems, made me determined to learn more. I began researching HIV extensively, from its virology and the mechanism of antiretroviral therapy to the global efforts in prevention and education. This experience opened my eyes not only to the science behind HIV treatment but also to the persistent stigma that prevents many from seeking care. I saw how misinformation and fear can be just as harmful as the virus itself, reinforcing my passion for public health and medical education. Studying the history of the HIV/AIDS epidemic further emphasised the transformative power of medicine – not just in saving lives but in challenging societal prejudices.

My brother's experience solidified my commitment to pursuing medicine, with a focus on advocacy, inclusivity, and ensuring that all patients receive compassionate, evidence-based care.

SECTION 2 [1173 characters]

A level maths has significantly enhanced my data interpretation skills, which were particularly evident when I participated in an interschool maths competition. The competition involved analysing patterns, interpreting complex data sets, and applying mathematical principles to solve challenging problems under timed conditions. This required precision, logical reasoning, and the ability to adapt quickly to unexpected scenarios. Collaborating with my team further refined my communication skills, as we had to clearly articulate our thought processes, share insights effectively, and reach consensus on problem-solving approaches. These experiences not only strengthened my analytical abilities but also taught me the importance of teamwork and perseverance when faced with demanding tasks. Such skills are directly relevant to studying medicine, where interpreting diagnostic data, such as laboratory results, imaging scans, and patient histories, is fundamental to forming accurate diagnoses and treatment plans. Furthermore, the ability to communicate findings clearly and collaborate with a multidisciplinary team is essential for providing comprehensive patient care.

SECTION 3 [1682 characters]

I have gained an appreciation for the work of medical staff and have an understanding of the importance of clear communication, constant support and superior patient care during my time as a hospital volunteer. The time that I have spent speaking with doctors, asking questions, discussing their specialties and the route they took to get there has further confirmed my aspiration to become a medical doctor. Last month I had the opportunity to observe and assist in the delivery of a baby. It stands out as one of the most exciting, exhilarating and moving experiences in my time as a hospital volunteer. I have had the privilege of serving patients in many different areas such as endoscopy, day surgery, long-term care and maternity. Each area has offered difficult challenges as well as joyful events and recoveries.

At the age of 25 I realise that I am classed as a mature student. However, I believe that there is great benefit in having studied at the prestigious London School of Economics, having worked hard in a commercial environment, having lived independently in an international setting and having had the experience of dealing with stress and personal challenge as well as meeting people from many different walks of life and many socio-economic classes.

I have developed strong communication skills through my experience in the corporate world and through the leadership roles I have been offered. I have held many responsibilities within my church, such as leading the hospitality team and organising women's events. Through these roles and leadership positions, I have not only learnt how to delegate, motivate and manage but also how to communicate and serve well.

11.74 A level entry — 3876 characters

SECTION 1 [883 characters]

While travelling in a rural area of Kenya, I witnessed the stark contrast between healthcare in developed and developing regions. Clinics were often understaffed and lacked essential medicines, making even basic treatments unavailable. This experience left a deep impression on me, as I saw first-hand how limited healthcare access can lead to preventable suffering. The absence of a robust healthcare system in remote areas sparked my desire to become a doctor who can contribute to improving healthcare delivery, particularly in underserved regions. I became determined to pursue a career in medicine with the aim of bridging these gaps and providing care to those who need it the most.

My experience made me realise how critical it is for healthcare professionals to not only provide treatment but also advocate for better infrastructure and resources in areas that need them most.

SECTION 2 [1269 characters]

Studying chemistry has helped me think clearly about key scientific principles, while the biology course has given me knowledge of the structure and function of many areas of the body. I have built on this by reading 'Mutants' by Armand Marie Leroi, which explores deviations from normal embryological development to explain genetic disorders. I also read 'Right Hand, Left Hand' by Chris McManus, which investigates the origins of handedness and puts forward a theory on why the right hand is dominant, questioning asymmetry in nature. Mathematics has enhanced my logic skills, and by studying German, I have become proficient in the language, constantly testing myself in a non-scientific setting.

Outside my A level studies, I took an Open University course in 'Molecules, Medicines, and Drugs', which I passed in June 2008. I was a finalist in a nationwide essay competition by the Royal College of Science Union. Furthermore, I am proud to have been part of a Young Enterprise company that reached the London finals. As the team's HR Director and Deputy Managing Director, I was responsible for team well-being and for ensuring effective communication. At school, I am a senior prefect in charge of charity events, practising my communication and leadership skills.

SECTION 3 [1724 characters]

My work experience has also aided me in my decision to study medicine. Most recently, I spent a week shadowing doctors on an infectious diseases ward, learning in the process about infection control procedures such as use of negative air pressure rooms to prevent the spread of infectious disease on the ward. During this period I also made time to talk to tuberculosis patients, and in doing so learnt a great deal about the management of this disease, including the use of many drugs together to combat antibiotic resistance.

In June of this year, I travelled to Aachen in Germany, where I undertook a week of work experience in a paediatrician's surgery. I learnt about the range of differences between paediatric and adult medicine, from the fairly mundane alterations to dosage to the more subtle changes in behaviour and tone of voice that the doctor adopts. The trip also allowed me to hone my communication skills, needing to address both children and adults in a foreign language and to use medical terminology not normally encountered in A level study of the language.

I am also volunteering at a care centre for multiple sclerosis sufferers for an afternoon each week. There is one visitor to the centre whom I have particularly bonded with, who has the primary progressive form of the disease. She is unable to speak, instead only mouthing words. Whilst, at first, communication was extraordinarily tough and left me wondering whether I was frustrating her, I eventually began to become accustomed to her way of communicating, and we play Scrabble each week with minimal trouble. Finally, my continuing work with St John Ambulance has trained me in first aid and given me an introduction to providing medical care.

11.75 A level entry — 3901 characters

SECTION 1 [680 characters]

Some people say they have always wanted to be doctors, but I have discovered my ambition more gradually. I became passionate about science when I was 14 and science at school became more interesting and challenging. I thought about a career in medical research but, after my work experience, I realised that by becoming a doctor I could combine my interest in science with my love of working with people and I could help patients first-hand. I know medicine would be the ideal career for me.

SECTION 2 [872 characters]

As I am inquisitive, in biology and chemistry I love doing practical investigations as well as learning the theory. I read 'New Scientist' to keep up with scientific developments and I am particularly interested in genetics, especially stem cell research and its use in regenerative medicine with the possibility of curing diseases such as Parkinson's. I am also interested in the psychological side of how genes affect personality, which I learnt about by reading 'Nature via Nurture' by Matt Ridley.

I enjoy maths and the satisfaction of solving problems so I think I will enjoy the diagnostic aspect of medicine. The combination of art with these scientific subjects has developed practical skills such as manual dexterity and time management. Critical thinking helped me understand the structure of arguments and this is useful in my A level subjects and other reading.

SECTION 3 [2349 characters]

Work experience at a unit of the John Radcliffe Hospital exposed me to departments which research cures for conditions such as cystic fibrosis and motor neurone disease. It was interesting to see the latest research and it taught me how important it is in medicine to work as a team and share ideas. Working there also raised ethical issues about vivisection. This inspired me to set up a medical ethics discussion group at school. I attended a Medlink conference in Nottingham and another medical conference at UCL, which gave me an insight into what it would be like to be a doctor, and the sort of commitment needed. Last summer I shadowed a GP in Bath and an orthopaedic surgeon at the John Radcliffe Hospital. At the GP surgery I sat in on consultations which showed me how varied the work is. I saw a hernia and skin cancer as well as minor ailments. I worked with the nurses and receptionists, and attended a practice meeting, which showed me how the surgery operates. In the hospital I saw a variety of patients, mainly with spinal problems. I particularly enjoyed working in paediatrics with children born with scoliosis and talking to patients in the wards. I have also participated in an experiment into psychosis involving a brain scan and psychological tests.

I find working with children very rewarding, and I teach swimming at a primary school and babysit regularly. Last Christmas I helped paint decorations for the Banbury Children's Hospital. In summer 2005 I went on a World Challenge expedition to Bolivia for a month which improved my teamwork and leadership skills. This included a week working in an orphanage, which was rewarding and made me more aware of how much I take for granted. I raised over GBP 3000 for this trip by working for the Cambridge School Classics Project and organising events such as a piano recital and a barn dance. I am grade 8 standard at the piano and also enjoy accompanying. I sing in the school choir and have performed in Mozart's 'Requiem' and Handel's 'Messiah'. I row at the City Of Oxford Rowing Club and I am working towards my gold Duke of Edinburgh award.

I know medicine would be the ideal career for me. I appreciate it will be very hard work, but I would love a stimulating and challenging job where I face new problems every day, and where I could use my knowledge to improve people's lives.

11.76 A level entry — 3947 characters

SECTION 1 [1170 characters]

Science helps me to rationalise and understand the world: it orientates the way I view and approach problems. Pure sciences have always excited me, but their application to the complex and diverse study of human health and illness offers my intellectual curiosity the greatest stimulation and compels me to pursue the study of medicine. A school project on neurones sparked my curiosity about the nervous system and how it influences health. Understanding how pain signals travel to the brain and how conditions like multiple sclerosis disrupt this process fascinated me. I explored the complexities of pain management, including how medication, psychological support, and innovative treatments like nerve stimulation play a role in patient care. This interest was further reinforced during my shadowing experience, where I observed a doctor explain chronic pain conditions to a patient with empathy and clarity. It made me realise that medicine is not just about treating symptoms but about understanding the root causes and improving patients' quality of life. I hope to use this knowledge to become a doctor who provides both medical expertise and compassionate care.

SECTION 2 [1119 characters]

My commitment to St Leonard's is not confined to the classroom. Elected Head Boy by my peers and teachers, I am relied upon to make important decisions when representing the school community, chairing the school council and ensuring the student voice is heard. Last year, I achieved a Gold Award for creativity in science and technology. Under the supervision of a consulting engineer, our team conducted basic research, wrote a detailed report, and gave a presentation on the construction of a dual carriageway bypass. Explaining complex engineering concepts to an uninformed audience was a challenge I relished.

As chair of the school council, I am entrusted with representing the school community and ensuring the student voice is heard. This responsibility has honed my decision-making and leadership skills, as I must navigate diverse perspectives, mediate discussions, and advocate for meaningful changes that benefit the student body. Chairing meetings requires effective communication, active listening, and the ability to build consensus, particularly when addressing sensitive issues or conflicting viewpoints.

SECTION 3 [1658 characters]

Work experience in a GP surgery earlier this year offered me insight into the doctor–patient relationship and the psychology of the sick. Hospital work experience has broadened my knowledge of the complexity of practising medicine whilst balancing treatment to meet patients' needs. I am attracted not by the routine, but the unpredictability, the uncertainty and the constantly developing nature of the profession. A summer job doing clerical work in a GP surgery taught me about the interactions between primary and secondary care, and made me aware of the behind-the-scenes working of general practice. I work regularly as a volunteer in an elderly care home, and this has opened my eyes to the needs of the many, highly dependent people in geriatric care. Developing personal relationships with many of them has made the impact of chronic disease on their lives evident. It made me realise that there are people whose medical needs cannot be met by science, but whose lives can be made easier by care and compassion.

Outside school, I enjoy playing a lot of sport. I have played club rugby and cricket for many years, and have captained my Durham City RUFC team for the past three seasons. I am now on the Durham County side. My adventures with the Duke of Edinburgh award scheme have developed my initiative, independence and motivation.

I have been selected by the charity Project Trust to go to Uganda for 12 months to teach underprivileged children. Whilst this will be a tough year, I am thoroughly looking forward to the challenge. I hope that the experience will broaden my perspective, and that I will enter university with a more mature outlook.

11.77 A level entry — 3606 characters

SECTION 1 [1025 characters]

Over the last few years, I have become increasingly absorbed by the links between biochemistry and physiology, for instance the Krebs cycle, involved in providing ATP, to sustain basic life processes. This interest led me to my first work experience placement at the Imperial College Hospital's Haematology department. I worked for three days alongside a senior consultant, shadowing, sitting in on a board meeting, and observing the extraction of two separate bone marrow samples for biopsy to test for Chronic Myelogenous Leukaemia (CML).

Whilst this helped to satisfy my desire for more depth than the A level course provided, what really captivated me were the ward rounds. These allowed me to talk to the patients and understand how their conditions affected their lives. It also allowed me to observe both the bedside manner of the doctors and to see how the patients listened, or in some cases still thought that they knew better. It was this that led me to the realisation that my true vocation was to become a doctor.

SECTION 2 [428 characters]

Having been involved with school CCF for two and a half years, I have now been promoted to a rank of Warrant Officer, as a senior NCO. This has opened up many experiences for me from leading sections of cadets on exercise, to mountaineering in the Swiss Alps, both of which I thoroughly enjoyed. In addition I am Deputy Head Boy at MCS. These roles both require me to demonstrate leadership, diplomacy and be a good team player.

SECTION 3 [2153 characters]

In order to understand some of the other roles of a doctor I spent two days working within my local surgery, shadowing two GPs and sitting in on a learning disability seminar. What really intrigued me was the extensive role of a GP within a community and the variety of issues they deal with. I also worked at Imperial College Hospital IVF unit for four days, observing theatre, including the reversal of a sterilisation, and also fertilisation by ICSI. I was also keen to gain first-hand experience of palliative care, and so currently I am working as a volunteer at Sobell House Hospice Day Centre with patients suffering from a variety of terminal illnesses. This is a truly humbling experience and I am inspired by the positive attitude of both the patients and the staff. I have learned to appreciate that in medicine sometimes you cannot save a life, and that it is then important to really consider how you can give them the best quality of life possible, for however short it may be.

I also gained a placement in the Weatherall Institute of Molecular Medicine, conducting my own Real-Time PCR; this helped me understand the role of laboratories in medical care. This summer I spent four weeks working in virology at Oxford Brookes University, infecting cells with viruses, transfecting with plasmids, before staining and viewing them on a confocal microscope, on which I have written a short thesis. I also enjoy reading for personal development. I subscribe to the 'New Scientist' and am currently reading James Le Fanu's 'The Rise and Fall of Modern Medicine'. I was also particularly enthralled by Richard Dawkins' genomic portrayal of natural selection in 'The Selfish Gene'.

I am also working for my Duke of Edinburgh Gold Award. I am a keen sportsman, representing the school in cricket, hockey, rowing and rugby. I am training for my karate black belt, and have recently competed in the Boston rowing marathon, which at 52km is the longest and toughest rowing race in Britain.

I am a highly motivated and determined scientist and I am confident I have the qualities it takes to both succeed in medical studies and become an excellent doctor.

11.78 A level entry — 3997 characters

SECTION 1 [994 characters]

Supporting my mum who has multiple sclerosis allowed me first-hand insight into the challenges patients face daily. Helping manage my mum's medications, accompanying them to doctor's appointments, and witnessing their struggles with pain and fatigue made me appreciate the resilience required to live with a long-term condition. I saw how medical professionals balanced scientific expertise with empathy, adjusting treatments to suit individual needs. This experience highlighted the importance of patient-centred care and problem-solving in medicine. I also recognised the emotional toll illness takes on families and the need for clear communication between doctors and patients. The way small interventions – whether a change in medication or simple lifestyle advice – could drastically improve my mum's quality of life reinforced my desire to be part of a profession that makes tangible differences in people's lives. This experience solidified my passion for medicine and patient advocacy.

SECTION 2 [1135 characters]

Studying A level physics and representing my college as part of a team of four at a national competition allowed me to apply experimental skills in a high-pressure environment, where precision and critical thinking were paramount. I developed a deep understanding of scientific principles through hands-on experiments and was responsible for designing, testing, and analysing results. Competing at a national level sharpened my problem-solving abilities and my capacity to work efficiently under time constraints. These experiences have been invaluable in refining my attention to detail, adaptability, and teamwork, skills that are essential in medicine, where accurate data interpretation, decision-making under pressure, and collaboration with multidisciplinary teams are crucial for patient care and medical research.

I am also fully involved in my school community. I mentored two Year Eleven students through their GCSEs and am currently producing and directing a school musical. All of this has given me sense of responsibility and ownership, has honed my ability to make decisions under pressure, and to show respect for others.

SECTION 3 [1868 characters]

I spent a week shadowing a consultant of respiratory medicine at St Mary's, London and Ealing Hospital. I witnessed many clinical consultations covering a wide range of respiratory and allergic disorders. I shadowed a palliative care team at Mount Vernon Hospital, observing their Multidisciplinary Team meeting, new admissions and ward rounds, which enabled me to see a very different aspect of medicine.

These experiences enabled me to appreciate the importance of teamwork within healthcare. They also made me acutely aware of the realities of medicine and the necessity for empathy and compassion within the profession, particularly when attending to the needs of terminally ill patients and their families. I have arranged a work-shadowing placement to experience primary care in a GP's surgery.

Through the Aim Higher Summer School Scheme I spent a week at The School of Pharmacy investigating 'The Science of Medicines', which included a visit to the pharmacy at Guy's and St Thomas' Hospital to see the production of chemotherapy drugs. This helped me understand the complexity of the treatment undergone by some of the cancer patients I see in my voluntary work. I also attended the 'Image your heart' conference at Imperial College, which increased my understanding of medical imaging. I am trained in first aid and infection control.

I enjoy serving my community as a member of the Hillingdon Youth Council. My involvement has helped my decision-making skills and heightened my awareness of public responsibility. I volunteer at my local palliative care centre, where I enjoy talking to the patients and staff.

I have been playing the violin and singing for nine years and find it an excellent source of relaxation. I am a member of Hillingdon Youth Choir and Symphony Orchestra, which bring the benefits of leadership qualities and a natural sense of teamwork.

11.79 Graduate entry — 3498 characters

SECTION 1 [952 characters]

Becoming a doctor will equip me with the skills to apply my experience in shaping health systems and my knowledge of health economics and policy.

While working with ministries of health in sub-Saharan Africa (SSA) has been rewarding, I want something more – a direct impact on patients. My desire to become a doctor was solidified by Michael, a homeless man I met while volunteering at San Francisco General Hospital's emergency department. The last time I saw him, he held my hand and told me he was tired of the pain and wanted to die. I stood silent, frustrated that I lacked the skills to help. Michael's suffering, like many in underserved communities, was shaped by his socio-economic environment. His story reinforced my belief that medicine requires both individual patient care and systemic change.

As a doctor, my duty will be to serve not only as a clinician but as a public servant, improving healthcare for individuals and communities alike.

SECTION 2 [879 characters]

In the third year of undergrad at the University of California at Berkeley, I read a book by Dr Paul Farmer that helped me cement the connection between health, society and economics. The book convinced me that I needed to be able to explain both a doctor's and a health system's behaviour in order to become effective at improving a person's health. While a chemistry major at the time, I was certain I wanted to become a doctor. But I kept feeling disconnected between what I was learning and how I could apply my scientific knowledge to improving a patient's and society's health. I immediately began to study public health.

Following college, I pursued a Master's degree at the London School of Economics in health economics and policy. My coursework focused on using economic principles to provide evidence and rationale in designing efficient and equitable health policies.

SECTION 3 [1625 characters]

I work in the Africa Human Development division on health for the World Bank. In striving for the Millennium Development Goals by 2015, many countries around the world, particularly in SSA, realise that reducing infant mortality, maternal mortality and preventing non-communicable diseases will take an appropriate health workforce with appropriate skills to fight the tasks ahead. While many SSA countries design plans to increase the stock, types, productivity and distribution of health workers, determining the costs for such plans has been out of reach. I've helped design and implement a model that puts a price on national human resources for health strategies and plans. In this way, I've helped health ministries in Ghana and Sierra Leone deliver healthcare in a more efficient way.

But despite all the work I've done for the World Bank, it was meeting a homeless man while volunteering at San Francisco General Hospital that had the biggest effect on me. It helped me realise that medicine was more than just the study of the body's biology. I've learned that medicine is the deep and intimate relationship between the body and its interaction with society: a society that is influenced by both politics and economics. I know that many will question why I'm shifting from working as a junior health economist into medicine. While effecting change at a health system's level is crucial to a sustainable public's health, I desire something more. Because of my health system's perspective and experience, taking this next step to become a doctor will lead to me making a positive and direct impact on a person's health.

11.80 Graduate entry — 3660 characters

SECTION 1 [925 characters]

Listening to a doctor share their journey on a podcast was a turning point in my decision to pursue medicine. They spoke about their experiences treating patients, the emotional highs and lows of the profession and the lifelong learning involved. What resonated most was their deep sense of purpose – how they found fulfilment not just in curing diseases but in supporting patients through vulnerable moments. Their stories of perseverance, teamwork and compassion gave me a new perspective on what it truly means to be a doctor.

Hearing first-hand about the challenges and rewards of medicine made me reflect on my own aspirations. I was particularly inspired by how they balanced scientific problem-solving with human connection, a combination that I find deeply compelling. Their passion for patient care reinforced my desire to pursue medicine, not just as a career, but as a vocation where I can make a meaningful impact.

SECTION 2 [562 characters]

My degree has let me explore my fascination of the molecular basis of life whilst developing skills of critical appraisal, time management and self-directed, didactic and group learning. I won the 2024 BBSRC scholarship, awarded to one student from KCL, for an 8-week project at the MRC-Asthma UK Centre in Allergic Mechanisms of Asthma. Applying the scientific method and using immunological techniques and rigorous data analysis, I wrote a report of a novel finding I made on IL-10-Treg cells. I hope to contribute to the advancement of medicine in the future.

SECTION 3 [2173 characters]

Volunteering weekly as a GP's receptionist for a year revealed the holistic approach and continuity of care provided at a community practice. I learnt about record-keeping, ethics and striking rapport with patients. Arranging multi-weeks at University College London Hospital and St George's Hospital presented the realities in specialties such as cardiology, paediatrics and A&E. The synergy within multidisciplinary teams, despite stressful conditions and tough expectations, was inspiring to see. I was intrigued by the competence and dexterity of physicians using in-depth knowledge and judgement to diagnose, treat and also counsel patients to alleviate anxieties. A consultant impressed on me his duties as a clinician as well as in research, teaching and management. Voluntary work for four months at an elderly home involved helping residents with tasks whilst appreciating the need for clear communication, patience and integrity. As well as supporting paramedics as a first-aider at events, I have cared for people when most vulnerable, which has amplified my desire for a humane vocation in medicine.

At university I am president of the snooker society, which requires me to multitask and use tact to negotiate with third parties, delegate tasks and raise funding. Selected as a Widening Participation Student Ambassador, my role has ranged from tutoring teenagers to delivering presentations at events of up to 150 people. Along with writing news articles published in the 'GKT Gazette', I have built extensive communication skills. I also regularly organise charity football with a team, which entails sharing ideas at meetings whilst respecting and adapting to views different to my own. Attending seminars and talking to junior medics clarified the commitment required to reach these roles and affirmed my resolve for such a varied profession embracing lifelong learning. Spending 3 months befriending patients with neurological damage at the Royal Hospital for Neuro-disability was humbling and at times disheartening. However, listening attentively to their concerns and showing empathy, veracity and support, I felt I made a difference at a personal level.

11.81 Graduate entry — 3781 characters

SECTION 1 [1414 characters]

"An individual has not started living until he can rise above the narrow confines of his individualistic concerns to the broader concerns of all humanity." Martin Luther King, Jr. My undergraduate degree has made me realise that my passion and interests lie not only in the mechanisms of human development, but also in the people in which these processes take place. Research is too impersonal; I want a career that combines the excitement of scientific investigation with human contact. Over the past three years I have worked as an auxiliary nurse. Duties require patience, a friendly and sympathetic manner, compassion and a mature attitude. Although hard work at times, the combined efforts of our multidisciplinary team made the satisfaction of it worthwhile. Much of my work has been on mental health wards, an area I find particularly rewarding, especially now that I understand more about the factors underlying dementia. As a nurse I recognise my limitations. However, my enquiring mind means that I would thrive on the challenge of diagnosis and deciding what treatment should be given. This summer I spent six weeks travelling through South America. In a place where the focus of people's lives is so different, I evaluated my career options and decided what I really want from life. I know I have the compassion, skills and determination to become a doctor, not just as a career, but as a life commitment.

SECTION 2 [1029 characters]

As a Diversity Ambassador Leader at university, I developed essential skills in empathy, leadership, and cultural competence that are directly relevant to a career in medicine. In this role, I led initiatives aimed at promoting inclusivity, raising awareness about diverse cultures, and fostering a sense of belonging. I worked closely with students and staff to create programmes and events that celebrated diversity, which required me to communicate effectively with individuals from various backgrounds and listen to their perspectives. This experience taught me the importance of understanding and respecting differences, as well as the value of creating an environment where everyone feels supported. These skills will be invaluable as a doctor, where cultural competence is essential for providing compassionate and effective care to patients from diverse backgrounds. I also developed my organisational, problem-solving, and teamworking abilities – key qualities for navigating the challenges of the healthcare profession.

SECTION 3 [1338 characters]

By completing a placement at Sheffield Fertility Clinic this summer, my perception of an embryo changed. I saw that the work done at the clinic was more significant than just whether an embryo was created; these tiny cells are the hope and fulfilment for so many couples whose whole reason for living is to have a child. Spending time in general practice meant that I learnt the value of conversational skills used during a consultation. My placement on a maternity ward showed me the excitement of birth. Being a doctor is not just about helping people, but being able to cope with unpleasant situations in everyday life. I have seen death as well as full recovery, and understand the range of emotions that are linked with people's suffering. Ethical dilemmas such as eugenics and euthanasia really concern me.

Over the past three years I have worked as a volunteer with Mencap. Working in a team taking care of a group of mentally handicapped adults proved to me the importance of good communication skills and patience. Voluntary work for the St John Ambulance service allowed me to show that I can act quickly under pressure in emergencies. I am heavily involved in the university rowing team. Last year I took on the role of UCL Women's Boat Club in which commitment, time management, and self-motivation were the essence of success.

11.82 Graduate entry — 3930 characters

SECTION 1 [772 characters]

My degree in pharmacology has solidified my passion for medicine by deepening my understanding of scientific principles and honing essential skills for clinical practice. Studying pharmacology has allowed me to rationally assess drug actions and anticipate potential side effects, reinforcing the importance of safe and effective prescribing. The psychology components of my degree have broadened my perspective on patient care, emphasising the significance of human behaviour in holistic treatment.

As a people's person, I have found myself more drawn towards the need to caring and not simply the scientific knowledge that comes with pharmacology. I enjoy learning about systems but crave patient contact, and I feel that a medical career would give me the right balance.

SECTION 2 [1004 characters]

Organising a medicine book club allowed me to deepen my understanding of healthcare while developing transferable skills essential for a career in medicine. I selected and facilitated discussions on books exploring medical ethics, patient experiences, and advancements in healthcare, encouraging participants to engage critically with complex topics. This role required effective communication, leadership, and the ability to foster an inclusive environment where diverse perspectives were valued. Analysing medical themes and ethical dilemmas enhanced my critical thinking and decision-making skills, as I reflected on the impact of these issues on patient care.

Additionally, managing the club taught me organisational and time-management skills, as I balanced planning sessions with my academic responsibilities. These experiences have prepared me for a career in medicine by strengthening my ability to communicate complex ideas, think critically about ethical challenges, and collaborate with others.

SECTION 3 [2154 characters]

Work experience has given me valuable insight into the medical field. I have shadowed two GPs and an SHO and was delighted to see theories applied to real life. During my placements, I attended doctors' meetings and witnessed an A&E trauma case, where consultants, nurses, radiologists and physiotherapists worked efficiently and cohesively together as an impressive team. These placements gave me a realistic perspective on hospital life which, although physically and emotionally challenging at times, confirmed beyond any doubt that this is where my future lies. I now understand the importance of compassion, effective communication and empathy for building effective relationships with patients and their families, a perspective further confirmed as a member of the Community Service Unit (CSU) for a year. I cared for people ranging from the elderly in nursing homes to young infants in a day nursery.

Last year, I visited a local nursing home weekly. I found the standard of care disappointing but appreciated the importance of palliative care. Brightening up their day and promoting the wellness of others was incredibly rewarding. I am also fortunate to distinguish the different perspective of hospitals in the Philippines compared with developed countries. Although the hospitals were busier with more physicians, their facilities are not as advanced. I feel my knowledge and appreciation of different cultures will enable me to treat patients from diverse backgrounds with the same level of understanding.

I balance academic studies with extracurricular activities by volunteering. In the 'Philippines Health Programme' based in Manila, I was privileged to help care for street children and teach them English. I assisted in giving out free vaccinations and raised awareness of the environment and health. I have also used my organisation skills to contribute to the King's College Christmas Charity and Fashion Show. To relax, I enjoy playing the piano and reading novels and medical literature. I am also a member of SIFE, Brentwood Badminton Club and the church choir, where I have organised charity events and have helped raise £200 for MS.

11.83 Graduate entry — 3988 characters

SECTION 1 [1287 characters]

It has always been my desire to become a doctor, and, although my A level grades prevented me from immediate entry to medical school, the ambition remained with me. I decided to undertake a degree in chemistry and have since graduated with first-class honours, which I believe demonstrates that I am well equipped for the academic rigours of medicine. During my time at university I have undergone a diverse range of experiences at home and abroad, and now I have the insight to understand why I have always been inclined to contribute to society through the practice of medicine.

My interest in medicine was actively stimulated through a voluntary research project I carried out during my third year of study at the prestigious University of Wollongong, Australia, 'Developing Novel Dual Action Anti-malarial Agents'. Two of the agents I designed and synthesised were sent to a biomedical laboratory in Bangkok, for their in vitro anti-malarial potency against a chloroquine-resistant parasite to be tested for. My interest, not only in people but the psychosocial impact of disease and illness on their lives, was manifested when I spent three weeks teaching orphans whose lives had been devastated by the AIDS virus, as well as Maasai tribesmen, during a voluntary project in Tanzania.

SECTION 2 [1281 characters]

Throughout my degree and particularly during the year-long research project I carried out as part of my Master's year, I have developed and applied skills of critical appraisal and have been trained to make decisions based upon scientific evidence, both of which have fundamental importance in evidence-based medicine.

I have always endeavoured to be a part of the community, from my position as Head of Year Council throughout secondary school, to my responsibility of Orientation Week Leader during my study year abroad, through to being a team captain of the Sheffield University Cheerleading Squad. I have gained essential leadership and teamwork skills along the way. As team captain of the cheerleading squad, I led a team with diverse abilities and personalities, which required me to motivate, inspire, and support each member, fostering a sense of unity and collaboration to achieve our shared goals. I was responsible for organising practices, choreographing routines, and managing logistical aspects of competitions, which enhanced my organisational and problem-solving abilities. Balancing these responsibilities alongside my academic commitments taught me the importance of time management and prioritisation, skills that are crucial for a demanding career like medicine.

SECTION 3 [1420 characters]

Through shadowing doctors in four specialities at a Sheffield Hospital, and two GPs, I developed an awareness of the realities of being a doctor in the modern NHS: I considered a patient's distress when their condition could not be treated and a doctor's frustration when he was unable to help his patient to be amongst the difficulties of the job. However, I feel that the excitement of taking on the challenge of a diagnosis using essential problem-solving and decision-making skills, coupled with the immense feeling of reward that comes by making a positive difference to people's lives, far outweighs these cons.

As a Relief Residential Social Care Worker for the Together Trust, and an employee of Bolton PCT Health Care Assistant Bank, I intend to further explore the healthcare profession during my gap year. Gaining practice of taking a patient-centred approach to situations and acquiring an understanding of the NHS are just some of the ways in which my gap year work will equip me well for medical school.

Activities such as boxing and running, which has helped me raise money for Cancer Research UK, help me to gain a balance between work and play, which is essential for coping with the demands and challenges of becoming a doctor. My ambitious nature and appreciation of diversity resulted in my backpacking around Australia independently, and spontaneously extending my travel to New Zealand and Thailand.

11.84 Graduate entry — 3742 characters

SECTION 1 [895 characters]

During my university years, I sought to contribute to the well-being of others through biomedical research. I spent two summers as a research student at the University of Toronto, investigating the signalling pathways in pre-eclamptic placental cells in a clinical molecular biology lab. My work involved genetic isolation, analysis techniques, and advanced microscopy for cell culture, offering invaluable hands-on experience in genetic medicine. This deepened my understanding of disease mechanisms and the potential for targeted therapies.

Collaborating with professional geneticists in a demanding lab setting highlighted both the challenges and rewards of research. The experience of seeing how research directly impacts patient care sparked my passion for medicine and confirmed my aspiration to combine scientific innovation with compassionate patient care to make a meaningful difference.

SECTION 2 [972 characters]

Initially, I pursued biomedical computing at university but soon realised that my true interests and strengths lay in the biological sciences. This shift is reflected in my academic performance in subsequent years. In my final year, I was encouraged to pursue a Master of Science, focusing on research aimed at enhancing farmed fish tissue growth to support both First- and Third-World populations. Through this work, I honed skills in patience, critical analysis of research papers, and meticulous attention to detail in designing research methodologies.

Alongside my lab work, I taught undergraduate students complex animal dissections and anatomy, thriving in the collaborative, peer-directed learning environment. This experience deepened my understanding of group dynamics and the value of mutual learning. I was honoured to receive the University Award for Excellence in Teaching, which reinforced my commitment to education and leadership within a scientific context.

SECTION 3 [1875 characters]

The first experience that influenced my career path was when I volunteered at my local hospital. I was able to share the view of medical care from the patient perspective and appreciate the hopes and anxieties involved in these encounters. I also interacted with many healthcare providers to gain an understanding of their roles. A high-school placement in general practice and a physiotherapy clinic further expanded my knowledge in this area.

Following this, during my first summer of university, I worked at Camp Kodiak – a wilderness boarding programme for children suffering immense physical and mental challenges. Working as a counsellor, I was directly responsible for the individual well-being of my campers 24 hours a day, including their ability to work with others, learning from their counsellors as well as attending to their medical needs. Mornings were often spent administering the medicines required to manage an extensive variety of conditions. The intimate level of involvement in each of these campers' daily routines gave me a deeper level of patience and understanding, in helping others negotiate immense challenges. In working directly with healthcare providers I gained valuable insight into the pharmacological and psychological elements of treatment. Personally, nothing that summer could compare to the satisfaction of knowing that I'd helped my campers through days of sports, life skills and fun that would translate into future achievement in their daily lives.

I am excited by the opportunities of a patient-focused career in medicine and new developments in healthcare based on the application of fundamental research. My time in the community, the classroom, the hospital and the research laboratory have, I believe, equipped me with the skill set to contribute to medical school, my peers and ultimately in the improvement of human health.

11.85 Graduate entry — 3898 characters

SECTION 1 [1458 characters]

From an early age, I have been passionate about medicine and its impact on society. Growing up in Bootle, one of the most deprived areas in the UK, I was surrounded by the challenges of chronic disease and poverty. My father, a senior partner at a local GP practice, and my mother, a nurse, both played pivotal roles in my understanding of healthcare. I saw first-hand the profound difference a compassionate doctor and nurse can make in the lives of those facing difficult circumstances.

While my desire to study medicine was strong, I initially chose to pursue a degree in pharmacology to understand the science behind medicine. I was fascinated by how drugs work in the body and their effects on patients. I also became intrigued by the placebo and nocebo effects, exploring the psychology and physiology behind these phenomena.

I graduated with a first-class honours degree, finishing in the top five out of fifty-five students. My dissertation was even nominated for the Science, Engineering, and Technology Awards in 2008, an accomplishment I am proud of. However, throughout my studies, I realised that my true passion lies in working directly with people in medicine. The parts of my course that fascinated me most were those that connected science with humanity. This is why I am now applying to study medicine, with the goal of becoming a GP, where I can combine my scientific knowledge with the opportunity to make a direct impact on people's lives.

SECTION 2 [637 characters]

My degree in pharmacology has helped understand drug mechanisms, pharmacokinetics and pharmacodynamics, drug interactions and side effects, and the importance of therapeutic drug monitoring. I have also gained experience in designing, conducting and interpreting clinical drug trials, and gained a good ability to critically evaluate and apply scientific literature to clinical questions. I also understand the role of genetics and patient variability in drug response, which is increasingly important in the development of personalised treatment plans. I feel my degree has given me a solid background in research and scientific rigour.

SECTION 3 [1803 characters]

I decided to take a gap year before entering university and I worked at my father's general practice, where I organised and ran my own respiratory clinic, seeing COPD and asthma patients on a one-to-one basis to test their lung function. Following every clinic, I would discuss the results I had obtained with the practice's respiratory disease coordinator, and decisions on diagnosis and treatment would be made. I enjoyed this work very much, especially working with the patients. I also undertook a number of interesting audits for the practice and the local commissioners. One such audit was carried out in conjunction with Aintree Hospital and attempted to find patients who may be unknowingly diabetic. The majority of my work experience has been in the primary care setting, where I shadowed two GPs in their respective surgeries. I have also shadowed the match doctors at Everton and Liverpool football clubs, giving me an insight into emergency medicine. This has been continued with my long-term commitment to St John Ambulance.

I currently work for Assura Medical in Liverpool auditing dermatology data. The cause and epidemiology of many of the dermatological problems I have encountered are difficult to establish, and it is this diversity that I find interesting.

While I was at school, I gained an Edmund Rice 6th Form Scholarship, was appointed deputy head boy and senior prefect, and completed my Duke of Edinburgh Gold Award. I am currently volunteering at my school, helping pupils who are participating in the Duke of Edinburgh Award. At university, I was a member of the Student Community Action volunteering service, and I enjoy playing tennis and badminton. I love to read, laugh and discuss issues with friends, and I have a passion for music – I am a grade 8 pianoforte student.

11.86 Graduate entry — 3978 characters

SECTION 1 [856 characters]

My decision to pursue a career in medicine is deeply rooted in my passion for science, my fascination with the human body, and a profound desire to help others. The pivotal moment in my journey toward this field occurred during my travels in South America, where I had the opportunity to observe medical practice on a ward in Peru. During my time there, I witnessed how healthcare professionals, despite working with limited resources, were able to make a significant impact on their patients' lives.

This experience profoundly reinforced my commitment to the medical profession. It was a powerful reminder of the transformative role that compassionate and skilled medical care plays in improving health and well-being, and it solidified my resolve to combine my scientific knowledge with a dedication to making a tangible difference in the lives of others.

SECTION 2 [686 characters]

During my undergraduate years, I developed strong time management skills, learning to prioritise tasks effectively in order to meet deadlines and achieve academic success. I am confident that the analytical, problem-solving, and computer literacy skills I gained through studying physics will serve as valuable assets in my medical career. For my research project, I critically appraised journal articles, delivered presentations, and engaged in meaningful collaboration with fellow researchers.

These experiences, coupled with my mature and reflective approach to independent learning, have equipped me with skills that will be invaluable as I embark on my journey as a medical student.

SECTION 3 [2436 characters]

To gain insight into medical practice, I undertook work experience with a general practitioner, consultant physician, and general surgeon. This experience deepened my understanding of how essential communication and multidisciplinary teamwork are in optimising healthcare. Observing doctor–patient relationships highlighted the importance of empathy and effective communication in medical practice. I also recognised that while medicine is an exciting and rewarding field, it can be demanding and emotionally taxing. One particular experience involved observing a surgical procedure followed by the compassionate delivery of bad news to a patient, which reinforced my understanding of the emotional complexities of medical care. These experiences confirmed my passion for medicine, and I have arranged further shadowing in a local hospital to continue gaining exposure to different aspects of the profession.

I have also volunteered at a nursing home, caring for an elderly relative with Alzheimer's disease. In this role, I assisted with daily activities, providing emotional support by reading and chatting with her. This experience taught me patience and compassion, and I found it deeply rewarding. Additionally, I led a local summer play scheme, where I developed my interpersonal, leadership, and communication skills, especially in handling delicate situations with sensitivity. These experiences have strengthened the foundation for the skills necessary in medicine.

Outside of academic and work commitments, I maintain a balanced life through my hobbies and interests. I am a dedicated musician, playing the violin, piano, and guitar, with grade eight and seven qualifications in violin and piano. As leader of the second violins in the North Wales Youth Orchestra, I honed my leadership abilities and continued to play in an ensemble. I also enjoy playing cricket and competitive football, thriving in team environments. Furthermore, I am passionate about climbing, and last year I summited Mount Kilimanjaro with my father. This challenging journey required perseverance and teamwork.

Having gained valuable experiences and insights, I am now certain that I want to pursue a career in medicine. I am fully aware of the academic, physical, and emotional challenges ahead, but I am confident that my enthusiasm, determination, resilience, and academic ability will enable me to succeed in this demanding and rewarding profession.

11.87 Graduate entry — 3647 characters

SECTION 1 [779 characters]

Before university, I hadn't fully grasped how deeply I wanted to become a doctor. To understand if dedicating my life to others was the right path, I undertook three long-term volunteering placements. The most pivotal was my role as a Ward Befriender on a renal ward at the Royal London Hospital. Each week, I visited patients at their bedside, engaging them in conversation and offering a compassionate ear. Although witnessing patients in pain or gradual decline was difficult, I stayed focused on providing a reassuring presence during challenging times.

This experience deepened my respect for nurses and gave me valuable insight into the collaborative nature of an NHS healthcare team. Ultimately, it was this role that confirmed my aspiration to pursue a career in medicine.

SECTION 2 [987 characters]

My degree in Medical Engineering has expanded my technical knowledge and deepened my interest in medicine. Starting with foundational engineering principles, I progressed to specialised topics, including urology and clinical ethics, which provided insight into the intersection of engineering and healthcare. The diverse teaching methods – self-study, group exercises, PBL, and hands-on laboratory work – challenged me to think critically.

A formative experience was our fourth-year project, where we worked with 'Actifuse', a proprietary bone substitute material for spinal fusion. This project was both challenging and rewarding, requiring us to apply theoretical knowledge to a real-world clinical solution. It sparked my desire to explore medicine further, encouraging me to read around the subject and consider my future contribution to the field. Reflecting on this, I realise my academic path has prepared me for medical engineering while fuelling my passion for pursuing medicine.

SECTION 3 [1881 characters]

In today's NHS, where doctors increasingly take on leadership roles, I have come to appreciate the value of management skills, which I have developed through various experiences. As a residential steward in university halls, I was responsible for the pastoral care of students and handling emergency situations like fire alarms. This role expanded when I became senior steward, managing a team and developing key leadership skills. These experiences proved valuable when I worked towards the leadership and management award, allowing me to reflect on my growing abilities in guiding and supporting others.

My academic journey has also equipped me with useful skills. The 'Insights' model helped me refine my study approach, ensuring I can cope with the demanding workload of a medical degree. Additionally, my NCFE qualification in Equality and Diversity has enabled me to work effectively with a diverse range of people, an essential skill in healthcare.

My extended work placements at hospitals further strengthened my desire to pursue medicine, offering me a first-hand look into the daily lives of healthcare professionals. I observed how doctors manage teams, communicate with patients and staff, and offer reassurance during difficult times. This reinforced my understanding that, beyond medical knowledge, the ability to lead with empathy and composure is crucial.

Volunteering with St John Ambulance has been another transformative experience. Treating patients at public events and earning four first aid certifications has deepened my passion for emergency medicine. It has taught me how to stay calm under pressure, assess situations methodically, and provide effective care when it's most needed. Finally, participating in the University of London Ski and Snowboard Club has helped me manage stress and stay physically active, essential qualities for a future in medicine.

11.88 Graduate entry — 3643 characters

SECTION 1 [1057 characters]

During the COVID-19 pandemic, I volunteered to support my community in various ways, including food distribution, assisting vulnerable individuals, and raising awareness about health and safety measures. I saw how the crisis worsened existing inequalities, with many struggling to access basic necessities and healthcare. This experience highlighted the profound impact small acts of service could have on people's well-being, strengthening my desire to pursue a career in medicine. Interacting with those affected by the pandemic revealed the emotional and psychological toll of illness and isolation. Many were not just fighting the virus but also dealing with fear, uncertainty, and loss.

This deepened my understanding of the need for holistic care that addresses both physical and mental health. Volunteering helped me develop problem-solving skills, resilience, and empathy – key qualities for a career in medicine. The dedication of healthcare workers further inspired me to not only provide treatment but also offer emotional support and reassurance.

SECTION 2 [1027 characters]

For the past two years, I have served as the Music Officer in sixth form, teaching piano lessons to younger students. This role required me to take initiative in lesson planning, researching effective teaching methods, and breaking down complex concepts for beginners. Patience and perseverance were key, especially when helping a pupil who initially struggled but eventually achieved Grade 1 – a moment I found deeply rewarding. This experience developed my communication and adaptability, as I tailored my teaching style to meet each student's needs. These skills are directly transferable to medicine, where clear and empathetic communication is essential when explaining diagnoses and treatments to patients.

Additionally, witnessing my pupils' progress reinforced the importance of encouragement and collaboration – values that are central to the doctor–patient relationship. Teaching piano has not only improved my ability to guide others but also underscored the satisfaction of helping people reach their full potential.

SECTION 3 [1559 characters]

Shadowing an ophthalmologist with a focus on surgery, medical care, and research provided me with valuable insight into one of the many specialties in medicine. Within a hospital dedicated to a single organ, I saw how effectively the consultant explained complex issues in a way that patients could understand. My work experience in a pharmacy department highlighted the importance of multidisciplinary teams, with doctors, pharmacists, nurses, and physiotherapists collaborating regularly. Spending a day with a GP revealed the variety of medical concerns encountered, from minor issues to home visits for complex, disabled patients. I observed the need to identify underlying problems and provide opportunities for health promotion.

Volunteering weekly on a cardiology ward for six months has deepened my understanding of team dynamics and the shared responsibility for patient care. A conversation with a patient recovering from a heart attack emphasised the significance of empathy in a doctor, particularly when a consultant's simple gesture of holding her hand made a world of difference. Since February, I've volunteered at a respite home for disabled adults, where I witnessed the challenges of daily tasks for those with disabilities and admired the resilience of patients and the quality of care provided by carers.

I also developed valuable skills supervising day trips, assisting with feeding patients, and communicating with individuals with speech impediments. These experiences have reinforced my desire to pursue a career in a caring profession.

11.89 Graduate entry — 3927 characters

SECTION 1 [1294 characters]

As a teenager, I never imagined that I would find myself assisting physicians with technical procedures like colonoscopies and venepunctures during my mother's extended hospital stays. I also took on the responsibility of helping her to the toilet during times of rectal bleeding, then reporting back to the nurses. These challenging and intimate experiences were pivotal in shaping my desire to pursue a career in medicine. They gave me a profound understanding of the physical and emotional toll of illness, as well as the vital role healthcare professionals play in both treating and supporting patients. Through these experiences, I learned the importance of staying calm and focused under pressure. I developed a deep appreciation for the complexity of diagnosing medical conditions, using scientific knowledge to make informed decisions, and helping patients recover not just physically but emotionally as well. It was during these times that I realised how deeply I wanted to contribute to the healing process, offering not only medical care but compassion and reassurance to those in need. These formative moments have reinforced my commitment to pursuing a career in medicine, where I hope to combine my scientific understanding with empathy, to make a difference in the lives of others.

SECTION 2 [983 characters]

Throughout my degree, I developed strong time management skills, which allowed me to balance various commitments, including my role as a customer assistant, my work as an A level tutor, and my passion for sketching and playing badminton at an advanced level in local clubs. This ability to juggle multiple responsibilities has been essential in managing my time effectively and maintaining a well-rounded lifestyle. I also have a naturally inquisitive mind, which drives me to stay informed about scientific and medical advancements. I regularly read journals such as the 'BMJ' to broaden my understanding of current issues in healthcare. Recently, I've been particularly focused on the topic of varenicline and suicidal behaviour, as it has sparked my interest in the intersection of pharmacology and mental health.

These experiences have only strengthened my resolve to pursue a career in medicine, and I am excited to continue working towards my goal of becoming Tomorrow's Doctor.

SECTION 3 [1650 characters]

Speaking four languages, along with my current studies in Arabic and British Sign Language, has greatly enhanced my ability to communicate with diverse patients. This skill proved invaluable during my placements at a GP surgery and as a member of St John Ambulance, where I developed my first aid abilities and learned to connect with patients at public events.

Volunteering as a ward befriender at the Royal London and Whipps Cross Hospitals gave me the chance to observe and learn from junior doctors about life as a medical student. I contributed to patient care and shadowed doctors as they took medical histories, conducted physical exams, and provided diagnoses and treatments. Attending an interdisciplinary meeting also highlighted the importance of teamwork, organisation, and communication in delivering quality patient care.

My placement with Whizz Kidz, working alongside physiotherapists, paediatric nurses, and wheelchair trainers, offered valuable insight into disability care. I supported children in gaining independence using wheelchairs, which was both rewarding and enlightening.

As a project leader for READ International, I honed my leadership skills by recruiting, managing, and motivating volunteers. I also had the opportunity to travel to Tanzania in 2020 to distribute books, an experience that broadened my cultural awareness and strengthened my sense of responsibility.

Mentoring undergraduates further developed my counselling and problem-solving skills. Additionally, volunteering in response to the 2023 earthquake, where I provided emotional support and counselling, deepened my understanding of trauma and mental health.

11.90 Graduate entry — 3767 characters

SECTION 1 [910 characters]

My desire to pursue medicine stems from a deep fascination with the science of life and its ability to meaningfully impact others. I first realised my calling during summers spent working at an IVF clinic in Athens, where I shadowed my uncle, an obstetrician-gynaecologist. I was captivated by the life-changing treatments offered to couples struggling with infertility – advancements unimaginable just a few decades ago. Interacting with patients daily, I witnessed the emotional toll of their treatment and saw first-hand the importance of communication, calmness, and psychological support in medicine.

These experiences, along with my work in stem cell research, reinforced my passion for a career that combines scientific discovery with compassionate patient care. I am eager to pursue medicine to make a tangible difference in patients' lives by offering both innovative treatments and empathetic support.

SECTION 2 [997 characters]

I am confident that studying biomedical sciences as my first degree was the right decision before applying to medical school. This degree provided me with a strong foundation in the scientific principles of medicine, deepening my understanding of human biology, disease mechanisms, and therapeutic interventions. Among the subjects I studied, cancer biology particularly fascinated me, as it allowed me to explore the complexities of oncogenesis, molecular signalling, and targeted treatments. My passion for this field grew through a second-year project on the role of oestrogens in breast cancer, followed by a final-year research project in cancer biology.

These experiences honed my analytical skills, critical thinking, and appreciation for the connection between research and clinical practice. While I valued the intellectual challenge of research, it was the human aspect of medicine that truly drew me in – the opportunity to apply scientific knowledge to directly improve patients' lives.

SECTION 3 [1860 characters]

My decision to pursue medicine was further solidified last summer during my month-long placement at Hammersmith Hospital. There, I had the opportunity to engage with various healthcare professionals, including house officers, nurses, and consultants, and gain a deeper understanding of their roles. I learned that the medical profession, while demanding and often frustrating, is ultimately fulfilling, as it combines scientific knowledge with a genuine desire to help others. One of the most important lessons I took from my time in the echocardiography department was the importance of a doctor not only being responsible and conscientious but also maintaining an enquiring mind – constantly seeking to analyse, update, and expand their knowledge.

In high school, I served as a student council representative and was a member of both the health and environmental education groups. These roles taught me valuable skills in teamwork, leadership, and decision-making. Through outdoor activities like hiking and rafting at summer camp, I learned how to face challenges in tough conditions, while my part-time job as a bookshop assistant helped me develop communication skills, especially with children.

Despite these extracurricular commitments, I ranked first in the nationwide entrance examinations, earning the National Scholarship Foundation Award and the University of Patras Award for being the top student. Although I was grateful for these achievements, I knew that the United Kingdom, with its globally recognised education system, was the ideal place for me to pursue my medical studies. In addition to English and Greek, I speak French fluently and am currently teaching myself Italian to further enhance my communication skills. I am eager to continue my journey in medicine, where I can combine my academic strengths with my passion for helping others.

11.91 Graduate entry — 3947 characters

SECTION 1 [855 characters]

Losing my brother to SCID at the age of 5 was a traumatic event and my first encounter with genetics and medicine. This experience, though painful, sparked an interest in pursuing a medical career. As I grew older, I discussed my options with my grandfather, a GP, and several other doctors I encountered while working as a medical team secretary. Through these conversations, I realised the importance of building a broad foundation for a career in medicine, one that would give me a well-rounded perspective and an appreciation for the wider healthcare environment. My passion for both medicine and genetics led me to choose a degree in human genetics, where I could combine these interests. I specifically selected modules related to medicine, such as developmental biology, to deepen my understanding of how genetics intersects with clinical practice.

SECTION 2 [1402 characters]

Studying developmental biology has equipped me with valuable skills for medicine, including attention to detail, critical thinking, and research proficiency. I learned to analyse complex biological processes, identifying how disruptions can lead to disease, which mirrors the diagnostic skills required in medicine. My experience in conducting experiments and interpreting data sharpened my ability to evaluate research, while communicating complex ideas has strengthened my ability to explain medical information clearly and empathetically.

Following university, I felt it was important to gain further skills in a non-medical background while utilising my degree specialty. Working as a forensic examiner provided me with invaluable experience in professional communication, problem-solving, and teamwork, particularly in the high-pressure environment of time-critical cases. I also developed a strong appreciation for the importance of confidentiality and professional integrity, as these were fundamental to my role. Despite working outside of traditional healthcare, I maintained a connection with medicine by interpreting medical reports for various cases and relating them to my own examinations. This exposure allowed me to appreciate the critical role of medical expertise in forensic investigations, reinforcing my understanding of how scientific knowledge is applied to real-world situations.

SECTION 3 [1690 characters]

I have worked at the Nottingham Access Centre, helping separated families interact in a neutral space, which taught me valuable skills in mediation, quick adaptation, and managing high-pressure situations while engaging with individuals of all ages. My most rewarding experience was volunteering with literacy volunteers, where I helped children improve their reading skills. This role challenged my communication styles, but by adapting my approach to each child's needs, I quickly built trust with them, their parents, and teachers.

I also gained insight into hospital laboratories and radiology at Kingsmill Hospital and developed my patient interaction skills as a volunteer at Queen's Medical Centre. Observing doctors and nurses first-hand, and assisting with daily ward duties, allowed me to connect with patients and understand their experiences, deepening my appreciation for the relationships between doctors, patients, and the NHS.

Additionally, I had the privilege of shadowing a consultant physician at Sherwood Day Hospital, where I witnessed medical cases like the TILT test and the management of MRSA patients. I interacted with patients, including those with speech difficulties and Parkinson's disease, and learned important lessons in being a caring listener, and the value of excellent communication and compassion in alleviating patients' and families' concerns.

Outside of medicine, I have diverse interests such as sports, travel, and reading. Having lived abroad and travelled extensively, I've developed an interest in different cultures and traditions, which has helped me refine my interpersonal skills and deepen my understanding of people from diverse backgrounds.

11.92 Graduate entry — 3988 characters

SECTION 1 [1233 characters]

My role as a Management Consultant for the NHS CfH Project, one of Deloitte's most prestigious engagements, sparked my initial interest in the health service. I thrived in this role, knowing that my work was contributing to improving healthcare delivery. However, as I became more involved, I realised that my future career should have a people focus rather than a financial one. This realisation led me to leave Deloitte and seek a more direct, emotionally rewarding experience in a caring environment.

I knew that I wanted to combine my desire to work within the NHS with my academic abilities and passion for science. Medicine became the natural choice, as it would allow me to blend my skills with a deeper, more personal connection to patients. To ensure that medicine was truly the right path for me, I made the difficult decision to leave my business career behind and gain hands-on experience in patient care. This step, though significant, solidified my commitment to pursuing a medical career and gave me the opportunity to immerse myself in the human side of healthcare. It was through these experiences that I found my true calling – working in medicine, where I could contribute directly to improving the lives of others.

SECTION 2 [1092 characters]

My studies in business and maths have provided me with a solid analytical foundation, developing my problem-solving skills and logical thinking – abilities that are essential in medicine. These subjects have taught me how to approach challenges systematically and make decisions based on evidence and data, skills that are directly transferable to diagnosing and treating patients. Alongside full-time work, I took the initiative to teach myself A level chemistry in just three months. I found it to be an engaging subject, one that I could relate to both my work in the hospital and everyday life. The practical application of chemical principles in medicine further sparked my interest. Currently, I am studying A level biology to deepen my understanding of human biology and disease mechanisms. While my studies are demanding, I recognise the importance of maintaining balance, ensuring that I take necessary breaks from both work and study to stay focused and energised. These experiences have prepared me for a career in medicine, blending analytical thinking with a passion for science.

SECTION 3 [1663 characters]

I have been working as a Healthcare Assistant on a surgical ward, where I greatly enjoyed interacting with patients and providing care. This role expanded my understanding of hospital procedures and highlighted the importance of interdisciplinary communication. I had the opportunity to shadow doctors on both surgical and orthopaedic wards, gaining valuable insight into the challenges and experiences of consultants. These experiences helped reinforce my career aspirations. My time on the ward was rewarding, as I could contribute to patient care while also observing various procedures in my free time.

Seeking broader experience, I currently work in an NHS day centre for adults with complex needs and learning disabilities. Here, I coordinate activity groups, assist with personal care, and serve as a keyworker, assessing and documenting well-being. I work closely with relevant parties to ensure care plans are tailored to each individual's needs, providing choice and flexibility. This role has been both challenging and fulfilling, offering the opportunity to observe review meetings with psychiatrists.

In addition, I take on bank shifts as a Senior Healthcare Assistant, extending my experience to medical, orthopaedic, and accident and emergency wards. To continue my development, I actively arrange doctor shadowing and plan to experience a different healthcare system in Canada later this year.

These diverse roles have deepened my desire to pursue a medical career and solidified my focus. With my life experience, maturity, and commitment, I believe I am well-prepared to embark on my medical studies and make a meaningful contribution to the field.

11.93 Graduate entry — 3691 characters

SECTION 1 [1018 characters]

From the age of 15, I've been fascinated by medicine, beginning with a work experience placement at my local hospital. That experience ignited my interest in healthcare and solidified my desire to pursue a career in this field. My academic path led me to achieve a Master's in physics at Oxford, where the intellectual challenge fuelled my ambition. However, over time, I realised that while the academic pursuit was rewarding, it did not satisfy my desire for human connection. As a natural people person, I craved an environment where I could not only engage in intellectual work but also collaborate with others and make a meaningful impact on people's lives.

I am drawn to medicine because it offers the perfect balance: a dynamic, diverse environment where I can work closely with others, solve complex problems, and contribute to society. After much reflection, I now understand that medicine is the career I have been seeking, one that aligns with both my intellectual strengths and my passion for helping others.

SECTION 2 [995 characters]

My Master's in physics has equipped me with several transferable skills that are highly relevant to a career in medicine. The rigorous problem-solving and analytical thinking required in physics have sharpened my ability to approach complex medical scenarios with a systematic mindset. I've learned to break down intricate problems, identify key variables, and apply theoretical knowledge to real-world situations – skills essential for diagnosing and treating patients. Furthermore, the research aspect of my degree honed my attention to detail and my ability to assess data critically, both of which are crucial when interpreting medical tests or clinical trials.

Working independently and in collaborative settings has also prepared me for teamwork in healthcare, where cooperation and clear communication are vital. Overall, my physics background has strengthened my resilience, adaptability, and intellectual curiosity – traits that will serve me well in the ever-evolving field of medicine.

SECTION 3 [1678 characters]

I have shadowed a stroke consultant, a GP, and a leading neuro-oncologist, gaining insight into three distinct areas of medicine. What connected them all was their ability to treat each patient as an individual. Whether delivering hope or bad news, they communicated effectively by being sensitive to each patient's unique illness, needs, and circumstances. I also volunteer at a local nursing home, where I feed residents. Building trust and understanding their habits is rewarding, and the personal satisfaction of helping someone eat a full meal or engage in a conversation, no matter how brief, is immense. Patience is key, as is seeing each person as a whole, listening for the unspoken, and addressing their needs beyond the physical ailment.

Additionally, I've volunteered on an outpatient tea trolley, attended NHS training courses, and am currently taking a geriatric feeding course at St George's, gaining hands-on experience in both NHS and private care settings. Through conversations with consultants, doctors, and students, I have gained an understanding of the challenges and rewards of a medical career. While the path to becoming a doctor is long and demanding, I've seen in others the same drive and determination I recognise in myself. Despite their frustrations, they wouldn't change their profession for anything.

I am a driven person, evident in both my academic and extracurricular achievements. As OUNC President, I led a committee, advocated for fairer legislation, and improved team morale and vision. My ability to balance leadership, responsibility, and academic rigour demonstrates my commitment to challenges and my desire to contribute meaningfully.

11.94 Graduate entry — 3974 characters

SECTION 1 [660 characters]

Medicine has always struck me as an exciting profession, positioned as it is at the very human interface between science and society. I am attracted to the need for lifelong learning, and the wide range of specialisations open to medics. It is a long-term interest of mine, which was originally sparked during my sixth form years by time spent volunteering at a school for children with learning difficulties.

With a challenging six months spent teaching English in China as well as three years of university behind me, I find myself in a carefully considered position, excited at feeling ready to enter such an intellectually and emotionally challenging field.

SECTION 2 [637 characters]

Since arriving at Oxford, I have thrived in a challenging academic environment and feel well prepared to face the demands of a rigorous medical degree. In my first year, I earned a distinction in my exams and received a scholarship in recognition of my academic performance.

The hands-on nature of my chemistry studies has honed my precision and attention to detail, skills that I believe will be invaluable in mastering practical medical procedures. Next year, I will undertake an independent year-long laboratory project, which will enhance my problem-solving abilities and further refine my capacity for independent research and study.

SECTION 3 [2677 characters]

To gain a deeper understanding of the realities of being a doctor, I undertook several work experience placements. My first experience was at a GP practice, where I observed consultations with doctors, spent time with the practice nurse, health visitor, and reception team. This exposure helped me appreciate the vital roles each member plays in a healthcare team. I was particularly drawn to the diagnostic aspect of medicine, but what I found most rewarding was witnessing the careful management of medications for patients with chronic conditions.

I then shadowed a psychiatrist at a Drug and Alcohol Service, which catered to individuals on methadone maintenance for heroin addiction. I was drawn to the social dimension of the work and saw the importance of a holistic approach to patient care. This placement also highlighted that healthcare aims not only to cure but also to improve quality of life and minimise harm. Further experience came from shadowing an F2 doctor on a psychiatric inpatient ward. This experience provided insight into the complexities of caring for psychotic patients and underscored the significance of thorough patient documentation. These notes were essential in recognising patterns of behaviour and understanding what treatments had been successful or not.

Beyond clinical settings, I have been active in my community through my role on the college welfare team. As a Peer Supporter, I completed training in supportive listening, learning the importance of trust and confidentiality while dealing with sensitive matters in a non-judgemental way. Recently, I began volunteering at a homeless centre, serving food and engaging with visitors. This experience challenged my perceptions of homelessness and reinforced my belief that working with vulnerable people can be both difficult and rewarding.

Last summer, I returned to China to work on an English language camp, where I was also involved in coordinating activities for 400 attendees. This role required strong organisational skills and enthusiasm. Living in China broadened my cultural awareness and made me more adaptable, as well as comfortable seeking assistance when needed.

At university, I have honed my time management skills by balancing academic demands with extracurricular activities. I've played for the women's football team, the college badminton and table tennis teams, and coxed the Men's Novice B rowing team. These experiences have reinforced the importance of teamwork, leadership, and commitment in achieving collective goals. Additionally, playing the violin and piano since the age of six has instilled in me the value of discipline and the joy of collaboration in music.

11.95 Graduate entry — 3958 characters

SECTION 1 [1595 characters]

As an identical twin, I have always been fascinated by genetics and heritability, which led me to pursue a degree in genetics. During my undergraduate studies, I engaged in laboratory-based research, but it was through this experience that I realised my career interests lay in a different direction. I particularly enjoyed researching dominant and recessive genetic disorders, such as sickle cell anaemia, PKU, and Fragile X syndrome, and I became intrigued by how certain families seem more vulnerable to specific conditions. This interest deepened after reading 'Is it in Your Genes?' by Philip Reilly, which explores the inheritance of family diseases. I am eager to continue studying and expand my scientific knowledge, particularly in the area of genetic heritage, to better understand the physiological effects of various diseases.

Since graduating, I have determined that a career in medicine is the intellectual and personal challenge I am seeking. This decision was solidified after attending a lecture by a clinical geneticist. Her insights and experiences helped me realise that the opportunity to work alongside people in both a scientific and compassionate role makes medicine the perfect fit for me. Additionally, I was inspired by my cousin, a surgeon, who performed my tonsillectomy. This experience, along with my shadowing of doctors at Leicester Royal Infirmary, has shown me the profound personal and professional rewards of a career dedicated to caring for and improving others' lives. I am fully committed to investing the time and effort needed to follow in their footsteps.

SECTION 2 [1075 characters]

My genetics degree has equipped me with a variety of valuable skills, including critical thinking, problem-solving, and research proficiency. Through analysing complex data and interpreting findings, I gained skills directly relevant to diagnosing and treating patients. The attention to detail and precision required in genetics research mirrors the accuracy needed in medical practice. I also developed strong communication skills through presenting research. Moreover, my understanding of genetic diseases and ethical considerations will inform my decision-making in medicine.

I am often described as compassionate, responsible, and approachable, qualities I demonstrated in roles such as school prefect and captain of my college basketball and volleyball teams, where we won a national gold medal in volleyball. In addition to still playing basketball, I have also held the responsible position of treasurer on the committee, which strengthened my organisational and financial management skills, further enhancing my ability to handle responsibilities in a medical career.

SECTION 3 [1288 characters]

During university, I volunteered to teach schoolchildren how to develop entrepreneurial skills, which then led to my involvement with Barnardo's CareFree programme. There, I support young carers in managing the challenges they face while caring for individuals with physical and mental illnesses. This experience has taught me valuable lessons in patience, tolerance, and effective listening, especially when working with those dealing with mental health issues. Shadowing doctors provided me with insight into the team dynamics essential for the smooth operation of a hospital. I also had the opportunity to speak with patients and observe the importance of positive, interactive relationships between patients and doctors, particularly when preparing patients for surgery, which I also understand personally through my own experiences.

Currently, I work full-time as a PA and part-time as a bartender, while actively seeking work experience as a healthcare assistant. I'm also saving to travel next summer and have two trips abroad planned for the next year. Additionally, I plan to pass my driving test soon. I believe this reflects my ability to balance the demands of a medical career, future studies, and personal interests, showing that I am a well-rounded and committed individual.

11.96 Graduate entry — 3876 characters

SECTION 1 [1181 characters]

My greatest ambition is to become a doctor, a field where I will constantly learn and challenge myself. I am motivated by the opportunity to use my knowledge and skills to positively impact people's lives, a responsibility I deeply value. I am fascinated by the human body and its processes, especially how disease arises when things break down. Though I know the journey to becoming a doctor will be tough, I am confident the rewards will make the effort worthwhile.

During university, I participated in a widening participation scheme at an inner-city school, where I worked with teenagers to help them raise their educational aspirations. This experience, though challenging, was rewarding and taught me patience, adaptability, and effective communication. Many students faced personal and social barriers, but by building trust and offering guidance, I helped some recognise their potential. This experience deepened my passion for working with people and inspired my interest in medicine, as I realised how essential qualities like empathy and support are in patient care. Just as I helped students overcome obstacles, I aim to support patients in overcoming health challenges.

SECTION 2 [1026 characters]

Through my degree in biomedical science, I developed a strong foundation in understanding human biology and disease mechanisms, which has greatly enhanced my critical thinking and problem-solving abilities. I learned to approach complex biological concepts with curiosity and rigour, skills that are directly transferable to the diagnostic process in medicine. During lab work, I honed my attention to detail and precision, as experiments often required accuracy to ensure valid results. This taught me the importance of reliability and consistency, qualities essential when working in a clinical setting. Furthermore, my research projects helped me develop resilience and adaptability, as they required me to troubleshoot and find solutions when things didn't go as planned. I also gained experience in teamwork, often collaborating with peers to interpret data and present findings, which reinforced my ability to communicate complex ideas effectively – a key skill for working with both patients and colleagues in medicine.

SECTION 3 [1669 characters]

To ensure that medicine is the right career path for me, I sought out various experiences within the medical field. I organised two months shadowing a vascular surgeon, where I observed major surgeries, such as a leg amputation, and attended ward rounds. This exposure highlighted the importance of effective communication, both with patients and the medical team. Engaging with fifth-year medical students allowed me to gain insights into their journey, while practising skills like taking blood reinforced my hands-on learning. I also arranged placements at two surgeries, shadowing GPs, participating in home visits, and attending team meetings. I witnessed how doctors addressed patient concerns with patience and empathy, deepening my understanding of communication in patient care.

Volunteering has been key to my development. In a postnatal well-being group, I listen to new mothers, offering support without judgement. At a hospice, my Sunday duties involve serving meals and providing companionship, highlighting the power of social interaction. As a Red Cross volunteer, I have learned life-saving skills and the value of teamwork. My role as a teaching assistant in a primary school taught me patience while supporting young learners, and my work with Cub Scouts has given me a sense of responsibility and the opportunity to be a role model.

University further shaped me. I stepped out of my comfort zone by joining salsa lessons, which helped build confidence and connections. I also enjoyed being part of an intermural netball team. My gap year, spent travelling solo across Asia and Africa, was an invaluable experience in self-reliance and personal growth.

11.97 Graduate entry — 3837 characters

SECTION 1 [1136 characters]

I initially chose to study biochemistry, believing it would provide a solid foundation in understanding the molecular mechanisms of life. Throughout my university years, I enjoyed the intellectual challenge of scientific discovery, but I soon realised I needed a career where my work directly impacted people's lives, rather than being limited to academic research. This became even clearer during a summer placement at Cancer Research UK, where I immersed myself in lab work. While I valued the technical skills and analytical thinking involved, I felt frustrated by the disconnect between basic research and real-world impact.

During this time, I met a physician in my lab who was training for her PhD. Conversations with her and other medical researchers opened my eyes to the career path of an academic doctor – a role that blends patient care, research, and teaching. The idea of applying scientific knowledge to improve lives while advancing medical research was incredibly inspiring. This experience solidified my decision to pursue medicine, where I could combine my passion for science with compassionate, hands-on patient care.

SECTION 2 [917 characters]

At university, I mentored first-year biochemistry students, leading tutorials and teaching sessions to support their academic development. This role required me to break down complex concepts, adapt my explanations to different learning styles, and offer constructive feedback to help students gain confidence and improve their understanding. It strengthened my communication, patience, and problem-solving skills as I tailored my approach to meet individual needs. Balancing these responsibilities with my own studies also honed my time management and organisational skills. Most importantly, I learned the value of empathy and encouragement in fostering growth – qualities essential for building trust with patients and collaborating with colleagues in medicine.

This experience reaffirmed my passion for teaching and supporting others, preparing me for the collaborative and educational aspects of a medical career.

SECTION 3 [1784 characters]

During my work experience with a consultant lipidologist and chemical pathologist, I gained valuable insights into the specialist's role in diagnosing and managing lipid disorders. I observed her consultations, learning how she thoroughly assessed patients' medical history, conducted tests, and developed personalised treatment plans. I also had the opportunity to observe laboratory work, understanding how biochemical analysis is used to interpret lipid profiles and guide clinical decisions. Her patient-centred approach and her ability to explain complex conditions with clarity inspired me, deepening my interest in the intersection of pathology and patient care.

I am an active individual involved in many university activities. Last year, I was elected president of the UCLU Volleyball Club, an incredibly educational experience. I learned to prioritise, be considerate of team members, and exercise patience with questions. In high school, I was vice president of the student body and a prefect, where I was responsible for the well-being of my dormitory's residents, ensuring they respected curfews and treated each other respectfully. These roles taught me how to understand people as individuals, develop listening and reasoning skills, and manage complaints and conflicts.

I also founded A.B.C. (A Brother's Care) to raise funds and awareness for Tibetan children's hardships. These leadership positions taught me to handle pressure, believe in myself, and maintain a positive attitude. I gained a wide range of experiences that allow me to interact effectively with others, and I am confident that these qualities will help me in patient care. Through these challenges, I developed patience, determination, and endurance, all of which are essential qualities for a doctor.

11.98 Graduate entry — 3755 characters

SECTION 1 [1157 characters]

In July, I graduated with a BSc (Hons) in biochemistry from Liverpool University, which has truly cemented my passion for pursuing a career in medicine. While I deeply enjoyed the intellectual challenges of my studies, particularly exploring the genetic causes of diseases like cancer and cystic fibrosis, I found myself more drawn to the human side of medicine. Understanding how tiny genetic changes can lead to life-changing conditions fascinated me, but I realised I wanted to be part of a profession where I could connect with people directly and make a real impact on their lives.

For my honours project, I used C. elegans worms to study the effects of genetic mutations on neuron development. While I loved the scientific exploration, I couldn't shake the feeling that I wanted to work in a more hands-on way with individuals. This experience, along with my growing desire to apply my scientific knowledge in a practical setting, made me realise that medicine is where I can combine my passion for science with my genuine desire to help others. I'm excited to pursue this path, where I can make a tangible difference in people's health and well-being.

SECTION 2 [530 characters]

Through my studies, I developed self-motivation, discipline, and organisation, which are critical for managing the demanding nature of medical training. I honed my written and oral communication skills, particularly when presenting complex scientific concepts in a clear and accessible way. My interest in genetics and disease, including modules on oncogenes and cystic fibrosis, has deepened my understanding of the molecular mechanisms behind health. My honours research improved my critical thinking and problem-solving skills.

SECTION 3 [2068 characters]

During my time at university, I worked part-time as a care assistant at a nursing and residential home in Liverpool. In this role, I assisted residents with mobility issues, toileting, and general care tasks, such as changing colostomy bags. This experience not only helped me refine my communication skills but also taught me the vital importance of patience and empathy. As the primary carer for two male residents, I learned how crucial it is to build strong, trusting relationships with both patients and their families. In addition, while completing my A levels, I volunteered as a classroom assistant at a local school for children with physical disabilities. Many of the students had conditions like autism, myotonic dystrophy, and ADHD. This experience highlighted the significance of specialised care and opened my eyes to the incredible resilience of children facing challenging circumstances.

After deferring university entry in 2004, I worked as a customer service officer at Lloyds TSB. This role not only helped me finance my travels but also allowed me to explore the South Pacific and South-East Asia for four months. It was a transformative experience that built my confidence and taught me to navigate a wide range of social situations.

Outside of academics, I was an active member of the Rankin halls football team, where I also served as social secretary. Organising football tours and securing sponsorships helped me develop strong leadership and organisational skills while strengthening my sense of teamwork.

A lifelong passion of mine is music – I play the piano at Grade 8 level, as well as the saxophone and bass guitar. Performing in various bands and local concerts has further nurtured my teamwork and discipline.

All these experiences, from caring roles to leadership positions and personal passions, have equipped me with the qualities of patience, understanding, initiative, and resilience. Combined with my scientific knowledge and enthusiasm, I feel well prepared to pursue a medical degree and make a meaningful contribution to the field.

11.99 Graduate entry — 3991 characters

SECTION 1 [1946 characters]

Six years ago, fresh-faced from university, I started my first graduate job working as an assay development scientist for a drug discovery company called Prolifix Ltd., at Harwell. Not long afterwards, the urge to travel took hold and I flew to Australia, where my part-time job as a synthetic chemist at Menai Organics Ltd. during university helped me gain a three-month position as a research assistant at the University of Sydney, School of Chemistry.

One year later, my daughter Lydia was born and I had the privilege of cutting the umbilical cord. At the time I was working in treasury management, where I learned two things: the importance of managing my finances effectively and that accountancy was not for me. With the intention of 'testing the water' for one or two weeks, an enquiry about work experience at a local veterinary practice resulted in a permanent position as a veterinary nursing assistant. I immediately knew that a career in a healthcare setting was right for me but soon realised that I would prefer to treat humans rather than animals.

Recently, I enrolled at the Open University to study 'Molecules in Medicine', a postgraduate course focusing on the molecular structure of drugs and how they interact with their target. Shortly afterwards, I was offered a position at the University of Oxford, as a medical laboratory scientific officer at CTSU (Clinical Trial Service Unit and Epidemiological Studies Unit), which is funded by the MRC, Cancer Research UK and the BHF, whose work primarily involves studies of the causes and treatment of chronic diseases, including cancer, heart attack and stroke. My primary responsibility is to analyse blood and urine samples for several randomised, controlled trials. I feel privileged to be involved with such a prestigious organisation, which has truly inspired me, not only to become a practising physician but perhaps also to be involved with clinical trials of the future.

SECTION 2 [1010 characters]

Winning the Project Conference Prize at university for the best presentation demonstrated my ability to communicate complex information effectively, a skill essential in medicine. Preparing and delivering the presentation required me to condense intricate concepts into clear, accessible points tailored to a diverse audience. This experience honed my ability to engage listeners, respond thoughtfully to questions, and adapt my delivery to meet individual needs – all of which are vital for patient care and teamwork. I also learned the importance of confidence, clarity, and empathy in communication, ensuring understanding and building trust.

These skills are directly transferable to a medical setting, where explaining diagnoses, discussing treatment options, and collaborating with colleagues require precise and considerate communication. Winning this prize affirmed my aptitude for connecting with others through clear, thoughtful dialogue, a quality I am eager to bring to my future career as a doctor.

SECTION 3 [1035 characters]

My veterinary practice experience was very rewarding and gave me the opportunity to perform anaesthesia and administer IV, IM and subcutaneous injections, practise suturing following postmortems and witness a variety of surgical procedures, from exploratory laparotomies to thyroidectomies.

Recently I used my savings to support myself whilst I volunteered full-time at the John Masefield Cheshire Home for the physically disabled, primarily assisting the physiotherapist with the residents' daily exercises, but also contributing to other events including fun days and excursions. My time there really opened my eyes to the reality of life in a care home and the difficulties faced by people suffering from conditions such as multiple sclerosis, Huntington's disease and Usher syndrome. In addition, I began to appreciate the demands placed upon the carers and nurses who looked after them, as well as the ongoing battle to treat these conditions. I developed a great rapport with the residents and staff and still help out when I can.

11.100 Graduate entry — 3780 characters

SECTION 1 [921 characters]

I am a very scientifically minded person and graduated with a BSc in genetics and microbiology. To further enhance my scientific understanding, I am currently pursuing an MSc in molecular medicine. Over the past few years, I have volunteered regularly at the North London Hospice, offering emotional and social support to patients and their families. This experience has allowed me to develop my communication skills while providing compassionate care.

I also worked for two years at Thermo Fisher Scientific, where I provided medical product support to hospitals and trained in the Biochemistry Laboratory at Queen Elizabeth's Hospital. Despite excelling in this role, I found the satisfaction of helping patients as a volunteer far more fulfilling. Becoming a doctor will enable me to combine my scientific knowledge with a genuine passion for patient care, allowing me to make a meaningful difference in people's lives.

SECTION 2 [1132 characters]

My studies in genetics and microbiology, culminating in a BSc with a first-class mark in my dissertation on 'Avian Influenza: Myths and Realities', provided me with a solid foundation in understanding the molecular mechanisms that underpin health and disease. Through my research, I developed strong analytical skills and an ability to critically evaluate complex scientific concepts, which are crucial for diagnosing and treating patients in a clinical setting.

Building on this foundation, my current MSc in molecular medicine is equipping me with advanced knowledge that is directly relevant to medicine. The course deepens my understanding of the molecular basis of diseases, therapeutic strategies, and drug development, all of which are integral to modern medical practice. This advanced medical knowledge will not only complement my medical studies but also enable me to bring a scientifically informed perspective to patient care. The analytical, research-driven skills I have honed throughout my academic career will support my ability to contribute meaningfully to both clinical practice and medical research in the future.

SECTION 3 [1727 characters]

I have undertaken work experience in the A&E department at Barnet Hospital, shadowing nurses, doctors and consultants. This provided me with an invaluable perspective on how challenging and rewarding the profession can be. I firmly believe my personal qualities, such as commitment, determination and empathy, are ideally suited to medicine.

I also enrolled in summer school at Luton and Dunstable Hospital, working in the Clean Surgery ward. This provided an insight into how healthcare workers come together to provide a patient-centred service. In addition to working alongside nurses to clean, dress and bathe patients, I also shadowed a junior doctor and observed a range of operations in the Orthopaedic Theatre. This illustrated the importance of precision and professionalism in the healthcare system.

In my free time, I have visited over 30 countries and love to immerse myself in different cultures. I have witnessed first-hand that, particularly in developing countries, basic knowledge of hygiene is often lacking and there is often a need for both improved healthcare and improved health education. One of my proudest personal achievements was to lose 6 stone in weight in a bid to raise awareness of diabetes within the South Asian ethnic community. My story will be published in the next edition of 'Asiana' lifestyle magazine.

My professional and personal life experiences, combined with my academic qualifications, make me highly suited to a career in medicine. I believe that my passion for caring for others, combined with my unfettered enthusiasm, will serve me well in this field. I look forward to continuing my personal and academic development, both during medical school and throughout my future career.

11.101 Graduate entry — 3877 characters

SECTION 1 [1156 characters]

Medicine is a challenging and demanding career, but the satisfaction and continuous learning it offers more than make up for the hard work. I have made an effort to gain as much experience as possible, to avoid any false impressions about the field.

My desire to become a doctor began after observing healthcare professionals in action. I spent a week at the Royal Victoria Infirmary, Newcastle, in the Care of the Elderly ward, where I admired the multidisciplinary team's dedication to patient care. Watching how consultants and junior doctors used their knowledge to make diagnoses and provide stability in such a demanding setting inspired me. I was fortunate to ask questions and observe various procedures.

My interest in medicine has been lifelong. I enjoy reading both fictional and non-fictional works on medicine, and I follow medical news and journals such as the 'Student BMJ'. I've attended lectures at the Centre for Life, including those by Nobel laureate James Watson, and participated in genetics workshops, where I learned valuable skills. Virtually every aspect of medicine excites me, and I can't wait to be part of the medical community.

SECTION 2 [1097 characters]

My current degree will definitely help me with graduate entry medicine, as it has prepared me not only for the majority of modules from the first two years of medicine but also made me familiar with the type of commitment, hard work and personal input required in a medical degree.

I take academics very seriously and have participated in science Olympiads, maths Olympiad and Maths Challenge (*Silver Award*). These have definitely improved my personal learning skills, and also made me very competitive. Within school I have been involved with debating, achieving a Best Debater Award (September 2003) in an interschool competition, as well as the Running Trophy.

I am also a Skills Trainer at my current Students' Union, where I deliver many skills sessions to the students to help develop areas like confidence, task management, presentation skills, leadership and teamwork skills, as well as more course-specific research and essay-writing techniques. Teaching these sessions has invaluably increased my own understanding of interpersonal qualities that will greatly help me in a medical career.

SECTION 3 [1624 characters]

Since last March I have gone on to volunteer at the Belsay Unit of the Newcastle General Hospital for Age Concern, helping patients in the wards and some outpatients carry out activities that would be hard to do themselves due to various motor disabilities. This has allowed me to talk to various patients about their experiences and get an outlook on continued patient care during their stay and after.

I also worked with St John Ambulance prior to my degree, where I was trained in first aid and basic anatomy. I have volunteered to help out at several public duties involving large numbers of people. This has helped me appreciate working in stressful conditions where time is of the essence, and the need to be calm, confident and level-headed while being thorough at the same time.

I was able to compare the different aspects of medicine from primary care to working in hospitals, as I have also spent two weeks with a health centre and two days with a GP surgery in Newcastle. I shadowed six general practitioners and several other specialists, seeing successful provision of comprehensive clinical care in primary care settings. The enthusiasm with which GPs enjoyed teaching a young student like me was infectious. I am currently coordinating a volunteer team to help out at St Oswald's Hospice by providing a day off to the dedicated members of staff there as a Project Manager at my university.

I enjoy music. I was part of the school chamber choir and also play many musical instruments. I love pursuing many extracurricular activities and am currently part of the university's spinning and mixed martial arts clubs.

11.102 Graduate entry — 3422 characters

SECTION 1 [1347 characters]

Wanting to pursue medicine stems from my passion for science and my instinct for human connection. Studying genetics has given me a strong foundation in scientific research and critical thinking, but I realised that I wanted a career where I could apply this knowledge in a more direct and personal way. My week shadowing a House Officer on the Nephrology ward at the University Hospital of Wales was a pivotal moment in confirming this. Observing dialysis treatments and witnessing the impact of ongoing care on patients' lives made me appreciate the intricate balance between scientific expertise and compassionate patient interaction. Seeing a biopsy procedure up close further highlighted the level of empathy and skill required in medicine – qualities I deeply admire and aspire to develop.

Following my scientific inclinations, I organised a fulfilling summer as a paid research intern studying plant genetics at the University of Missouri. It afforded me the challenging opportunity to conduct research, which has unquestionably improved my analytical technique. Whilst there I attended a wide array of scientific lectures with peers: topics ranged from osteopenia in cyclists to controversial chemical usage in food packaging. I came away from the experience deeply committed to combining science and compassion in my future academic career.

SECTION 2 [813 characters]

As treasurer of the University Biomolecular Society, I combine financial management with scientific advocacy, engaging with public biological issues. My role involves organising events and discussions on key biological topics, requiring clear communication and fostering productive dialogue. Managing the society's finances has strengthened my organisational and problem-solving skills, ensuring effective resource allocation to meet our goals. Collaborating with members from various academic backgrounds has enhanced my teamwork and communication abilities, helping me balance different perspectives and priorities. These skills are directly relevant to medicine, where clear communication, resource management, and teamwork are essential in addressing complex health challenges and providing high-quality care.

SECTION 3 [1262 characters]

I have found great fulfilment in dedicating my time to various volunteer causes, which has significantly boosted my confidence. In roles such as supervising at a local primary after-school club and assisting in the reception class, I developed strong connections with young children. Currently, I volunteer weekly at a rehabilitation centre for patients with serious head injuries. While each afternoon can be emotionally and physically draining, the sense of purpose I gain from this work is immeasurable.

This summer, I am organising work experience in Nepal, aiming to gain insights into a healthcare system with fewer resources. In the future, I plan to combine my passion for French and my love for charity work, potentially in an African Francophone country.

I manage a busy schedule by staying active through middle-distance charity runs, playing squash, and surfing. One of my proudest accomplishments was completing a challenging 3-day cycle ride from South to North Wales. I also volunteer with Oxfam at music festivals and have completed a basic first aid course with the Red Cross. In keeping myself informed with some of the more contentious issues related to my current field of study, I have become increasingly drawn to the study of medical ethics.

11.103 Graduate entry — 3817 characters

SECTION 1 [855 characters]

My interest in medicine was first sparked at the age of 12 when my grandmother was diagnosed with cancer. At the time, I viewed doctors as almost magical figures who could cure even the most devastating illnesses, and I dreamed of doing the same. As I matured, I came to understand the complexities and challenges of medicine, yet my fascination and desire to pursue it only grew stronger. While I initially passed the Belgian medical entrance exam and was accepted to study medicine, I decided to defer my place to ensure I fully understood the realities of the profession. Instead, I chose to study Biochemistry at UCL, a subject I knew I would enjoy and that would provide a strong scientific foundation for a future medical career. I really enjoyed the rigour and process of UCL, and I am keen to not just study medicine, but do so in a UK university.

SECTION 2 [1411 characters]

At university, my endeavours have led me to be added to the Dean's List as well as being awarded the Sir Jack Drummond prize for outstanding academic performance in my second year. As the student with the top marks in the Life Sciences Faculty, I have also been honoured with a scholarship. These are testimony to my relentless efforts to do well, leave no stone unturned, and my resilience when faced with self-doubt.

As a Student Ambassador for the Widening Participation Scheme, I host group visits to UCL, introducing prospective students to university life and encouraging them to pursue higher education. This role has strengthened my ability to communicate clearly and adapt my approach to engage with individuals from diverse backgrounds. Guiding groups through activities and addressing their questions required patience, empathy, and the ability to explain complex information in an accessible way. Managing these visits alongside my academic commitments has also enhanced my organisational and time management skills. Most importantly, this experience has taught me the importance of creating a supportive and inclusive environment, a quality that is essential for building trust and rapport with patients. By fostering understanding and confidence in others, I have developed skills directly transferable to medicine, where educating and empowering patients is a key part of providing effective care.

SECTION 3 [1551 characters]

Over the past two years, various work placements have given me a realistic insight into medicine. My experiences in the Neurology Department at Antwerp's Middelheim Hospital, Radiology at the Royal London, pathology at Neotia Hospital, and a paediatric clinic in Kolkata all confirmed my commitment to this field.

In Neurology, each day brought something new – from the high-pressure handling of a stroke patient to the routine of taking histories and blood pressure. At Neotia and Royal London, I saw how essential diagnostic tests and imaging are for accurate and prompt diagnoses.

During a summer internship with Cancer Research UK (studying how the protein kidins220 interacts with dynein), I worked with a dynamic scientific team, learnt experimental techniques, and enhanced my practical dexterity. Patience and perseverance are key in my role as a Peer Assisted Learning mentor, a continuation of my school tutoring. As Student Representative for the Life Sciences Faculty, I gained experience in student union governance, echoing the bureaucratic side of medicine.

I co-lead 'Junk In The Trunk', a student halls recycling initiative, managing volunteer recruitment, promotion and finance. These responsibilities sharpened my time management, organisational skills and composure under pressure – qualities vital in medicine.

As founder and president of the UCL Chocolate Society, I strive to be both decisive and approachable. Open to new ideas but capable of making the final call, I believe these leadership traits will serve me well as a doctor.

11.104 Graduate entry — 3905 characters

SECTION 1 [1070 characters]

The idea of being a doctor always appealed to me, but I initially dismissed it as an idealistic wish to save lives. Still, science was the class I enjoyed most. At 15, I devised a project on the effects of food and sport on fitness and ran the Paris Marathon in the top 10%, proving my physical and mental toughness. I chose to study physics at university for its intellectual challenge, but realised I needed a more people-oriented path. I explored business, and a six-week PwC Personal Development Course sharpened skills like teamwork, adaptability, and stress management, which are also vital for doctors.

However, I found the business world didn't align with my goal of making a positive change. I turned to my caring side and became a football trainer at 16, learning the balance of leadership and friendship. I later worked as a private academic tutor, where clear communication and patience were essential. Volunteering at a retirement home further solidified my desire to help others. All these experiences led me to medicine as my true, albeit belated, calling.

SECTION 2 [679 characters]

My physics studies have provided me with valuable skills directly applicable to medicine, particularly in problem-solving, analytical thinking, and data interpretation. One project involved using principles of fluid dynamics to study blood flow in arteries, where I applied mathematical models to simulate cardiovascular conditions. This experience sharpened my ability to analyse complex systems and draw accurate conclusions, skills essential in diagnosing and treating medical conditions. Furthermore, my lab work required precision, attention to detail, and effective teamwork, all of which are vital in the clinical environment, where accuracy and collaboration are crucial.

SECTION 3 [2156 characters]

Currently, I am volunteering in a hospital. This gives me the certainty that I love caring for others. It started off with patient transport, which was great as my first patient contact. From other volunteers, some with 25 years' experience, I learnt the skills necessary: compassion, listening, and comfort. When a nurse said I was naturally talented with patients, it delighted me more than any compliment could have done. I gained more responsibilities such as teaching new protocols, and shadowing doctors in areas including diagnostics, the OR, therapy, and casting. Apart from seeing the real-life procedures, I learnt most by talking to doctors. They warned me of the downsides including exhausting work hours, the huge responsibility of patient trust, and the stress this brings. However, I have not heard of a field where everyone is unanimously positive. Once, when a patient feared for her life from a gastroscopy, I used empathy combined with the knowledge of the procedure to calm her. Events in my personal life helped me gain this caring asset. My brother has autism and needs extra care, which I helped provide with his support network. My grandfather had a major stroke, and I always find it touching to watch his children care for him daily. A specific interest in medicine came from my sister's PhD research into the metastasis of prostate and breast cancer. Related is the promising drug abiraterone – only medicine could bring such exciting developments!

Still, without having a way to unwind, a doctor can underperform, with severe consequences. I stay calm and focused by playing team sports, guitar, and trying out new activities – last year being Kundalini yoga. The Manchester Leadership programme, which entailed 60 hours' volunteering in the community, and learning about the role of leaders in society, including doctors, illustrated the social responsibilities. A doctor I shadowed put this in a practical way: 'Put yourself in their shoes – if they come in with only a broken ankle, you shouldn't be bored by it, but understand that this makes a huge difference to their life.' A great doctor needs to see this bigger picture.

11.105 Graduate entry — 3664 characters

SECTION 1 [859 characters]

My personal experience with tinnitus has deeply influenced my desire to pursue medicine. Struggling with the condition, I initially found it challenging to find effective solutions. This led me to conduct my own research into tinnitus, exploring the latest treatments and scientific understanding of the condition. I became fascinated by the complexity of hearing disorders and the impact they have on patients' quality of life. During my research, I discovered the pivotal role of the ENT team in diagnosing and managing such conditions, witnessing first-hand their comprehensive approach to patient care, from providing tailored treatments to offering emotional support.

This ignited my passion for medicine, particularly in the field of audiology and ENT, and strengthened my desire to pursue a career where I can help others with similar health challenges.

SECTION 2 [849 characters]

For my EPQ, I investigated the effectiveness of antidepressants in treating depression, which provided me with invaluable research skills. Undertaking this project involved conducting a thorough literature search, critically assessing existing studies, and synthesising information to form a balanced perspective. I also learned how to analyse data and draw evidence-based conclusions, skills that are directly applicable to medicine. In clinical practice, a doctor must constantly evaluate the latest research, assess treatment options, and tailor approaches to meet individual patient needs.

This experience has reinforced my understanding of how research underpins medical decision-making and has equipped me with the analytical and critical thinking skills necessary for evaluating clinical evidence and delivering informed, patient-centred care.

SECTION 3 [1956 characters]

During my week in A&E at Addenbrooke's Hospital, I witnessed the treatment of a patient who had fallen from a multi-storey building. The A&E and intensive care teams worked together under immense pressure, making crucial decisions. This highlighted the importance of clear communication, teamwork, and composure in high-stress environments. I also spent a week in cardiology, where a doctor performed surgery to stop and restart a patient's heart to check an implanted defibrillator. The surgeon's sustained focus and the life-changing impact of the surgery reinforced my desire to pursue medicine.

Volunteering in geriatric wards over six months deepened my understanding of the emotional challenges faced by elderly patients. Small gestures, such as a conversation or a cup of tea, helped alleviate feelings of loneliness. Observing staffing shortages and bed allocation issues gave me insight into the pressures on our healthcare system. Volunteering for St John Ambulance for a year demonstrated how basic first aid can have life-changing effects in emergencies.

I completed a week in an audiology department, shadowing audiologists during consultations and observing hearing loss tests. I was struck by the patience needed to communicate with elderly patients who struggled with their condition. This experience reinforced my appreciation for clear communication in healthcare and the importance of multidisciplinary teamwork, as audiologists worked with ENT specialists to provide care.

As chair of the sixth form charities committee, I organised fundraising events for a local charity supporting teenage mental health. This role helped me develop leadership, communication, and listening skills. My paid work at a dispensary in my local GP surgery enhanced my organisational abilities and confidence in interacting with patients and staff. These experiences have given me the empathy, resilience, and teamwork skills essential for a career in medicine.

11.106 Graduate entry — 3457 characters

SECTION 1 [922 characters]

Reading 'Genome' by Matt Ridley deeply influenced my interest in genetic medicine, igniting my fascination with how advances in genetics can revolutionise patient care. The book provided me with a deeper understanding of the role genetics plays in disease, inspiring me to pursue a career where I could be part of this transformative field.

However, it was my grandmother's experience in the hospital that solidified my commitment to medicine. While the medical advancements she received were impressive, it was the compassionate care and communication from her doctors that truly made a difference in her recovery. Her treatment showed me that, regardless of technological progress, the patient–doctor relationship is foundational to effective healthcare. This combination of scientific interest and the importance of human connection is what drives me to study medicine and strive for a career where I can integrate both.

SECTION 2 [1059 characters]

Being part of the student advisory panel for King's College Muscle Lab has been a transformative experience, bridging my understanding of research and patient-centred communication. In this role, I attend sessions where respiratory medicine academics present their latest findings and contribute by writing blogs and simplifying technical research papers into language patients can easily understand.

One such project involved summarising research on ankle dorsiflexor muscles, their role in balance and walking, and how COPD may weaken them. This work highlighted the importance of doctors balancing technical expertise with clear and empathetic communication to ensure patients fully grasp their conditions and treatment options. Collaborating with researchers has deepened my appreciation for how research informs clinical practice, while refining my ability to convert complex medical information into accessible insights. These skills are crucial for fostering trust and understanding in patient care, and I am eager to build upon them as a future doctor.

SECTION 3 [1476 characters]

During my work experience with a vascular surgeon and a cardiologist, I observed how essential it is for doctors to tailor treatments to individual patients. I saw how similar medical conditions were treated differently, depending on factors such as age, lifestyle, and patient compliance. I was particularly impressed by the collaborative nature of the multidisciplinary team, where diverse perspectives helped shape decisions. In one case, a team member identified a crucial detail on an angiogram that had been overlooked, highlighting the importance of teamwork in patient care.

Volunteering at a care home with residents suffering from dementia and physical disabilities gave me a deeper understanding of the challenges faced by the elderly. I learned that, alongside medical care, meaningful activities and a supportive network are vital for enhancing the quality of life in later years.

Joining St John Ambulance was another valuable experience. Although I was initially apprehensive about medical emergencies, the first aid training and teamwork built my confidence in helping others during critical moments. Outside of my academic life, I have also developed my communication skills by attending The Spanish Institute, where I interact with adults from various professional backgrounds. Additionally, running weekly youth groups for my Duke of Edinburgh Awards allowed me to strengthen my leadership and delegation skills, further preparing me for a career in medicine.

11.107 Graduate entry — 3698 characters

SECTION 1 [1008 characters]

My interest in medicine started with a fascination for the human body and a desire to apply science meaningfully. This grew during my EPQ on nutrition and health, where I explored the link between diet and disease, deepening my appreciation for research in healthcare. Volunteering at a homeless shelter from age 14 exposed me to the intersection of social issues and healthcare. I saw how unstable housing, poor nutrition, and lack of medical care contribute to chronic illnesses and mental health struggles. Many individuals faced significant barriers to receiving even basic medical attention due to financial constraints, stigma, or logistical challenges.

This reinforced my belief that healthcare should be accessible to everyone, regardless of their status. It deepened my understanding of the importance of preventative care, mental health support, and community-based initiatives, inspiring me to pursue medicine with a focus on healthcare disparities and advocating for inclusive, compassionate care.

SECTION 2 [1021 characters]

For four years, I have been a committed member of my university athletics team, progressing from a dedicated athlete competing at regional level to serving as president of the society. This role involved managing team logistics, fostering a sense of community, and balancing responsibilities with my own training. More recently, I have taken on the role of assisting in coaching young athletes, which has allowed me to further develop my leadership and communication skills, particularly when working with new students. Adapting my coaching approach to suit each athlete's needs has honed my ability to listen, provide clear guidance, and motivate others effectively.

These experiences resonate with the skills required in medicine, where teamwork, clear communication, and individualised patient care are essential. Coaching has also deepened my understanding of the importance of empathy, encouragement, and resilience – qualities I believe are vital in building trust and fostering positive outcomes as a future doctor.

SECTION 3 [1669 characters]

I have completed clinical placements in a medical lab, assisting technicians with patient sample tests, and at a paediatric ward for a year, where I often translated between Arabic-speaking parents and English-speaking nurses. This experience highlighted the importance of clear communication, especially with a language barrier. I also supported procedures such as cannulation and nebulisation by comforting children and parents. One impactful case was a six-week-old child with head lesions undergoing cannulation before surgery. Witnessing the mother's positive experience underscored the emotional impact of medicine.

I was an avid participant in team sports in school, including playing in basketball games for the school U18 team and attending swim practice weekly before school as part of the school's swim team, competing nationally. Maintaining this alongside my studies required discipline and time management, both necessary qualities for a medical student. During my gap year, aside from improving interview skills, I hope to tutor, to contribute to my community and improve my people skills. I have already acquired students and begun to teach lessons. I have also started a paid language teaching job at a local education centre, which has strengthened my organisation and improvisation.

I am fully aware that studying medicine is not easy, however, I am prepared to face these challenges for the immense interpersonal rewards that the profession yields. The prospect of having a rigorous science education followed by years of training and constant learning is incredibly enticing, and I hope to make full use of my education to become an excellent doctor.

12 Power words

VERBS

Abbreviated	Abolished	Abridged	Absolved
Absorbed	Accelerated	Acclimated	Accompanied
Achieved	Acquired	Acted	Activated
Actuated	Adapted	Added	Addressed
Adhered	Adjusted	Administered	Admitted
Adopted	Advanced	Advertised	Advised
Advocated	Affected	Aided	Aired
Allocated	Altered	Amended	Amplified
Analysed	Answered	Anticipated	Applied
Appointed	Appraised	Approached	Approved
Arbitrated	Arranged	Articulated	Ascertained
Asked	Assembled	Assessed	Assigned
Assisted	Assumed	Attained	Attracted
Audited	Augmented	Authored	Authorised
Awarded	Balanced	Began	Benchmarked
Benefited	Bid	Billed	Blocked
Boosted	Borrowed	Bought	Branded
Bridged	Broadened	Brought	Budgeted
Built	Calculated	Canvassed	Captured
Cared	Cast	Catalogued	Categorised
Centralised	Chaired	Challenged	Changed
Channelled	Charged	Charted	Checked
Circulated	Clarified	Classified	Cleared
Closed	Coached	Co-authored	Collaborated
Collected	Combined	Commissioned	Committed
Communicated	Compared	Compiled	Completed
Complied	Composed	Computed	Conceived
Conceptualised	Condensed	Conducted	Conserved
Consolidated	Constructed	Consulted	Contacted
Contributed	Controlled	Converted	Conveyed
Convinced	Coordinated	Copyrighted	Corrected

Corresponded	Counselled	Created	Critiqued
Cultivated	Customised	Cut	Dealt
Debated	Debugged	Decentralised	Decreased
Deferred	Defined	Delegated	Delivered
Demonstrated	Depreciated	Described	Designated
Designed	Detected	Determined	Developed
Devised	Diagnosed	Directed	Discovered
Dispatched	Dissembled	Distinguished	Distributed
Diversified	Divested	Documented	Doubled
Drove	Earned	Eased	Edited
Educated	Effected	Elicited	Eliminated
Emphasised	Empowered	Enabled	Encouraged
Endorsed	Enforced	Engaged	Engineered
Enhanced	Enlarged	Enlisted	Enriched
Ensured	Escalated	Established	Estimated
Evaluated	Examined	Exceeded	Exchanged
Executed	Exempted	Expanded	Expedited
Experienced	Explained	Explored	Exposed
Extended	Extracted	Fabricated	Facilitated
Fashioned	Fielded	Financed	Fired
Flagged	Focused	Forecasted	Formalised
Formatted	Formed	Formulated	Fortified
Founded	Fulfilled	Furnished	Furthered
Gained	Gathered	Gauged	Generated
Governed	Graded	Granted	Greeted
Grouped	Guided	Handled	Headed
Helped	Hired	Hosted	Identified
Ignited	Illuminated	Illustrated	Impacted
Implemented	Improved	Improvised	Inaugurated
Incorporated	Increased	Incurred	Individualised
Indoctrinated	Induced	Influenced	Initiated
Innovated	Inquired	Inspected	Inspired
Installed	Instigated	Instilled	Instituted
Instructed	Insured	Integrated	Interacted
Interpreted	Intervened	Interviewed	Introduced
Invented	Inventoried	Invested	Investigated
Invited	Involved	Isolated	Issued
Joined	Judged	Justified	Kept
Launched	Lectured	Led	Lightened
Liquidated	Litigated	Lobbied	Localised
Located	Logged	Maintained	Managed
Manufactured	Mapped	Marketed	Maximised

Measured	Mediated	Mentored	Merchandised
Merged	Minimised	Modelled	Moderated
Modernised	Modified	Monitored	Motivated
Moved	Multiplied	Named	Narrated
Navigated	Negotiated	Netted	Noticed
Nourished	Nursed	Nurtured	Observed
Obtained	Offered	Opened	Operated
Orchestrated	Ordered	Organised	Oriented
Originated	Overhauled	Oversaw	Participated
Patented	Patterned	Performed	Persuaded
Phased	Photographed	Pinpointed	Pioneered
Placed	Planned	Polled	Posted
Prepared	Presented	Preserved	Presided
Prevented	Processed	Procured	Produced
Profiled	Programmed	Projected	Promoted
Prompted	Proposed	Prospected	Protected
Proved	Provided	Publicised	Published
Purchased	Pursued	Qualified	Quantified
Quoted	Raised	Ranked	Rated
Received	Recognised	Recommended	Reconciled
Recorded	Recovered	Recruited	Rectified
Redesigned	Reduced	Referred	Refined
Regained	Registered	Regulated	Rehabilitated
Reinforced	Reinstated	Rejected	Remedied
Remodelled	Renegotiated	Reorganised	Repaired
Replaced	Reported	Represented	Rescued
Researched	Resolved	Responded	Restored
Restructured	Resulted	Retained	Retrieved
Revamped	Revealed	Reversed	Reviewed
Revised	Revitalised	Rewarded	Safeguarded
Salvaged	Saved	Scheduled	Screened
Secured	Segmented	Selected	Separated
Served	Serviced	Settled	Shaped
Shortened	Shrank	Signed	Simplified
Simulated	Sold	Solidified	Solved
Spearheaded	Specialised	Specified	Speculated
Spoke	Spread	Stabilised	Staffed
Staged	Standardised	Steered	Stimulated
Strategised	Streamlined	Strengthened	Stressed
Structured	Studied	Submitted	Substantiated
Substituted	Suggested	Superseded	Supervised
Supplied	Supported	Surpassed	Surveyed

Synchronised	Systematised	Tabulated	Tailored
Targeted	Taught	Tested	Tightened
Took	Traced	Tracked	Traded
Trained	Transacted	Transcribed	Transferred
Transformed	Translated	Transmitted	Transported
Treated	Tripled	Troubleshot	Tutored
Uncovered	Underlined	Undertook	Unified
United	Updated	Upgraded	Urged
Used	Utilised	Validated	Valued
Verbalised	Verified	Viewed	Visited
Visualised	Voiced	Volunteered	Weathered
Weighed	Welcomed	Widened	Withstood
Witnessed	Won	Worked	Wrote

NOUNS

Accountability	Accuracy	Adaptability	Advocacy
Altruism	Ambition	Aspiration	Attentiveness
Authority	Autonomy	Awareness	Backbone
Balance	Belonging	Bravery	Camaraderie
Care	Clarity	Collaboration	Command
Comfort	Compassion	Comprehension	Competence
Confidence	Confidentiality	Connection	Consent
Contribution	Courage	Curiosity	Decency
Decision-making	Dedication	Delegation	Dependability
Depth	Determination	Devotion	Dignity
Direction	Discovery	Discipline	Drive
Efficiency	Empathy	Encouragement	Endurance
Engagement	Equity	Ethics	Excellence
Example-setting	Evolution	Fairness	Focus
Follow-through	Fortitude	Framework	Generosity
Governance	Gratitude	Grit	Growth
Guidance	Harmony	Healing	Honesty
Humaneness	Humility	Identity	Independence
Influence	Informed consent	Ingenuity	Initiative
Inclusion	Insight	Insightfulness	Intellect
Intuition	Judgement	Kindness	Knowledge
Learning	Maturity	Mediation	Mindset

Motivation	Multi-disciplinarity	Mutuality	Neatness
Observation	Open-mindedness	Organisation	Originality
Ownership	Patience	Perseverance	Perspective
Presence	Preparation	Precision	Proficiency
Productivity	Prognosis	Punctuality	Purpose
Rapport	Realisation	Reasoning	Reassurance
Reciprocity	Recovery	Reflection	Reliability
Representation	Resilience	Resolve	Respect
Respectfulness	Responsibility	Restraint	Rigorousness
Sanctity	Safeguarding	Self-awareness	Self-discipline
Self-improvement	Sensitivity	Service	Sociability
Stability	Stewardship	Structure	Support
Synergy	Sympathy	Synthesis	Temperance
Tenacity	Thoroughness	Thoughtfulness	Transformation
Treatment	Trust	Understanding	Vigilance
Vision	Vulnerability	Well-being	Zeal

ADJECTIVES

Accountable	Accurate	Adaptable	Altruistic
Ambitious	Analytical	Approachable	Aspirational
Astute	Attentive	Aware	Balanced
Bold	Brave	Caring	Clear
Collaborative	Comfortable	Companionable	Compassionate
Competent	Comprehending	Confident	Confidential
Connected	Consensual	Considerate	Consistent
Creative	Critical	Curious	Decent
Decisive	Dedicated	Delegative	Dependable
Determined	Devoted	Dignified	Disciplined
Discerning	Driven	Efficient	Empathetic
Encouraging	Engaged	Engaging	Ethical
Excellent	Exemplary	Explorative	Fair
Focused	Friendly	Generous	Grateful
Gritty	Grounded	Guiding	Harmonious
Healing	Honest	Humane	Humble
Imaginative	Inclusive	Independent	Ingenious
Innovative	Insightful	Intellectual	Intuitive
Judicious	Kind	Knowledgeable	Logical
Mature	Mediative	Methodical	Mindful

Motivated	Motivational	Multidisciplinary	Mutual
Neat	Observant	Objective	Open-minded
Organised	Original	Patient	Perceptive
Persistent	Prepared	Precise	Proactive
Proficient	Productive	Prognostic	Purposeful
Rational	Realistic	Reassuring	Reciprocal
Reflective	Reliable	Representative	Resolute
Respectful	Responsible	Restrained	Rigorous
Sacred	Self-aware	Self-disciplined	Self-improving
Sensitive	Service-oriented	Sincere	Sociable
Stable	Strategic	Structured	Supportive
Sympathetic	Synthesising	Synergistic	Tactful
Temperate	Tenacious	Thoughtful	Transformative
Trusting	Trustworthy	Understanding	Visionary
Vigilant	Vulnerable	Welcoming	Zealous

MEDICAL SCHOOL INTERVIEWS

A practical guide to help you get that place at medical school

Over 150 questions analysed includes Multiple Mini Interviews (MMI)

THIRD EDITION

Published October 2025
Scan QR code to order online